The Ballad of Winston,

the wandering trader

BOOKS 1-5

(an unofficial Minecraft series)

(**illustrated** edition)

By,

DR. BLOCK

Copyright © 2020-2021 by Dr. Block and Eclectic Esquire Media, LLC

ISBN: 978-1-951728-90-8

No part of this publication may be reproduced, distributed, or transmitted in any form or by any means, without the prior written permission of the publisher, except in the case of brief quotations embodied in critical reviews and certain other noncommercial uses permitted by copyright law.

This UNOFFICIAL Minecraft-inspired book is an original work of fan fiction which is NOT OFFICIAL MINECRAFT PRODUCT. NOT APPROVED BY OR ASSOCIATED WITH MOJANG.

Minecraft is a registered trademark of, and owned by, Mojang AB, and its respective owners, which do not sponsor, authorize, or endorse this book. All characters, names, places, and other aspects of the game described herein are trademarked and owned by their respective owners.

Published by Eclectic Esquire Media, LLC
P.O. Box 235094
Encinitas, CA 92023-5094

Inquiries and Information: drblockbooks@gmail.com

Table of Contents

Introduction 1

Book 1.. **2**
   Chapter 1 3
   Chapter 2 10
   Chapter 3 16
   Chapter 4 22
   Chapter 5 27
   Chapter 6 33
   Chapter 7 39
   Chapter 8 48
   Chapter 9 55
   Chapter 10 61
   Chapter 11 74
   Chapter 12 82

Book 2... **88**
   Chapter 1 89
   Chapter 2 93
   Chapter 3 98
   Chapter 4 103
   Chapter 5 106
   Chapter 6 109
   Chapter 7 116
   Chapter 8 122
   Chapter 9 125
   Chapter 10 131

Chapter 11 139
Chapter 12 143
Chapter 13 146
Chapter 14 152
Chapter 15 163

Book 3 .... **168**
Chapter 1 169
Chapter 2 176
Chapter 3 180
Chapter 4 186
Chapter 5 190
Chapter 6 195
Chapter 7 203
Chapter 8 209
Chapter 9 214
Chapter 10 221
Chapter 11 226
Chapter 12 230
Chapter 13 236
Chapter 14 240
Chapter 15 244

Book 4 .... **249**
Chapter 1 250
Chapter 2 258
Chapter 3 264
Chapter 4 271
Chapter 5 276
Chapter 6 285
Chapter 7 291
Chapter 8 297

Chapter 9	302
Chapter 10	309
Chapter 11	319
Chapter 12	334

Book 5 .... **340**

Chapter 1	341
Chapter 2	346
Chapter 3	349
Chapter 4	355
Chapter 5	361
Chapter 6	366
Chapter 7	374
Chapter 8	381
Chapter 9	388
Chapter 10	394
Chapter 11	400
Chapter 12	405
Chapter 13	412
Chapter 14	415
Chapter 15	422
Chapter 16	425
Chapter 17	429
Chapter 18	435
Chapter 19	438
Chapter 20	442
A Note from Dr. Block	448
Coloring Book for Minecrafters	450
Also by Dr. Block	451

Introduction

Hey, guys! Dr. Block here. I wanted to start this book with a quick note to let you know about a couple of things.

First, the *Ballad of Winston* takes place in the same universe as my *Diary of a Surfer Villager* series. However, there are no overlapping events. In fact, the *Winston* series starts approximately 50 years prior to the *Surfer Villager* series. This means also that in the *Winston* series, there is no netherite and the Nether consists of only one biome.

Second, I wanted to mention the illustrations in this book. You will notice that some of the villagers have smaller noses than others. The villagers with small noses are female. Also, some of the villagers in this book have hair, while others don't.

If you've never read my *Winston* series, I hope you enjoy this collection of the first five books. If you have read these books before, I hope you enjoy the new illustrations.

Dr. Block
10 November 2021

Book 1

Chapter 1

My name is Winston, and I'm a wandering trader. I'm an old man now. There will probably be a price on my head for writing my life story, revealing all of the secrets that I intend to reveal.

But I don't care anymore.

The consequences of some of my choices have been so horrific, so burdensome, that this is the only way I can free my mind from the horrors of what my life has become. But it wasn't always that way. I wasn't always a wandering trader.

Most people don't know this, but a significant minority of wandering traders are not spawned as wandering traders. They joined the Guild of the wandering traders voluntarily ... well, more or less voluntarily, anyway. And by joining, they submit to the creed of the wandering trader, known as the Way.

By submitting to that creed, they knowingly – or in my case, unknowingly – joined a secret society, involved in pulling the strings of many of the most significant events in the world of Minecraft.

But, I'll get to that later.

* * *

For now, I need to tell you something about my childhood.

I spawned as a desert villager child. I was given the name of Kevin by my parents, Dale and Barbara. My parents were typical desert villagers. They had a well-built, modest home. They traded with players who visited the village. My father was a leather worker, so he was able to earn emeralds fairly easily, selling leather armor and saddles.

My recollection, vague as it may be, is that we lived a rather comfortable lifestyle. My family was not rich by any means, but I don't ever remember feeling hungry. I don't ever remember feeling scared. Well, not very often.

There was this one time a group of about a dozen husks wandered into our village one late afternoon. It was a surprise because husks normally wandered in one or two at a time, and were fairly easy to avoid. They killed one of my neighbors, an old man who was in his front yard smelling a flower. The husks snuck up behind him – he couldn't hear very well – and ate him while he was just trying to enjoy the scent of a flower.

Savage.

His screams alerted the village. Within seconds, about a dozen men in the village were able to gather weapons and dispatch the husks, though several were injured in the battle. That was the only time I remember my mom being frightened. Because she was frightened, I felt frightened too.

I had lots of friends in my village. My best friend was named Bart. He was a mischievous kid. He was always playing practical jokes on people. He pulled chairs out from underneath adults so they would fall flat on their butts. Everyone would laugh, kids and adults alike. Sometimes he would paint pigs funny colors and make them run through town.

I miss Bart.

I can recall going to school for a few years between the ages of six and ten. I do not recall any details about my teachers; they must have been fairly average or else I would expect to have a memory of them.

In school, I learned how to read and write. I learned basic mathematics. I was beginning to learn how to build villager dwelling structures, which is an important class, when I turned ten years old. The final day I attended school was on my tenth birthday; I would never go back to my school again.

I remember my ten-year-old birthday party vividly. My parents had invited all my friends. There were about fifteen kids there, including Bart. Bart put a booger on my dad's glass of water while my dad was doing something. The booger stuck to my dad's hand. Bart and I laughed. My dad was upset, I could tell, but he laughed along with us so as not to ruin my birthday party.

My friends gave me some pretty cool presents. A bag of chorus fruit, an eye of ender, an atlas of the Overworld. My parents gave me a creeper action figure. I named him Creepy.

We played games like pin-the-tail-on-the-mooshroom, hide-n-go creep, and Tic-tac-TNT. It was a fun day. After all the kids went home, I ate dinner with my parents and they made it clear that I needed to go to bed early that night.

"Kevin, your mom and I are really tired. I think you need to go to sleep," said my dad, yawning.

"I don't want to," I whined. "I wanna play with my creeper action figure."

Creepy

My mom laughed. "Why don't you take it to bed with you? You can pretend it exploded on your pillow or something."

"That's boring, Mom. I want to make Creepy blow up some players."

My dad chuckled. "Now, now, Son. Without players we couldn't trade. And without trade we wouldn't have any emeralds to buy the things we need."

I shrugged. "Yeah, I suppose. But still, it's pretty cool that creepers explode when they see players."

My parents looked at each other with a slight bit of concern in their eyes. I could tell they were thinking something like, *is our son psychopath?* But I wasn't. I was just a typical ten-year-old villager boy who thought explosions were cool.

"Anyway, Son, it's time for bed. Go brush your teeth and then Mom and I will come up and tuck you in."

I stood up and said, "Awww, man. Okay." Then I went upstairs and brushed my teeth and got into my bed.

My parents came up a few minutes later and tucked me in. I had my creeper action figure next to me, and I fully intended on acting out all sorts of vicious, explosive scenarios before I went to sleep, but the day finally caught up with me and I passed out.

Chapter 2

I would like to tell you that I had a peaceful slumber and that I dreamed of Creepy and all the players he killed, but it wouldn't be true. Well, actually, I did have a short dream about Creepy. He blew up a couple of mean players who had been trying to make bad trades with a villager. And then, he respawned so he could do it again. It was very satisfying!

Anyway, when I woke up, it was still dark. This was unusual because I usually slept through the night. But, waking up in the darkness was not the most unusual thing. The most unusual thing was ... the screams.

I heard the sound of men, women, and children screaming. People running through the streets yelling with fear. The hollow THUD of bodies falling on the street.

I sat up in bed filled with anxiety. I grabbed Creepy and held him close to me for protection. As I sat in bed shivering, the door burst open.

"Kevin! We need to go. Now!" said my dad as he took three huge strides to my bedside and grabbed me. We ran downstairs and my mom was there waiting for us by the door. She was holding a chest in which she had packed some food.

"What's happening, Mommy?"

I could tell by the look in her eyes, it was something very, very bad. "It's the pillagers. They've come."

Now, I don't know what you know about pillagers, hurrr, and I didn't know much when I was ten, but I did know this: Pillagers were evil. They killed *for the fun of it*. When they showed up in a village you had to run and hide or you would be dead. Every villager kid knows that.

From the time we can communicate we are told that over and over again. If you see a pillager, you run, and you keep on running until the threat is over. And so I knew what we had to do.

My dad cracked open the front door and looked out. He leaned back in and whispered, "It looks like the coast is clear. If we run as fast as we can to the north, we should be able to get to that little nearby cave where we found that piece of diamond ore that one time. We should be safe there."

My mom nodded. I clutched my creeper action figure closer to my chest. Creepy and I were ready to run.

"On the count of three, I will push open the door and we will run as fast as we can. Okay?" said my dad.

"Okay," I said. My mom nodded her head.

My dad peeked through the crack in the door again and then he began to count. "One. Two. Three." My dad pushed open the door, and we ran as fast as we could, my dad leading the way, I was in the middle, and my mom running right behind me.

As we were running, we heard more and more screams. I heard the sound of crossbow arrows going into the flesh of my fellow villagers. It was a sickening sound. A sound no ten-year-old should hear. We turned the corner and ran up the street. We had to go just three more blocks and we would be outside of the village boundaries and then on the way to the cave.

As we ran down the street, there were drop piles and pillager arrows everywhere. My mom tried to cover my eyes, but it didn't work because it slowed us down and in any event, I had already seen more than I needed to or should have.

We had just arrived at the end of the street and were about to step onto the desert sands when I heard my mom scream. I turned around and saw a pillager's crossbow arrow sticking out of her back!

"Mommy!" I screamed. She looked at me with sad eyes before she flashed red and disappeared in a puff of smoke.

My dad stopped and turned back. I saw the sadness and anguish in his face. He grabbed me by the shoulder. "Come on, Kevin. There's nothing we can do. She would want us to escape."

But I was frozen. I couldn't move.

My dad finally had to pick me up. But when he turned around and began to run for the cave again, an arrow went into his back. He fell forward and dropped me. I was about two blocks away from him when he looked at me, reached out with his arm, pointed to the north, and muttered, "Run." Then, he flashed red and disappeared into a puff of smoke.

I was still frozen.

What would a ten-year-old do without his parents?

I looked up and saw a pillager slowly approaching me. I began to cry. He began to laugh. I began to cry more. He laughed harder and louder.

I watched as he reloaded his crossbow. He lifted it up and took aim. I was ready to die. I held Creepy tight. *What could I do?*

Than a strange look crossed the pillager's face. A look of surprise. And then of shock. And then of fear.

He dropped to his knees, the crossbow slipping out of his hands and falling harmlessly to the ground. He then leaned forward and put both his hands on the ground as if trying to support himself.

That's when I saw the giant diamond axe stuck in his back. The pillager tried to reach behind himself, as if he might pull the axe out of his back and somehow survive. But, as he reached back, he blinked red and disappeared into a puff of smoke. The axe fell to the ground.

I sat there clutching Creepy and sobbing. I was mentally destroyed by everything that had happened and everything that I had just seen.

And then, I saw him.

A wandering trader walked out of the shadows between two alleyways, picked up the axe, and tucked it back into his inventory. He walked up to me. He was a looming figure. He seemed as if he were thirty blocks tall and ten blocks wide. He was a hero, a god. He had just saved my life.

He stood in front of me and reached out his hand. "My name is Wolf. Come with me if you want to live."

Chapter 3

I was so stunned the only thing I could do was go with him. Wolf picked me up and carried me around the corner. His two trading llamas were tied to a post. He put me on the back of one of them and said, "Hold on."

Wolf then grabbed the leads of the llamas and began walking away from the village. To my surprise, the pillagers did not follow us. I could have sworn we walked directly across their fields of vision, but it was as if they did not see us.

Wolf and his llamas moved slowly and methodically across the landscape. After about fifteen minutes, we came to a small cave at the base of a hill. (No, it was not the same cave to which my father had tried to take us.) Wolf took a couple of quick glances over his shoulders and, after assuring himself that we had not been followed, we walked into the cave.

Once we were inside the cave, Wolf removed some cobblestones from his inventory and blocked up the entrance. He then ignited several torches and placed them on the wall, revealing a large room containing a bed and campfire. He walked over to the llama on which I was riding and lifted me up and set me down on the ground.

"Are you hungry, child?"

I shook my head. I was too in shock to have an appetite. Plus, it was still nighttime. I should have been asleep. My parents should have been asleep. My parents should have been alive.

"Would you like a drink of water?"

I nodded my head. Wolf handed me a bottle of water and I drank a few sips and then handed it back.

Wolf looked at me with a kind expression and smiled. "I see you got a creeper action figure there."

I had forgotten I was holding it in my hand the entire time. I nodded my head. "I got it for my birthday," I said, barely able to whisper the words aloud.

Wolf smiled. "I haven't had a birthday party in a long time. Was it a good birthday?"

I nodded my head as tears streamed down my face. "It was until…."

Wolf took a deep breath and sighed. "We don't have to talk anymore about that. Here, why don't you lie down and go to sleep? In the morning we can talk about what to do with you."

*What to **do** with me?*

I sniffed and nodded my head. Wolf pulled a small bed out of his inventory and put it on the ground. It had sheets, a blanket, and a pillow. I laid down on the bed. It was almost as comfortable as my bed at home. I wanted my mom and dad to tuck me in. But that would never happen again.

I cried myself to sleep.

* * *

When I woke up, the door to the cave had been unsealed and I saw that Wolf's llamas were standing outside the door of the cave eating grass. Wolf was leaning against the rock at the cave entrance. He was casually chewing a piece of grass, looking out to the horizon, scanning for something. Maybe for a potential trading partner. Maybe for pillagers.

I lay in bed staring at him. I had not realized that wandering traders were so good with weapons. But, I was only ten years old. What did I know about life?

Not much, I thought as I clutched Creepy closer to me, *but I had sure learned a lot about death.* I began to cry. The realization that my parents would never be there again finally hitting home.

Without warning I felt Wolf's comforting hand on my shoulder. I looked up at him and wiped the tears from my face. I wanted to say something to him but I didn't know what. I was just a ten-year-old kid dealing with something terrible. My brain could barely function.

Wolf crouched down next to me and looked me in the face. "Kid, I'm sorry about what happened. But you need to know that **you are alive**. Make yourself a good life. Don't forget that."

I nodded my head, not really understanding, but wanting to give some acknowledgment that his words had penetrated my eardrums and made it into my brain.

Wolf took a deep breath and sighed. "Look, Kid, I saved you so I am responsible for you. That is the Way. I can offer you one of two things. Option one. I can take you to this nice orphanage I know in Capitol City. The villagers who run it are good, kind people. If you stay there, I'm sure you'll never want for anything. You'll probably end up going to college or trade school and having a decent life."

Wolf paused for a moment, looking down at the ground. He scratched the dirt with his fingers for a few moments before looking back up. "Option two. You can become a wandering trader like me. You can join us. Learn the Way of the Wanderer. It can be a lonely life, but you don't have to depend on anyone. You just have to follow the Way."

I heard all of Wolf's words. I knew that this was a monumental moment in my life. One day earlier, I had a safe home and parents who loved me. Now, I was basically an adult, deciding what was going to happen for the rest of my life.

"Why don't you think about it for a bit, Kid. I'll make some breakfast. But by noon, I've got to get going. So ... hurrr ... I hate to do this to you, but you'll have to decide by then."

Wolf stood up and began to walk away. I watched him, thinking about the two choices he had just given me. I clutched Creepy again. If I were a creeper, I would have walked up to those stupid pillagers attacking my parents and blown myself up and killed them. That would've been the honorable thing for a creeper to do.

Wolf stopped about halfway between my bed and the campfire where he was going to cook breakfast. He turned around and looked at me. "And, if you decide to become a wandering trader, I'll help you get revenge on the pillagers who killed your parents and destroyed your village."

With that handful of words, my decision had been made for me.

Chapter 4

Around midday I was sitting on the back of one of Wolf's llamas. We were headed in a northerly direction.

"Kid, I just want to make sure you're okay with this decision of yours to become a wandering trader and submit to the Way."

"I'm fine with it," I said, trying to sound emotionless and hard, but sounding exactly like a scared little kid who had just lost his parents.

"Here's the thing, there's a lot of stuff about wandering traders the average person doesn't know. The things we have to do to survive. To follow the Way. When you're a member of the Way of the wandering trader, sometimes we have to ... hurrr ... do some things the average person might find to be ... unsavory." Wolf paused for a moment and looked off in the distance. "You'll get used to it. Most of us do, anyway."

I wasn't quite sure what he was implying with this line of talk, but the thought of revenge against the pillagers who murdered my parents and destroyed my village was consuming me.

"So, like, sometimes you aren't actually wandering? You're like going on missions and stuff?"

Wolf nodded his head. "We transmit messages. To particular people for particular purposes. We ensure that certain items are delivered to particular places at particular times. There are other things too, but you will learn about those later."

We continued on in silence for a while until we came to the edge of a forest. Wolf brought his llamas to a halt. He looked at me dead center in the eyes. "Here's the deal, Kid. We're almost to the wandering trader headquarters. Once you see the place, your only option is to become a wandering trader or die trying. There's no getting out. So think about it really hard. We can still go to that orphanage. You can still live a relatively normal villager life if you want to."

I was about to respond when in the distance two players emerged from the forest. Wolf looked at me. "I'll be right back."

I watched as Wolf stealthily made his way toward the players. Even though he was clearly in their field of vision, it was as if they didn't see him. Suddenly he took a step in front of them and the two players acted shocked at his appearance.

"Bro, where did you come from?" said one of the players, wearing a mismatched set of leather and iron armor.

"Yeah, you wandering traders give me the creeps," said the other player, wearing a full set of iron armor.

Wolf smiled and bowed low. "I am a wandering trader. I appear when I am needed. Is there anything you would like to trade for? Perhaps a pair of iron armor pants? Or a suit of diamond armor?"

"Yeah, how much is the diamond armor?" said the player with the mismatched armor.

Wolf smiled. "Only one hundred and fifty emeralds."

"What a rip-off!" said the player. "What about the pair of iron armor pants?"

Wolf smiled again. "Those are a real bargain. Only ten emeralds."

The player nodded his head and reached into his inventory and pulled out ten emeralds. He handed them to Wolf who took them and said, "I'll be right back. The item is on one of my pack llamas."

Wolf walked back over to where I was sitting on his llama and reached into the storage bags. He rummaged around and finally found the iron armor pants. He winked at me and then walked back to the two players. He handed the iron armor pants to the player who purchased them.

"Anything else I can help you with?" The players each shook their heads.

"By the way," said the player who had been wearing the full set of iron armor from the beginning, "why is there a villager kid riding on your llama?"

Wolf shook his head. "That's none of your concern."

"Ha ha ha. You just got dissed by a wandering trader, bro," said the other player.

"Whatever, bro. Wandering traders are lame."

Wolf stood there calmly absorbing the abuse as the two players walked away from the edge of the forest. Once the players were out of earshot, Wolf took the leads of the llamas and looked at me. "So? Did you change your mind? Do you want to go to the orphanage now?"

I shook my head. "I want to learn the Way of the Wanderer. I want revenge for my parents' deaths and the destruction of my village. I want to be independent and self-reliant, like you are. I can't get close to anyone until I know that I can defend them."

Wolf seemed surprised by my words. "That's pretty deep for a ten-year-old. Okay then, once you cross into the forest, there's no going back. Are you sure?"

"I'm as sure as the sun is square."

Chapter 5

Before we entered the cave, Wolf told me to get off the llama and walk. As we entered the cave and the light of the sun became dimmer, Wolf ignited two torches and handed one to me. "Be on the lookout for creepers."

I clutched my creeper action figure closer to me. Creepers were cool – in theory – but I wasn't ready to meet one in reality. "Should I put Creepy away?"

Wolf looked at the toy. "Probably a good idea. If we have to run, you don't want to drop him."

I reluctantly tucked Creepy into my inventory and then held my torch aloft with both hands. I was surprised at how heavy it was. I walked to the left side of Wolf as he held his torch aloft in his left hand and pulled the llamas with his right hand.

We walked in the cave for several minutes. I heard the skittering sounds of strange cave creatures and mobs. I felt the soft breath of the earth rising from the bottom of the cave. For a moment I thought I heard the hissing of a creeper. I tensed. But it was nothing.

Eventually, we came to a dead-end. For a moment I thought maybe Wolf had changed his mind about allowing me to become a wandering trader. I thought maybe he was going to kill me. In that moment, it seemed like a logical conclusion, one my frightened ten-year-old mind came to very quickly.

Wolf looked at me and said, "I'm going to reveal the secret entrance to the headquarters. Like I said before, there is no going back. Are you ready?"

I nodded my head resolutely. I was ready. Well, as ready as a ten-year-old can think he is for a choice that was going to affect the remainder of his life.

"Here, hold the leads," said Wolf as he handed me the ropes attached to the llamas. I felt proud. One day, I would have my own pair of llamas.

Wolf walked over to what appeared to be natural cobblestone. He punched it and once he had gathered the small floating cobblestone into his inventory, I could see there was a lever behind it. Wolf pulled the lever and a small slot opened in the middle of the wall. Wolf quickly replaced the cobblestone in front of the lever and walked over to the slot. He stood there for five seconds before we heard, "Password?"

"Straight is the gate, and narrow the way, and few there be that find it," said Wolf.

There was a brief pause before the slot in the wall slid shut. A few more seconds passed and then the door in the wall swung inward.

Wolf looked down at me. "Give me those leads back. Welcome to wandering trader headquarters."

As we walked in through the passage, two wandering traders with spears leveled them at me and yelled, "Halt!"

"It's okay, fellas," said Wolf. "He's a foundling. He wants to join the Way."

One of the guards looked at Wolf and said, "Does he know the consequences of changing his mind?"

Wolf nodded his head. "I have asked him multiple times. He has never wavered."

The guards seemed satisfied and removed their spears from in front of me, permitting me to proceed. I wiped the sweat from my brow and trotted alongside of Wolf. "What was that all about?"

"I told you. The wandering traders are very secretive. Unless you are a wandering trader or are planning to become one, if you stumble upon this place ... hurrr ... you die."

I was surprised by the complexity of the wandering trader organization. *Like, they had a HQ and a secret password and guards and everything!*

I have to admit, I had always thought of wandering traders as ... well ... losers. They didn't have a permanent place to live and they didn't have any family or friends. But maybe I was wrong. Maybe this cave was their place to live and their fellow traders were family? Plus, any group of people who can keep a secret like this certainly weren't losers. But I suppose they could have still been very lonely.

Wolf led me down a few twists and turns inside the cave until we arrived at a large stable where Wolf deposited his two llamas. It looked to me like there were stalls for at least two hundred llamas, maybe more. However, only a small percentage of the stalls were in use. The rest of the llamas must have been out wandering with their handlers.

"Do you own your llamas?"

Wolf shook his head. "The Guild owns them. We are each assigned a pair to use. If they are hurt, lost, or killed, we have to pay for their care or replacement. And, if one of us dies, the llamas are handed down to the next wandering trader."

"So, when I become an official wandering trader, I'll get my own pair of llamas?" I said hopefully.

"Yes."

After we finished cleaning and feeding the llamas, we left the stable and walked through passageways for another few minutes. Wolf greeted people here and there before we came to a long passageway lined with doors. We walked past more than a dozen doors before Wolf stopped in front of one. "This is my room. Let me go put on some clean clothes and then I will take you to Wickham. He's our leader."

I was about to ask him more about Wickham when he slammed the door to his room in my face. I stood in the long curved hallway, brightly lit with torches. There were dozens of doors regularly spaced along the hallway. I assumed each of them housed a wandering trader. During the minute or so that I stood outside the door while Wolf changed his clothes, I didn't see or hear anyone else.

When Wolf emerged from his room, he was wearing a clean and better smelling outfit which was otherwise identical to the dirty and smelly one he had been wearing moments before. "Life on the road can get a bit dusty and dank, if you know what I mean. Feels good to put on clean clothes."

I nodded like I knew what he meant, but I had no idea. I had never even been on a camping trip with my parents. "Cool. Anyway, are we going to see this Wickham person now?"

Wolf nodded. "Just be polite and respectful. As I said, Wickham is our leader. You are new and you're a kid, so he'll let you make a few mistakes. But don't let that lull you into a sense of false security."

Had I made a big mistake? I was starting to feel really nervous and scared.

"I understand."

Wolf smiled and tousled my hair. "Okay, Kid, let's go."

Chapter 6

Wolf led me through numerous passages up and down and around. We passed a few dozen wandering traders here and there going about their various tasks. It seemed like some were cleaning the passageways, others were doing laundry, and others were making different types of food. It seemed strange to me. Prior to arriving at this place, the only thing I knew about wandering traders was what I'd seen on the surface of the Overworld: Some guy pulling a couple of llamas and trading. It seemed there was **a lot** more to it than that.

Eventually we came to a long flight of stairs leading upward. We climbed the stairs for what seemed like several minutes. My legs were tired by the time we made it the top. "Are we going to go back to the surface of the Overworld? This is crazy."

Wolf laughed. "It feels like it, doesn't it? It is a few hundred steps."

When we *finally* got to the top of the ridiculous stairs, there were two guards standing in front of a large oaken door. The guards crossed their spears in front of the door and one of them said, "State your business."

Wolf sighed. "Wayne, it's Wolf. You know me. I'm here with a foundling. He wants to join the Way."

Wayne looked annoyed at Wolf because he had used his name instead of addressing him more formally, but he raised his spear and said, "Proceed Trader Wolf with your objective." The door then opened as if by magic and we walked inside.

Inside the room was a humble table and several chairs. Sitting in one of the chairs was an old man. He had once been very strong and powerful, I'm sure. He still appeared very tall, even sitting down. He had gray hair and a long, thick gray beard. His eyes twinkled, but it looked as though they might not focus as well as they had in the past.

When we entered, he stood up from the chair, verifying his above-average height, despite the slight stoop in his back. "Wolf! Welcome back. Good to see you." Upon noticing me, he raised an eyebrow and then looked back at Wolf. "I see you've brought a new recruit with you?"

Wolf nodded politely. "Yes, great Wickham. This child's village was being destroyed by pillagers. I saw them kill his parents right in front of him. I put a stop to it. After questioning, he said he wanted to become a wandering trader."

Wickham stroked his gray beard thoughtfully. "Is this true, child?"

"Yes, it is," I said in a shaky voice.

Wickham chuckled. "You don't seem so certain."

I shrugged. "I'm just a bit nervous. Wolf said you are a really formal person."

Wolf shot me a look.

"Did he now?" said Wickham. "Well, I suppose in most cases I am. But let's do away with the formalities just for today, shall we?"

I took a deep breath and sighed. "That would make me feel a lot better, I think," I said.

Wickham smiled and approached me. "Why do you want to become a wandering trader?"

"I don't know. I mean, my parents are dead," I said, fighting back tears. "I am alone now. And, Wolf says he will help me get revenge on the pillagers once I pass the training."

Wickham shot a quick side-eyed glance at Wolf and then looked back at me. "Vengeance is a powerful motivator. But if you don't control it, it can overtake you."

I really had no idea what he meant by that but I said, "I see."

"You understand that the training in the Way takes several years, do you not?" asked Wickham.

"I remember Wolf saying something like that."

"And you also know that once you join the Way of the Wanderer, you have to follow the Way or else be **removed** from the Way."

"I think I heard something about that too."

"And you know you have to obey any directive given to you by a superior, including me, right?"

"Yeah, that makes sense, I guess."

I looked over at Wolf. There was some concern in his eyes as he watched the interaction between Wickham and me. I wouldn't understand what that concern meant for many years.

Wickham smiled. "Then it is settled. You can begin the training. But first, what is your name?"

"Kevin."

A look of disappointment and perhaps even disgust crossed Wickham's face. "Oh, no, no, no. That will not do. Your name must begin with a W. Are you willing to relinquish your birth name to become a wandering trader?"

I shrugged. Kevin was an okay name, but I never was really attached to it one way or the other. "Yeah, sure, I guess."

"Excellent," said Wickham as he walked over to his bookshelf and pulled out a book. I saw a bookmark sticking out the top of the book; Wickham turned to the marked page. "Let's see. What is the next available name on the list? Ah, here it is. Winston. Your name is now Winston the wandering trader."

"Winston," I said, trying it out. "I like it."

Wickham smiled, drew a line through the name "Winston" in the naming book, and placed the book back in the bookshelf. "I'm glad you like it. You'll never have another one."

Chapter 7

I was placed into a dormitory with six other initiates varying in age from eleven to fifteen. All the recruits except one had been training for nearly a year. I didn't spend much time with them except at mealtimes and bedtime. Everyone seemed pretty cool. I was expecting there to be some bullying behavior, but apparently the training in the Way removed that and no one bullied anyone.

There was one of the initiates who had only been at HQ for a couple of weeks. His new name was Wynter, spelled with a Y instead of an I.

Wynter was eleven years old and had a story similar to mine. He and his parents had been at a neighbor's house for a late supper. As they walked home after dark, two skeletons began to attack them. His parents were killed and he survived only when a player happened along and killed the two skeletons.

Wynter initially went to an orphanage in Capitol City, but didn't like it very much. He was complaining about it to another kid in the streets when a wandering trader overheard him and made him an offer to begin the training in the Way.

The first morning of my training, I put on my wandering trader robes, and waited for instructions. I was surprised when they came from Wynter himself.

"Winston, I was instructed to have you come with me. We're going to work at the same task."

I smiled. "Okay. That's great."

Wynter rolled his eyes. "Maybe. You'll see."

I followed Wynter for a few minutes until we came to a familiar room. The llama stable. Winter pointed to a shovel on the wall. "Grab one. We have to clean up the llama poop."

I slumped my shoulders in defeat. I knew there was no way of getting out of this. I walked over to the wall and grabbed a shovel. "How long do we have to do this?"

"All day. Wickham wants all the new recruits to shovel llama poop all day long until he feels we are ready for the next step in our learning process."

*Maybe I **had** made a bad decision about becoming a wandering trader?*

I will spare you the details of cleaning the llama stables. But I will tell you that I had to do it for three straight months. In the final month, I had to do it all alone, because Wynter had progressed to the next stage of his training.

When Wickham had decided I had learned enough humility by shoveling literal metric tons of llama poop, I was permitted to move on to the next training: stealth and sneaking.

In that class I learned why it was that Wolf seemed to be able to walk without being seen in the field of vision of the pillagers and those players on our way to wandering trader HQ. We were taught certain ways to hold our body and move our feet and hands. Ways to hold our robes. The colors chosen for the wandering trader robes specifically create a type of visual blindness in others observing it at certain angles. It wouldn't seem that way at first glance, given that the robes are blue, red, and yellow, but the camouflage is effective if you use the right techniques.

After several months of stealth training, I was permitted to go out with Wolf on a wander. The point of my presence was to observe his behavior from a distance without being seen and for me to attempt to walk in the field of vision of players without being spotted by them.

On the day we left headquarters, it was raining. "Aww, man! I've been inside that stupid cave for almost a year and I have to come out to this?" I whined.

Wolf snapped his head around at me. "Winston. Complaining is not acceptable within the Way."

I took a deep breath and calmed myself. "Of course, you are correct. I apologize."

That was something else I had been taught. In all the classes the teachers constantly emphasized that the Way is about sacrifice, the greater good, selflessness, and most importantly, obedience. When I remembered to focus on those things instead of my own ego, I felt calm and centered. I felt like my life mattered and didn't, all at the same time. If my life is to serve the Way, which is a greater purpose, then minor problems like a cold rain are easily endured.

After leaving the entrance to HQ, we wandered for several hours before we spotted a player walking along the side of a creek holding a fishing rod. "Okay, Winston. Let's give it a shot. I want you to go to the other side of the creek and hide behind a rock. When I appear to the player and begin interacting with him, I want you to emerge from behind the rock and walk along the creek for twenty paces before hiding behind another rock. If the player doesn't see you, it will be a success."

I nodded my head. "I'm on my way." I trotted down to a narrow part of the creek and crossed it. Then, I walked up to an area just outside of the player's field of vision and hid behind a rock. I then watched as Wolf slowly approached the player and then stood in front of him.

The player gasped in surprise. "Where did you come from?"

"I come to those who need me. Can I interest you in a trade?" asked Wolf.

That was my cue. I stood up and, using the techniques I had been taught, made my way slowly along the opposite side of the creek, plainly in view of the player and Wolf. Nevertheless, walking in the required position with the robes held at correct angles, I made it the required twenty paces and hid behind a rock without being detected.

I pumped my fist in silence. *Yes! I rule!* As I leaned against the rock, I had a big smile on my face. I had succeeded in my first test. Soon enough, I would be able to get my revenge on those pillagers.

After Wolf had completed his trade with the player, we continued on. In between the time we left the prior player and found another player with whom to trade, I asked Wolf about his life. He didn't answer all my questions but he answered some of them.

"What's the coolest thing you've ever done as a wandering trader?" I asked.

"I suppose that depends on your definition of cool. But, there was this one time I was wandering around in the snow biome. A polar bear and her cubs are wandering just off in the distance. Using my stealth, I was able to get within two blocks of the cubs and observe them. Eventually, they detected my scent and ran off."

I shook my head. "Are you telling me that you were able to approach two polar bear clubs in an all-white environment wearing your wandering trader clothes? Is that even possible?"

Wolf smiled. "I didn't think it was possible either. That is why I tried to do it."

I didn't know if I believed him. I still didn't think you could get that close to polar bears unless you were wearing an all-white outfit or a polar bear skin or something. But the sentiment made sense. Just because people tell you it's impossible doesn't mean it is. And you never know unless you try.

Eventually, we came to another player. This player looked fairly dominant. The player was wearing full diamond armor and had an enchanted sword. When we came upon him, he was attending to his large farm near his well-built home.

"Okay, Winston, this time I want you to go around the back of that hill over there and then wait for one minute. By then I will be engaged in trade with the player. I want you to stand up and walk over the top of the hill down to the bottom and then walk back behind it. You'll be in plain view of the player for at least thirty seconds. If he doesn't see you, you'll be making very good progress."

I smiled. I could totally do this.

I trotted off and hid behind the hill and then counted the seconds until one minute had passed. Then, I stood up and walked over the top of the hill. I could see Wolf was indeed trying to talk the player into a trade.

I began to move slowly down the hill, using the stealth movements I had been taught. I was varying my walking gait and changing the course of my path. I held my cloak perfectly. It was going very well until I struck my toe on a rock. I didn't scream out or anything, but there was a slight hitch in my step which must have drawn the player's attention.

I saw the player point and shout, "Is that a little kid wandering trader? I didn't know there was such a thing."

Wolf looked over and tried to cover for me. "I don't see anything."

"Are you blind as well as stupid?" said the player. "He's standing right there. He's walking down the hill directly at us."

I could see Wolf in the distance sigh and shake his head. I was trying to regain my stealth, but it apparently had been lost completely. Wolf reached into his inventory and pulled out his enchanted axe and chopped off the player's head. The player disappeared into a puff of smoke.

I screamed, "What are you doing?!?" I rushed toward Wolf. "Why would you kill a player just because he saw me?"

"That is the Way. No one is aware that there are wandering trader trainees. If word of this got out, I would be executed for betraying the Way, and so would you."

This is as crazy as a mushroom and carrot cookie.

"What are you talking about? What have I gotten myself into?"

Wolf sighed and shook his head. "I told you. There's no going back. You could've lived a fine life as an orphan, but you chose this Way. Now you know what it is truly like: Bloody and uncompromising."

I stood and looked at the drop pile left by the player. I'd only been in training for about eleven months. I still wasn't even eleven years old, and now my small mistake cost a player's life and all his wealth. I looked up at Wolf. "So the price of my failure is the death of someone else? That doesn't make any sense."

"That is the Way," said Wolf flatly.

I sucked my teeth and then inhaled deeply through my nostrils. I held my breath. And then I slowly exhaled. "In that case, I shall never fail again."

Chapter 8

My stealth and sneaking training continued for another six months, including weekly outings with Wolf and occasionally with other wandering traders. I did not have any failures that resulted in the deaths of players, except one. I was recovering from an illness and I probably should not have gone out that day, but I did.

I was attempting to sneak near a noob player who was talking to Wolf. It should have been easy to walk past him without him noticing, but I sneezed. Obviously, my stealth was lost. Wolf made me kill the player, as a lesson for my foolishness.

I was only eleven years old.

That player was the first **anything** I had ever killed. It was hard, doing the same thing that the pillagers had done to my family and to the members of my village. And yet ... it was at the same time so very easy. The noob only had leather pants and a T-shirt. The sword Wolf gave me easily killed him.

I felt sad but then Wolf told me that players can respawn. At worst, the player would lose all his possessions. But, because he was a noob, he would not have many and it would not be difficult to start over.

Wolf's revelation about the reincarnation of players gave me a sudden hope. "Do villagers respawn? Are my mom and dad alive somewhere?" I reached my hand into my inventory and gave Creepy a brief squeeze. (I carried him with me everywhere.)

Wolf shook his head. "I've never heard of anything like that."

* * *

I completed my sneaking and stealth training when I was about eleven and one-half years old. After that, I began to learn self-defense skills. These included grappling, karate, muay thai, jujitsu, and several others. That was another year of training. It included excursions to fight skeletons and zombies using only my hands. I was severely wounded several times at the beginning, but Wolf or another wandering trader trainer was always there with a healing potion and a quick sword just in case.

Once we were skilled in the art of self-defense, we learned the art of attacking with weapons. We began with the standard basic stuff, learning swordplay, bows and crossbows. We graduated to tridents and spears and explosives. That all seemed fairly normal. But then we began to learn the skills of the ninja and assassination.

By now, I was fourteen years old and beginning to question things, including my decision to join the Way. Once I learned that I was being trained to assassinate people, I pulled Wolf aside and asked him about it. "Are wandering traders assassins?"

By his expression I could tell Wolf was measuring his words carefully. He thought for nearly ten seconds before he spoke. "Wandering traders occupy a space that no one else can in the world of Minecraft. We are between everything and beholden to no one. Sometimes ... hurrr ... we have to act decisively."

*That was a very vague and diplomatic way of saying **nothing**, I think?*

"So you're saying that sometimes wandering traders *are* assassins?"

Wolf looked side-to-side to make sure we were alone and said, "Perhaps. You will learn more about that later. In the political training. That comes at the end."

And so I continued my assassination and ninja training, which combined the previous stealth and weapons trainings, but added strategy, subterfuge, traps, and poisons to the arsenal. Although I wasn't quite happy with the thought of assassinating people – especially if I didn't know for what purpose I was killing them – these swift and silent killing abilities likely would come in handy when I got my revenge on the pillagers.

To practice assassination, we would sneak up on various mobs, especially skeletons and zombies and husks, in the Overworld and occasionally would travel to the Nether to attack zombie pigmen and, when we got very advanced, blazes.

I'm not trying to say I was some sort of super dominant beast, but by the time I was fifteen, I could handle myself against just about anything the world of Minecraft could throw at me. At least on an individual level. (Of course, I had never faced a wither or the ender dragon.)

And then, finally we came to the "political training," as Wolf had called it. This was conducted by Wickham himself. There were only two of us in the class at this time, Wynter and myself. Everyone else being either older and already past this training or younger and not ready for the training.

On the appointed day, we were directed to Wickham's chambers, where I had first met him years ago and where he had given me my name. Wynter and I sat down in uncomfortable chairs while Wickham, looking increasingly hunched over and ever-closer to death, explained to us the purpose of the wandering trader organization.

"When wandering traders first appeared in the world of Minecraft, they were indeed merely that ... wandering traders, lost souls trying to scrape together a living. They were made fun of by villagers and players alike. They were attacked mercilessly by mobs during the day and the night.

"But then one of them, our first leader, Walter, convinced several of his fellow wandering traders to band together as a group. They wandered together to trade as a group for safety purposes. After a few years of growing success, many groups of settled villagers got upset. They thought maybe the wandering traders were going to be able to provide all the needs of the players and take away emeralds from the established villagers. And so an army – more of a mob, really – of villagers attacked the wandering traders and broke them up, forcing them to trade alone once more.

"Walter pretended to acquiesce, but instead formed a secret society. He first built this room in which you are now sitting. He and his fellow wandering traders dug the first passages of what is now this monumental headquarters underground.

"And, Walter himself created our creed. A wandering trader may wander alone but is never alone. A wandering trader who follows the Way is always protected. A wandering trader will never be weak again.

"And so that is what we do. We perform as individuals, but always putting the greater good ahead of everything else. The greater good includes the requirement that you obey everything I say or, upon my death, which my successor says. That is how we maintain our order and our strength."

Wickham paused, allowing us to absorb what he had just said. It also seemed that he was waiting for questions, so I asked one.

"So do you control the items we are allowed to trade?"

Wickham smiled. "No. You can trade whatever you want, unless I issue a prohibition. But I have never done that. I think in the history of the wandering trader Guild there has only been one such proclamation ... to prevent the extinction of a particular flower, if I recall correctly."

Wynter asked the next question. "How long has the wandering trader Guild existed?"

"Several generations," said Wickham. "And for several generations it has remained hidden from the rest of Minecraft. We need to keep it that way."

I wasn't sure if I should ask the next question. But Wolf told me this was the time I would learn. So I had to know. "Are we assassins? Hired killers?"

Wickham leaned back in his chair and tapped his fingers together. "I'm not surprised to get this question. In fact, I was surprised it wasn't the first question. The short answer is ... 'sometimes'."

"Why?" I asked.

"Sometimes, in order to secure economic stability, certain ... hurrr ... roadblocks must be eliminated."

"Who decides what is a roadblock?" asked Wynter.

Wickham leaned back in his chair and contemplated his answer for a few seconds. "Usually it is I who makes such decisions. But sometimes others make suggestions, and we agree."

"Others? Like who?" I asked.

Wickham shook his head. "That is not something to be shared with those of you who interface with the world at large."

I knew he was hiding something. I also knew he wasn't going to reveal that information to a fifteen-year-old trainee. I would figure it out eventually, I was certain. But for now, I just had to accept it.

"Are there any more questions?"

Wynter shrugged and shook his head. I said, "No."

"In that case, please go meet with your mentors. They will take you into the Overworld for one final test. If you succeed, you will be allowed to become a wandering trader by yourself."

Chapter 9

Early the next morning, before the sun had fully risen, there was a knock on my door. (I had been given an individual room in the dormitory about a year ago.) I stumbled out of bed and tossed on my wandering trader robes. When I opened the door, I saw Wolf standing there.

"Let's go."

I rubbed my eyes. "I thought we weren't leaving for like an hour?"

"We aren't," said Wolf. "But we have to select your llama team."

I totally forgot about that. If I were going to wander, I would need my own pair of llamas. Every prior wander, I had always been with a wandering trader who used his own pair of llamas. I was actually pretty excited. It almost felt like Notchmas.

"So, do I have to buy them?"

Wolf chuckled. "No. The wandering trader Guild owns all of the llamas. But, if they die or wander off while you have them in the Overworld, you're responsible for the cost of acquiring and raising another team of llamas."

Wolf led the way to the llama stable. When we got there, he led me to a section of the stable where there were three pairs of llamas in adjacent pens. Wolf swept his hand across the three pairs and said, "Check it out. You can have whichever pair you want. But choose carefully. You'll be stuck with that pair until they die ... or you do."

I looked at Wolf. "Is there really much difference amongst llamas?"

Wolf nodded his head. "Any llama can carry your goods for you. But some are better at protecting you than others. Some can be stubborn. You want the protective, obedient kind."

This would've been so much easier if llamas could talk. I could have given each a job interview or something.

"So where did all these pairs of llamas come from?"

"Well the first two pairs used to belong to wandering traders who were killed by vicious players. The llamas wandered back to HQ of their own accord as they have been trained to do. The third pair is untested. They have been raised by the Guild since they were spawned, but they have not gone out to the world."

I walked up to the first pair and saw from their nametags they were called Patricia and Victoria. Those were kind of boring names, but this was not a name contest. I walked around the llamas and inspected them. They seemed okay. I petted Patricia, and she seemed to like it. When I petted Victoria, she tried to kick me in the head. I backed away from her and as I did, I stepped in a big llama poop.

"Ha ha," laughed Wolf as he pointed to my foot. "You need to be more careful."

I walked out of the llama pen with a scowl on my face and wiped the poop off using the poop wiping stick which was conveniently located outside each stall. I looked at Wolf. "I don't want those two, especially not that Victoria."

Wolf smiled and moved on to the next pen. These two llamas were named Buffy and Felicity. At first glance, they looked a bit shabby. Like the prior owner had not taken good care of them or they were just getting old. I walked up to Buffy and pulled open her mouth to inspect her teeth. They were starting to look a little cracked. I walked over to Felicity and noticed that her stomach was bit flabby, like she hadn't been used as a pack animal in a long time.

I looked over my shoulder and asked Wolf, "When was the last time anyone used this pair?"

Wolf leaned forward and grabbed the chart attached to the pen and flipped through it. "Wow! It says here that the last time this pair was used was two years ago."

"No wonder this one is getting so fat," I said as I walked out of the pen. "Anyway, I guess they'd be all right but I would prefer if they were in better shape. Let's check out the third pair."

I walked into the third pen and saw that the young, newly-trained llamas were very excited. Their names were Sunny and Pippa. I walked up to Sunny and the hackle on her back stood up! *What?* I realized she was scared of me, or maybe just having an anxiety attack. But, once I started to pet her, she calmed down and tried to lick me in the face. I wasn't having any of that.

"Eww. Gross," I said as I gently pushed her face away from me.

I then looked at Pippa. When I petted her, her hair felt startlingly soft, especially for a llama. She had a kind of dopey look in her eyes and her tongue was hanging out of her mouth, but she seemed nice and compliant.

I walked around and inspected both of the llamas. Because they were young, they didn't have any obvious physical defects or excess weight on them. It might be a risk using an untested llama team, but they were definitely the best physical specimens of the three pairs. I walked out of the pen and said to Wolf, "I'll take these two."

Wolf smiled. "Great. Grab the leads and we will check them out with the stable hands."

I grabbed the leads. Sunny and Pippa came willingly and followed me as we headed for the exit of the stable.

The stable was being administered at that early hour by a wandering trader trainee who was a year younger than I was. We had hung out a few times. He was kind of a jerk. His name was Wes. As I signed the paperwork to take responsibility for this pair of llamas, Wes said bitterly, "I wanted that pair. I did half the training myself."

I shrugged. "Sorry man. First-come first-served."

"You're stupid, Winston."

"Maybe, but I am also about to become a full-fledged wandering trader, while you're stuck scooping llama poop."

Wes stood up and pulled a sword from his inventory. "You take that back!"

Wolf quickly grabbed Wes' hand and pulled the sword from it. "Enough of this. If one of you speaks another ill word, I'll report you to Wickham."

At that moment, I realized what Wes had been trying to do. He wanted me to lash out at him, and be punished so that I wouldn't pass my test. Instead of saying anything back, I just calmly smiled at him as I pulled Sunny and Pippa away from the stable and out into the world.

Chapter 10

Wolf and I had been walking for about an hour away from headquarters when I realized I had no direction or purpose. "Is there anywhere I'm supposed to go for this test? I mean, I know this is a final test of everything," I said.

Wolf shrugged. "Well, your test is whether you can be a wandering trader, so we are just wandering. Where we wander is up to you."

I nodded my head. It made sense in a bizarre sort of way. "But, I *am* supposed to *trade*, right? So, is there anywhere I should go to make it more likely to meet players?"

Wolf smiled. "You are thinking like a true wandering trader. I would suggest heading toward the village of Zombie Bane. It's about a day and a half walk from here. It's a fairly large village and I know a lot of players visit it for supplies. It has a fairly robust economy on its own, but you should be able to catch some players coming and going."

I smiled. "That sounds good." I reached into my inventory, pulled out my map, and held it in front of Wolf. "Where is Zombie Bane on the map?" Wolf pointed out the location of the village and we began to walk in that direction.

* * *

After some time had passed, I began quizzing Wolf about what he would be looking for when grading me. "I mean, do I have to make a certain number of trades? Do I have to avoid being seen by players at certain moments? What's the story?"

Wolf chuckled and shook his head. "I'm telling you, it's pretty simple. You just have to wander for a while and make some trades. As long as you do things the way a wandering trader would do them, you'll pass."

I was feeling very anxious and excited. I reached in my inventory again and gave Creepy a squeeze. I know it seems weird for a nearly sixteen-year-old who was about to become a wandering trader to need to squeeze his creeper action figure to keep himself comfortable, but it was my coping mechanism. Don't judge.

As we were wandering through a ravine carved over the years by a small stream, we spotted a player at the far end. Wolf tapped me on the shoulder and said, "I'm going to go hide and observe. Try to make a trade."

Wolf vanished and I continued forward, exercising my stealth in order to try to get the element of surprise with the player. One thing we were taught is that when a person is surprised, the person tends to lower his defenses, making it easier to trade with him and to make worse trades with him for your benefit. I stealthily moved amongst the rocks and boulders, concealing myself until I was just a few blocks away from the player. The player was wearing a full suit of iron armor and was leading a horse behind him.

"A good day to you, player," I said. "Have you a need for anything? I am a wandering trader who can provide it for you."

The player looked at me with angry eyes. "You guys stink. I hate you and your trades."

I smiled in the face of these insults. "But you have not seen my stock yet. Perhaps you would like to see it?"

The player shook his head. "Get out of my way, freak. I'm going diamond mining today."

"Perhaps a strong pickaxe then?"

"Go. Away. Loser."

I felt that this was my first real test. I could keep pushing him and trying to get him to buy something, which could lead to him lashing out and trying to kill me. The other option was to simply back away. Feeling that discretion was the better part of valor and killing the first player I ran into during my test was probably not what Wolf wanted to see, I stepped aside and allowed the player to continue.

"Good day to you, sir. Should you ever need anything in the future, keep an eye out for your friendly wandering trader."

"Go to the Nether, freak," said the player as he moved past me.

A few minutes later Wolf joined me. "Don't worry. You'll meet a lot of players like that," he said. "I think you handled it right. I sensed he was about to kill you ... or at least try. We know what would've happened...."

I smiled. As a villager growing up, I never wanted to be a hard-edged killer, and I still didn't, but it was nice to have the ability to kill or at least defend myself if necessary.

"Yeah, we do know what was going to happen," I said confidently.

Wolf smiled. "Let's get going. You haven't passed your test yet."

I suppose I could describe the next couple days in this diary, but I will spare you the agony. Hours of wandering aimlessly and then running into a player here and there. I made half a dozen trades by the time I arrived outside Zombie Bane and had half a dozen encounters with angry players who hated me and my kind.

In order to avoid possible hostility from its residents, we didn't go into Zombie Bane. I was impressed by its size. The village in which I had grown up housed maybe fifty families. Zombie Bane appeared to be a small city to me, housing hundreds if not thousands of families.

As Wolf and I sat on a hilltop overlooking Zombie Bane, Wolf said, "Have you ever heard the story of Cornelius, Bane of Zombies?"

I shook my head.

"Apparently, a bunch of zombies entered the town one evening about one hundred years ago. This Cornelius character actually got a sword and went out killed them all. He is some sort of folk hero among these villagers. They've got a whole cottage industry of souvenirs and such devoted to his memory. Apparently, villagers from throughout the Overworld like to come here to pay homage to Cornelius."

I nodded my head as I scratched the dirt with a stick. "My village could've used a Cornelius type when it was attacked by those pillagers."

Wolf reached out and put his hand on my shoulder. "I don't think even a Cornelius could've stopped those guys. You would've needed at least a dozen wandering trader assassins to stop that raid."

I took a deep breath and sighed. "I really hope I pass this test, Wolf. I want to get my revenge. It has been years deferred."

Wolf moved his hand off my shoulder and smiled. "You're passing so far. And, during the past few weeks, I have been doing some reconnaissance on the pillager outpost from which the raid came. We will get them all right. Just don't do anything stupid between now and the time we get back to HQ and we can go get our revenge as soon as you want."

I smiled. "Thanks, Wolf."

The sun was beginning to set, so we found a small wooded area and put our beds down in between the trees. We strung some ropes around the trees, enclosing the area where we were going to sleep in order to form a makeshift corral for my llamas.

We ate a simple dinner of bread, dried meat, and apples, washed down with a bottle of water. As our campfire began to burn low, we punched our beds. There were no monsters nearby, so we were able to fall asleep.

* * *

When we woke up the next morning, I told Wolf that I wanted to begin wandering back to headquarters. He said that was fine and would comply with the parameters of the test. "Just be sure to take a different route back than the one we took to get here," he said.

On the way back, I made multiple trades with various players and also encountered several of the typical angry players. I was able to diffuse or avoid all of these situations ... except for one.

I spotted a player who was fishing in a river. I stealthily snuck up next to him and then made myself visible right next to him. "Good day to you, sir. I'm here to trade."

The player yanked his fishing pole out of the water and threw on the ground. He pointed a finger in my face and said, "How dare you disturb me when I'm fishing?!? I hate you guys."

I took a step back from the very angry player and said, "Perhaps I could interest you in a cookie? That might make you feel better."

Without a word the player reached into his inventory and pulled out a diamond sword. He pulled it back and slashed at me. I deftly stepped out of the way of the blade, much to the surprise of the player.

"Hold still so I can kill you!" He shouted with rage.

This was the test. *Did I kill the player as I knew I could or did I try to diffuse the situation and risk injury? Or, I could use the third option which I had never used before other than a couple of times in a classroom setting.*

The player pulled his sword back again was about to slash at me when I quickly drank a potion of invisibility and then took five steps back so that I was nowhere near his sword as it sliced through the empty air.

"Where did you go?!? Come back here so I can kill you like the dog that you are!" said the player.

I continued backing away, leading the llamas with me. When the player noticed the llamas wandering away, I could see in his face that he got an idea. "Well, if you are too much of a coward to face me, then your llamas are going to suffer the consequences." He rushed toward the llamas to strike them down, but as he got close to the rear end of Sunny, she kicked him in the head and knocked him out.

I heard belly laughing coming from behind a large rock where Wolf had hidden to observe this interaction. I started laughing too.

Wolf came out from behind the rock and walked up to me. "That player was a real pain. I wonder what he so angry about?"

I shook my head even though I was still invisible and Wolf couldn't see it. "I don't know. It seems like about one-third of players are really angry at wandering traders for some reason. It's like, what did we ever do to you?"

"Players are weird, man. I think that's why the wandering traders have expanded into methods of earning money beyond trading, as a way to diversify their income stream."

Now that I had been out in the world with these players all by myself, his statement made some sense. "But hey, Wolf, when I was training with you, it didn't seem like the players got angry with you very often. What's your secret?"

"You know, I think maybe you're trying to sell too hard. I like to just kind of appear and stand still. Once I make eye contact if they don't say anything, then I offer a trade. Maybe you are just coming on a little too strong?"

I nodded my head. I looked down at my body and saw that I had finally begun to return to visibility. "Maybe you're right."

We left the unconscious the player on the ground and wandered away.

* * *

After another day and night of relatively uneventful wandering during which I made five trades and avoided upsetting any players, we arrived back at HQ. We returned my llamas to the stable and checked them in with the stable hand. Wes the jerk was gone and it was an older wandering trader who was running the stable.

No llama drama this time.

After the llamas had been cleaned and bedded down, Wolf took me to see Wickham and announced that I had passed the test.

Wickham smiled broadly at the news. "Congratulations, Winston. You are now officially a wandering trader."

"Cool! Do I get a diploma or something?"

"There is nothing to give you. You already wear the robes of the wandering trader. You don't get a diploma or a gift certificate or a ring or necklace or a key fob or anything like that. You just now have all the privileges of the wandering trader and it will be known throughout the Guild that you have shown the knowledge to wander in the Way."

I smiled. "Thank you, Wickham." I wanted to ask him something else but I thought it was kind of silly so I didn't.

"Winston, I can tell you have something on your mind," said Wickham. "Spit it out."

"Do I get a room away from the student dormitory now?"

Wickham and Wolf both chuckled. "I can remember feeling that way too," said Wolf.

"As do I," said Wickham. "Yes, you will get a new room within the next few weeks. For now, you'll have to make do with your room in the dormitory, but you can come eat with the wandering traders and not the students if you'd like."

"Thank you," I said as I bowed and then backed away from Wickham.

Wolf and I walked down the long flight of stairs from Wickham's chamber. As we were walking down the stairs, I said to Wolf, "I want to get my revenge tomorrow. Does that work for you?"

Wolf looked at me and smiled. Torch light gleamed off his teeth. "Perfectly."

Chapter 11

Wolf and I left at first light the next morning. We did not take any llamas with us. Wolf had been planning this for a long time, anticipating that when I passed my test I would want to seek revenge as soon as possible. He was right.

Before we left, I stopped at Wolf's room and he showed me the array of weapons and explosives he had been gathering for the past few months. "Pack as much of that TNT into your inventory as you can. You are going to need it."

I managed to fit nearly one hundred blocks of TNT in my inventory. "Just blow them all up and call it good? Is that the plan?" I asked.

"It might be a wee bit more complicated than that," said Wolf. "Grab a bow and some arrows. I enchanted the bows so they will shoot flaming arrows. And make sure you have several swords. Whoever survives the initial attack is going to be angry and coming at us. Hard."

I nodded my head. "I guess I get to test out my training for real." Wolf didn't say anything.

Within a few minutes we had completed our packing, and walked to the cave exit of HQ. The guard on duty asked us if we had forgotten our llamas.

"No, we haven't, Wenceslaus. Just going on a ... hurrr ... personal errand," said Wolf.

Wenceslaus shrugged his shoulders and opened the door to the cave. "In that case, have fun."

"I will," I said with menace.

We traveled quickly, wanting to get to the pillager outpost before nightfall so we could assess the current situation there. We didn't stop walking all day, we ate and drank as we moved. My feet hurt, but I shrugged it off. It was time for payback.

When we were within sight of the outpost, we found a hidden spot on the top of the hill. Wolf explained his plan. I liked it.

"When do we execute the plan?"

Wolf looked at the horizon. "It will be pitch black in about an hour. Let's ready our weapons, relax for a bit, and have a bite to eat. Once it's pure night, we strike."

* * *

An hour later Wolf and I were sneaking towards the outpost. There were several pillager guards wandering around the outpost, but not paying particular attention. It was easy to sneak past them using our techniques. Then, we each stealthily climbed up the walls of the outpost, planting TNT blocks at particular intervals and at the intersections of support beams. This took about twenty minutes. When we had finished, we climbed down and snuck away from the outpost.

Wolf looked at me. "Okay. I am going to ask you this one last time. Are you sure you want to kill all these pillagers? Personally, I am ambivalent."

"Absolutely. Revenge is a dish best served cold."

"In that case, ready your enchanted bow and get ready to shoot the TNT blocks. Let me go around the other side and get into position first."

I removed my bow, squeezing Creepy for good luck, and then removed a dozen arrows. It took about two minutes for Wolf to get into position on the other side of the outpost. When he gave me the signal – a brief howl – I notched my first arrow.

It had been a while since I'd practiced with a bow, so my first shot missed the TNT block and stuck into the side of the outpost, its small flame burning ineffectually. But, someone inside the outpost must have heard the impact because I saw a pillager stick his head out a window and look around.

At that moment, my second arrow flew true, landing in a TNT block and causing a massive explosion which killed the pillager looking out the window and then caused a chain reaction explosion up the side of the outpost.

On the other side, Wolf was having similar luck, his arrows landing home and causing a chain reaction explosion. Within ten seconds, the entire outpost had collapsed, killing at least half the pillagers instantly. The remainder of the pillagers were confused, running around looking for the source of the attack. In their confusion, Wolf and I were able to shoot another dozen of them with arrows, killing them. Finally there were only about eight pillagers remaining. They found us. Four came after me and four went after Wolf. I knew Wolf could handle himself and so I began to fight.

As the pillagers rushed toward me, I drank a potion of invisibility. The onrushing pillagers nearly collided with each other where I had been standing. I jumped behind one of the pillagers and slashed hard, cutting off his head. He flashed red and disappeared in a puff of smoke.

I may have been invisible but my sword wasn't. The pillagers rushed toward the floating sword and began to strike at the empty space behind it. I dropped the sword but not before I felt the felt the fire of a pillager blade entering the flesh of my left arm.

I rushed backward and pulled a TNT block from my inventory, ignited it, and tossed it toward the pillagers. They dove away from it, but not quickly enough. When the TNT exploded, one of the remaining pillagers was vaporized and one of the others suffered an arm injury. I rushed forward and stabbed the injured pillager to death.

I noticed my invisibility was beginning to wear off. I turned around and saw the final pillager. "Why are you attacking us?" asked the pillager. "We have a truce with the Guild."

That was news to me. Wickham cannot find out what I've done.

"This isn't a Guild matter," I said. "This is revenge for your attack on my village six years ago."

The pillager squinted at me. "You were once a villager?"

I nodded my head. "A desert villager. One of your men killed my parents right in front of me. I would be dead too if I hadn't been rescued by a wandering trader."

The pillager laughed. "I guess dying six years delayed is better than not dying at all. But after I kill you, there will be a rich price to pay by the Guild for this treason against the pillagers!"

I laughed. "Try it."

We rushed toward each other with our swords drawn, colliding with force, sparks flying and grunts issuing from our mouths. The pillager was extremely strong, but I was fast. I began to slash at him and was able to find home with my sword on his shoulder and then his side. He screamed in agony but continue to fight, slashing at me in a controlled, powerful way.

I was able to deflect his blows but then I heard Wolf scream in the distance where he was fighting. I was slightly distracted by the scream and the pillager managed to stab me in the upper chest, his sword going all the way through my body. I screamed and fell to the ground. I grabbed my shoulder trying to stop the flow of blood.

The pillager walked forward and stood over me, blood dripping from his wounds onto my cloak. "I thought you had me. But now, I have you. Any last words?"

I couldn't believe it had come to this. After all that training. All that practice. All this anticipation of my revenge. I got distracted by my friend's scream, and now I was going to die. But then, I had an idea.

"I just want to say goodbye to my creeper action figure," I said, purposefully trying to sound like a toddler.

The pillager laughed. "What a pathetic wimp. Okay, go ahead and say goodbye to your stupid doll."

I reached into my inventory and removed Creepy. I hugged it, pretending it was my baby.

"That's disgusting," said the pillager.

I looked at the pillager, hate in my eyes, and then smiled. "Creepy is not a doll; he's an action figure!" Then, I threw Creepy in the pillager's face, causing him to stumble backwards. This created just enough of a distraction that I could reach back into my inventory and pull out a splash potion of harming which I tossed right into the pillager's face. He screamed in pain and began slashing blindly with his sword, but I had already run away. I gave myself sufficient distance and removed a TNT block and tossed it at the pillager's feet. Then I quickly shot it with a fire arrow, causing an explosion. The pillager was gone.

I rushed toward where I had heard Wolf scream. I was expecting the worst, but that's not what I found. Wolf was standing there his hands on his knees panting, nearly out of breath. He looked up at me and smiled. He was breathing so hard that he could not speak, but managed to give me a thumbs up sign.

"Are they all dead?" I asked.

Wolf regained his ability to speak by then and said, "All of mine are."

I smiled. "Mine too."

Wolf straightened up and stretched his back. "So, how does revenge feel, kid?"

I took a deep breath and looked around at the destruction we had wrought. The entire outpost destroyed. Explosive craters everywhere. Pillager drop piles. "It feels great."

Chapter 12

After searching through the rubble to make sure we really had killed every last pillager, we collected any useful drops. I found Creepy on the ground, slightly singed from an explosion, but otherwise intact. We then returned to our camp site at the top of the hill. We took turns standing watch, just in case another group of pillagers might show up and search the area. But none did.

During my turn at watch, I reflected on my vengeance. Sure, it felt good to rid the Overworld of the scum that had killed my parents and destroyed my native village, but I had begun to feel uneasy about so much killing.

Would another group of pillagers try to track me down and get their revenge on me? Where would it stop?

I looked at the moon and the stars. I wondered what it would be like to visit the moon. I wondered if a villager or player would ever make it there.

I thought back to what the final pillager had said about working with the Guild. I was completely unaware of this alliance and it disturbed me.

When morning came, Wolf and I packed our belongings and then ate breakfast. As I chewed some bread, I asked, "Is there an alliance between the pillagers and wandering traders?"

Wolf stopped chewing for a moment before continuing. He swallowed what was in his mouth and took a long drink of water. "They have been known to help with transmitting messages and the occasional assassination. They only work for money. They have no honor."

I felt my face flush. I was getting angry. "Why didn't you tell me this before? I might not have become a wandering trader if I knew you worked with those murderous freaks."

"Calm down. When I rescued you, the Guild was not yet working with the pillagers. It is a recent development orchestrated by Wickham. I don't know the details."

"Any other scum working with the Guild?"

Wolf shrugged. "I don't know if I would call them 'scum,' but we have working relationships with the Wolf King and the Spider Queen."

I was shocked. "Relationships?!? So, can mobs talk?"

"When they want to. You'll see. They like to talk to wandering traders."

"Is there anything else you aren't telling me that I should know?" I asked.

Wolf smiled. "Probably, but I can't think of what it is right now."

I believed Wolf. I didn't think he was trying to hide anything from me. But, it was clear that the Guild, and more specifically, Wickham, was trying to hide things from me. *In what other nefarious plans and alliances were they involved?*

We finished breakfast and began our return trip to headquarters. It was an uneventful trip until we were about halfway home. We heard a couple of players laughing at something nearby. We snuck closer to the area from where the noise was coming until we could make out words.

"Come on, Bob, kill it!"

"I'm trying, Tom. It won't stop moving."

I looked at Wolf and whispered, "What do you think they are trying to kill?"

Wolf shrugged. "Let's go check it out."

We snuck forward until we could get a visual on what was happening. We saw that there were two large slimes and one baby slime. Judging by the way the large slimes were protecting the baby, I assumed it was their child rather than a random baby slime.

The two players were slashing at the large slimes who were trying to defend themselves but failing. Eventually the players chopped the two large slimes into medium slimes, then into small slimes until they had finally killed all the pieces. That left the baby slime all alone.

Bob and Tom looked at each other. "I think we should kill it," said Tom. "Otherwise, it's going to grow into an adult slime and try to get its revenge on us."

Where have I heard this story before?

Bob laughed. "Slimes are stupid. It won't be able to get revenge because it will be dead."

The players began to move forward to the baby slime. And that's when something snapped in me. I was reminded of the night my parents sacrificed their lives for me. I couldn't let this baby slime be killed.

I jumped up and rushed to the players. Wolf shout-whispered, "No! Don't do it!"

I didn't care. I ran up to the two players and without giving them a chance to surrender, mercilessly assassinated them.

The baby slime looked at me with fear in its eyes and backed away, fearful that I would kill it too. But I didn't. I put my sword back into my inventory and reached down and gently picked up the slime.

"Can you talk?" I asked. The slime made cooing and booping noises, but apparently was too young to be able to speak yet. "I wish I could talk to you, Child. I would tell you that everything is going to be alright. I'll be your new guardian."

Wolf arrived by my side a moment later. "It's not part of the Way to kill players unless the killing falls under a specific rule or arises from self-defense."

I shot a look at Wolf. "I was defending the life of another. Is that not the same as self-defense?"

"I guess, but it's ... hurrr ... it's a slime."

"Are you saying a slime has less right to be alive than us?"

"I'm not saying that, but now that you mention it...."

"Shut up. I'm taking charge of this child."

Wolf shook his head. "You realize that according to the Way, if you take the life of an orphan into your hands you have to protect it and see that it makes it to adulthood, just as I have with you."

I nodded my head. "I understand. Slimy here is going to be my traveling companion as I wander the surface of the Overworld."

Wolf rolled his eyes. "Suit yourself. Let's get back to headquarters. I've got a mission I need to take care of in the next couple of days, and you should probably relax for a couple days before you go out on your first required wandering."

I smiled. "Sounds good to me. Plus, I can get to know Slimy a little better."

"How do you think Creepy's going to react to having a little brother?" said Wolf with a chuckle.

I gave Wolf an angry, side-eyed look as I clutched Slimy to my chest. "You don't have to be rude."

Wolf chuckled again. "Come on. Let's get back to headquarters."

End of Book 1 of
The Ballad of Winston, the Wandering Trader

Book 2

Chapter 1

When Wolf and I returned to the wandering trader headquarters after completing my revenge against the pillagers, Wolf said goodbye to me and my new charge, Slimy. "See you later. I need to rest before I go on my assignment."

"What do you have to do?" I asked.

Wolf shook his head. "I never disclose my missions until after I'm done."

I felt as though he had assaulted me mentally. "You don't trust me? I'm not going to blow your cover. I can keep a secret."

Wolf shook his head again. "Trust has nothing to do with it. I wouldn't tell anyone. Even people I've known my entire life. It's just how I operate. I would suggest you do the same." He paused for a moment. "You know what the Great Walter the Wanderer said."

"Um, actually, I don't."

"He said that the best person is one who has cut off ties, gotten rid of chance, and renounced desires." Wolf paused for effect. "And, that is how I behave immediately before a mission so that I can be the *best person* when I conduct my mission."

I took a deep breath and sighed. "Okay, I get it. Still, it would be interesting to know what you're doing."

Wolf smiled and nodded his head. "I'm sure it would. And, well, this one is going to be pretty gnarly. You might hear about it before I even get back to HQ. It's going to be ... newsworthy."

"Oh, come on. Tell me."

Wolf chuckled. "You are persistent, at least. That trait will serve you well. Now, go get some rest. It looks like Slimy is about to fall asleep."

I looked at Slimy and saw that his eyes were beginning to close. "I guess you're right."

Wolf shook his head sadly. "Being a new dad is tiring. I'm not sure you made the best choice."

I clutched Slimy closer to myself. "I couldn't let him just be murdered."

Wolf shrugged. "Mobs are killed all the time in Minecraft. It's just part of life. That is the Way."

I knew he was correct, of course, but in the few brief hours that I had been Slimy's protector, I had grown very close to him. I didn't want anything to happen to him. I wondered if this was how my parents felt. Why they sacrificed their lives so that I would have a chance to live my own life.

"Anyway, see you later, Kid," said Wolf as he turned and walked away.

I waved goodbye to Wolf and then glanced at Slimy. He had fallen asleep now. I held him in the crook of my arm and began walking through the hallways back to my room. Several wandering traders walked past me and looked at the slime with confused looks on their face.

"Why do you have a slime?"

"Ewww, that's gross."

"Is he your new friend?"

I ignored all the insults and the questions and just kept walking. Within a few minutes I arrived at the door to my new single room. Unfortunately, Wes was standing there. Ever since I selected Sunny and Pippa as my llamas, he had hated me.

"What you got there, Winston?" he asked with a sneer.

"None of your business," I said.

"Looks like a disgusting little slime to me," said Wes.

"Aren't you still a trainee? What are you doing here in the **real** wandering trader quarters?" I asked.

Wes was taken aback by my statement. But, he realized that I was right and that he had no reason to be here and especially no reason to insult a full-fledged member of the Guild of the Wandering Traders.

I could see his eyes twitching back and forth as he thought about what he should do and considered the consequences of his stupidity by choosing to come here to taunt me. And then, his training in the Way kicked in and he stood ramrod straight and said, "I'm sorry, wandering trader Winston. I should not have come."

I squinted my eyes at him as I clutched Slimy to my chest. "That's right. Now, go away and leave me and Slimy alone."

Chapter 2

Once I was alone in my room, I put Slimy down on my bed. I then quickly crafted a small bed for Slimy and moved him onto it. I put a railing around the side so that he couldn't fall off at night when he was sleeping. It looked just like a baby's crib. As you may know, slimes, when they are sleeping, tend to quiver and bounce, running the risk of falling down from a high spot on which they may find themselves. I wanted to ensure that Slimy would be safe while he slept.

With Slimy safe in his new crib, I sat down at the small desk in my sparsely furnished room. I pulled out a notebook and recorded a summary of the events that recently had occurred to me. I included my passing of the wandering trader examination and the revenge raid on the pillager outpost. I also included a few paragraphs about rescuing Slimy and agreeing to be his protector. I was jotting down these notes in the hopes of one day writing a diary or a memoir in my old age. (Obviously, that is what you are reading now.)

I believe it is important to remember your life. No one else will ever care about those memories as much as you do.

After I had finished writing my notes, I checked on Slimy and saw that he was still sleeping. I decided to take a quick nap so that I would have energy to play with Slimy when he woke up later. I lay down on my bed and fell asleep quickly.

Unfortunately, about thirty minutes later there was a sharp knocking on my door which awakened me prematurely from my nap. I cracked my eyes open and sat up on the edge of the bed. I rubbed my face a couple times and tried to smooth out my hair before I put on my wandering trader robe. I walked to the door and opened it.

"Winston! Did you pass?" It was Wynter. I hadn't seen him since our final political education class with Wickham. I knew he had been about to take his wandering trader final exam as well.

I smiled. "I sure did. It didn't really seem all that difficult, did it?"

Wynter shook his head. "No. It seemed almost too easy. After all those years of training, I guess it should be."

I nodded my head. "It was fun to wander around while leading the llamas, especially because Wolf was still with me. I'm a bit worried that once I begin wandering around by myself, I will be bored and maybe even a bit lonely."

Wynter spotted Slimy sleeping in his little crib. "You won't get lonely while you have your squishy green traveling companion with you," he joked.

I looked over my shoulder and smiled at sleeping Slimy. I felt happy to see him safe. I was glad that I had chosen to save him. "Yeah, but he can't talk yet, so he can be a bit dull. At this time, he is more work than fun."

Wynter stepped through the door into my room without asking permission. It was a bit rude, but no big deal. I was informal. "So, what's the story with him? What was the situation when you encountered him?" asked Wynter.

I quickly explained how Wolf and I had stumbled upon two players mercilessly killing Slimy's parents. I told him about how I couldn't stand to watch such slaughter without doing something about it. And then how I killed the two players and rescued Slimy.

"Whoa, that sounds pretty intense! I'm not sure I would've saved the slime," said Wynter.

"We just have to do what will allow us to sleep at night, right?" I said, partly to let Wynter off the hook and partly to shame him for not caring enough about helping a defenseless baby mob.

Wynter looked slightly confused and ashamed. "Yeah," he said as he scratched the toe of his shoe against the floor. "I guess that's exactly what we have to do. Unless, of course, we are obeying the orders of one of our superiors."

"That is the Way," I intoned.

"Truly, it is," replied Wynter.

"So, when are you going on your first official solo wander?" I asked.

Wynter smiled at the thought. "In a couple of days. My training trader, Walden, told me I should relax a bit.

He says it can be a bit stressful being out there by yourself the first time."

I nodded my head. "Wolf said something similar. I also will be going out in a couple days. But, before then, I'm going to relax, eat a lot of food, and hang out with Slimy. I probably will spend most of my time in my room, so feel free to come by once in a while if you want to."

"Okay," said Wynter nodding his head. Something caught his eye and he looked over at the crib. "Say, it looks like the little booger boy is about to wake up. I had better bail."

"Dude. Booger boy?!? His name is **Slimy**. You can call him Slimy or the boy or the child, whichever you prefer, but not booger boy."

His name is *Slimy.*

Wynter rubbed his chin and looked up at the ceiling in thought. "I think I will call him Slimy. Easy to remember."

I rolled my eyes. "See you later, Wynter."
"Peace."

Chapter 3

The next couple of days were rather uneventful. I spent the majority of my time playing with Slimy, sleeping, and readying my supplies for my first solo wander.

I had decided that I would wander in the direction of a fairly large city called Creeper Junction. It was located about a day and a half to two days away from wandering trader headquarters. After speaking with several other traders, they said there were often players coming and going from the city who are amenable to trades. Furthermore, the city was big enough that they did not have any beef with wandering traders coming in and making trades on the streets of the city, unlike smaller villages where the residents believed wandering traders took away revenue.

I showed the map to Slimy and pointed at Creeper Junction. "What do you think about that, little guy? We're going to go to Creeper Junction."

Slimy, still too young to speak, said, "Beep. Boop."

I nodded my head. "That's what I thought. Anyway, I think we should leave first thing tomorrow morning. I've got Sunny and Pippa all loaded up with supplies and goods to trade. According to the map, there's a cave about halfway between here and Creeper Junction. If we leave early in the morning, we should arrive at the cave just before nightfall."

"Boop boop," said Slimy.

I laughed. "When are you going to learn how to speak properly?"

"Beep. Meep," said Slimy.

I laughed again. "You're no help."

At that moment there was a knocking on my door. I wasn't expecting anyone so I thought it might be Wynter again. I got up, walked to the door and opened it. It was Wayne, one of Wickham's guards.

"Winston, you are directed to come with me."

"Why?"

"You do not have the right to ask why. I am your superior," said Wayne, puffing out his chest. "However, I will tell you that Wickham wishes to speak with you." He looked over my shoulder and saw Slimy hopping around on the floor. "And bring that ... thing with you."

Rude.

"Fine. Do I need to bring anything else with me?"

Wayne shook his head. "Just you and the slime."

I walked over and scooped up Slimy. He had gotten a bit wound up when Wayne arrived, but he calmed down as I patted him on the head.

"That's disgusting," said Wayne.

I ignored his hateful comments and walked past him out the door, slamming it behind me.

* * *

We walked in silence to Wickham's chambers, up the long, ridiculous flight of stairs before arriving at the front door.

"Wait here," demanded Wayne.

Wayne walked up to the door and knocked softly and walked in. I heard voices before the door opened again and Wayne motioned me to enter. I walked up the final couple of stairs to the door and walked in.

"Winston, thank you for coming. And ... you've brought a friend," said Wickham.

I nodded my head. "You're welcome. This is Slimy."

Wickham looked at Wayne and said, "Leave us." Wayne obeyed, backing out the door before shutting it. After the door was secured, Wickham continued. "I heard the rumors that you had brought a slime baby into the headquarters, but I didn't believe them until now."

Slimy was twitching in my arms, so I patted his head to calm him. "I sure did. I rescued him from being killed by a couple of brutal players."

"Indeed," said Wickham rubbing his cheek. "You realize you will have to provide for the slime yourself. That is the Way. Do not expect any assistance from the Guild."

I nodded my head. "I understand. Wolf explained that to me."

Wickham nodded. "I'm surprised Wolf didn't discourage you from keeping the slime."

"Actually, he did. Not forcefully, but he did try to convince me not to keep it."

Wickham nodded. "Good. I had worried that maybe he was ... slipping."

An ominous statement?

"Well, I guess you don't have to worry about Wolf now, right?"

Wickham smiled. But it was not a smile of happiness or kindness. It was perfunctory, mechanical. There was something malicious behind it. "Indeed."

For the next minute, Wickham sat there just breathing and staring at me and Slimy. I could tell he was judging us. The longer he sat there in silence, the more creepy it became. But I didn't want to say anything and risk upsetting him. Finally, he said, "So, are you ready for your first solo wander?"

I nodded my head. "I sure am. I'm going to leave in a couple days at first light."

"Excellent. Where are you planning to wander?"

"I am going to head in the direction of Creeper Junction. I've heard it's a good area for trades. And then, if I have time, I'm going to explore the city a little bit."

Wickham nodded. "That's an easy first wander. I did that myself when I was about your age." Wickham paused again and stared at me. This time, thankfully it only lasted about ten seconds before he spoke again. "And I suppose you're taking the slime with you?"

I nodded my head. "Yes. I made a special little saddle for him so that he can ride on the back of one of my llamas. He won't be any trouble."

Winston narrowed his eyes into slits and stared at Slimy. He looked like a predator. "I'm sure of that."

Chapter 4

Two days later, I woke up before sunrise. I double checked to make sure Creepy – my good luck charm, comfort companion, and reminder of my parents – was still in my inventory. After confirming Creepy was with me, I scooped up Slimy from his little crib and put him on my bed. Then, I punched his crib to break it down and put it in my inventory. That done, I picked up sleeping Slimy. I was hoping he would stay asleep until we had departed from the wandering trader headquarters.

I walked through the hallway down to the llama stables. Unfortunately, Wes the idiot was working. "Come to get the llama team you stole from me?" asked Wes with a sneer.

I didn't bother to speak to him. I knew that if I gave him the silent treatment, it would make him much more upset than anything I could possibly say. I walked past him and to the corral where Sunny and Pippa were housed.

I entered the corral, checking carefully to make sure I did not step on any llama poop. Once I made it to Pippa, I placed a small, specially-designed saddle on her back. Then, I put Slimy into the saddle. I had learned during my wandering trader final examination that Pippa was much calmer than Sunny, so I assumed she would be the best llama to carry a sleeping baby slime.

I grabbed the leads of both llamas and walked up to the desk where Wes was working in order to check them out of the stables. He scowled at me but wordlessly handed me the required paperwork. I wrote down what I needed to and checked a few boxes. Then I handed the paperwork back to Wes. He looked over it before looking up at me. "Creeper Junction? Five to ten days?"

I nodded my head. "Correct on both counts."

"You may go," said Wes grudgingly.

I turned and led my two llamas along the corridor to the exit. An elderly trader I'd never seen before was sitting by the door. He wasn't much of a guard.

"Hey, kid, you going out for a wander?" he said in a cracking old man voice.

"I sure am, sir. My name is Winston. What's yours?"

The man laughed and I saw that he was missing all but one of his teeth. "My name is Wit. You spell it like it sounds. W-I-T."

What a strange character!

"Does that mean you use lots of quick comebacks and puns when you speak?"

He laughed again. I could smell his breath even from several blocks away. I wondered when the last time was that he had brushed his teeth. Or should I say his *tooth*.

"No, Wit isn't funny at all. Wit is just very pale. Very very pale."

Why was he talking in the third-person?

I wasn't quite sure what he meant by that. "Okay, thanks for the ... hurrr ... explanation. Anyway, can you open the door please?"

Wit chuckled. "Of course, I can. But the question is, will I?"

I did not want to deal with this foolishness on the morning of my first wander. I took a deep breath and sighed "Well, will you?"

Wit opened his mouth and flicked his one remaining tooth with his index finger. It made a hollow clicking noise. I was worried he was going to knock the tooth right out of his head.

"I think I will open it. You seem like a nice young man. Have a good wander," he said as he pulled the lever to open the door.

I walked out followed by my llamas, venturing into the Overworld for the first time ever in my life all by myself.

Chapter 5

My wander from headquarters to Creeper Junction was for the most part uneventful. After I had been wondering about an hour from headquarters, I ran into my first player. I made a trade for an iron shovel and an empty glass bottle. The player, who seemed relatively inexperienced, was very happy.

"I'm so glad you came by when you did," the player said. "I'm having a hard time figuring out how to craft things."

"Perhaps I could interest you in a crafting handbook then?"

The player smiled and rapidly nodded his head. "How much would that be?"

"Twenty emeralds," I said, doubling the price I needed to charge to make a profit because I sensed desperation in him.

The player, so thrilled about finally being able to learn how to craft things properly, excitedly reached into his inventory and quickly gathered twenty emeralds and handed them to me. I passed along the crafting handbook.

"Thank you," he said as he sat down upon a rock and began reading through it.

"You're welcome. If you ever need anything, just look for Winston the wandering trader," I said.

The player did not respond. He was already too engrossed in the contents of the book I had just sold him for an exorbitant price.

I continued wandering.

* * *

Several hours had passed. Slimy and I had taken a break to eat lunch underneath an oak tree near a stream. It was beautiful and serene.

* * *

Several more hours passed, and it was now nearing sunset and, according to my map, I was quite close to the cave where I intended to spend the night. As the sun began to set, I spotted a player nearby. I used my stealth and sneaking to walk into his line of vision when he was least expecting it. He shuddered and reached for his sword before realizing I wasn't a threat. Or at least, he didn't think I was.

"Why do you guys always do that?" said the player.

"Do what?" I said, playing coy.

"Never mind. Have you any good trades?" asked the player.

I showed him my list of available trades. "And, if what you want is not on the list, let me know. I might have something else you could use."

The player looked through the list of trades and didn't find anything he wanted. As he was handing the list back to me, he noticed the slime saddle on the back of Pippa. "What are you doing caring a slime around? Seems kind of weird."

"He's my ... um ... pet," I said, lying in order to conceal the fact that I had killed two players in order to save Slimy's life and to conceal the fact that a slime could ever be more than a pet.

"Why not get a dog or a cat or something?"

I shrugged. "I have two llamas. I don't need any more four-legged pets."

The player considered my words for a moment and said, "Makes sense, I guess. Anyway, thanks for stopping by. Sorry I didn't need anything."

I shrugged. "I'm easy like Sunday morning. No big deal," I said as I pulled on the leads of my two llamas and headed towards the entrance to the cave.

Chapter 6

About five minutes later, I easily found the entrance to the cave and walked inside, leading my two llamas behind me. I ignited a torch and held it aloft.

Before I left headquarters, I had asked several wandering traders about staying in the cave. They told me that it was a typical stop off point. They also said I should go into the cave for some distance, and not stay too close to the entrance in case some players might stumble upon me at night and murder me in my sleep. With that advice in mind I went down several passageways until I found a small unoccupied alcove in the cave.

I noticed that Slimy was looking all around, an expression of wonder on his face. "What do you think about this, Slimy? Does it look like a good place to sleep for the night?"

"Beep. Boop. Slurp."

"I agree. Let me get you down from there," I said as I reached up and lifted Slimy out of his saddle. I put him on the ground and he hopped around excitedly, glad to be out of the confines of the small saddle.

I reached into my inventory and pulled out some cobblestone and sealed the entrance to the alcove, ensuring that nothing would get in without having to break the blocks which would make enough noise that it would wake us up. I then affixed several torches to the walls to prevent any mobs from spawning in the darkness. I quickly set up my bed and Slimy's crib and then started a cook fire. Over the past couple of days I'd come to discover that Slimy would eat just about anything. This was actually good because I didn't have to pack a special baby slime food for the trip.

I cooked a couple of pieces of raw chicken meat and heated up a few bread rolls. Slimy had a little bit of both. Then I drank some milk and gave a little water to Slimy.

After dinner, Slimy entertained himself by bouncing around the small alcove for about fifteen minutes until he wore himself out and fell asleep on the floor of the cave. I picked him up and put him in his crib. Watching him sleep, I thought back to my own childhood, before the pillager raid, before I was orphaned, and before I became a wandering trader. I wished for a moment that I could have those days back again.

Then, the day caught up with me and I yawned. I walked over to my bed, got under the covers, and promptly fell asleep.

* * *

When I woke up, I could not tell what time it was because I was inside of a sealed chamber illuminated only by torchlight. Slimy was hopping up and down in his crib, straining at the guard rails, wanting to get out. I rubbed the sleep from my eyes and got up and stumbled over to Slimy's crib.

"You want out?"

"Beep. Beep," he said excitedly.

I lifted him out of his crib and watched as he hopped over to the entrance I had sealed last night. He was bouncing against the door. "Beep. Boo-boo. Beep. Boo-boo."

Given the sound of his words, it seemed to indicate he was repeating himself. "What is he trying to say?" He repeated the same series of sounds again and again.

Well, whatever it was, I had no idea. "Slimy, just let me pack all of our stuff back on the llamas and then we can open the door and go out."

Slimy kept bouncing against the door. I packed our things and then grabbed the leads to the llamas and walked over to the door. I picked up Slimy and put him in his saddle. He didn't like it. He started to cry.

"Blubber. Whah. Gurggg."

I tried to ignore him. I grabbed my pickaxe and broke down the cobblestone to unseal the entrance. As I was gathering the broken cobblestone to put back in my inventory, a giant cave spider stepped in front of me.

"Aaaaah," I screamed.

"Do not fear, wandering trader. Your people have an alliance with my Queen. Otherwise, you would be dead already," said the large and very confident spider.

"Netherrack," I swore as I reached into my inventory to stroke Creepy to help me calm down. "I never thought I would ever hear a spider talk."

"You should be honored. We do not talk to players or villagers and the like under normal circumstances. Only because of our alliance with Wickham do I deign to speak to you."

Wickham and his alliances. *Was this one of his sinister power plays that he was working on? Something he kept hidden from everyone else?*

"Well, then, I'm glad I am a wandering trader today and not just a villager or a player. Anyway, do you have something to tell me, or did you just happen to be passing by?"

"As a matter of fact, I was here to deliver some spider string for you to trade with," said the spider.

"You were expecting me?" I asked in shock.

The spider shook its head. "No, but many wandering traders stay in this cave. You are the one who happens to be here today."

I nodded my head. "I see. But, um, I didn't realize you might be here to give me something, so I don't think I have anything to give you in exchange."

The spider hissed and chuckled. "The spider strings are payment for wandering trader services given to us by Wickham. I do not expect any payment from you today," said the spider as he held out a large quantity of spider strings.

I took the spider strings and tucked them into one of the bags on Sunny's back. "Thank you. I'll be sure to let Wickham know that you delivered the spider strings."

The spider nodded his head. "Thank you. By the way, my name is Oculus, what is yours? I've never seen you before."

"Nice to meet you, Oculus. My name is Winston. I just became an official wandering trader a few weeks ago."

Oculus looked confused. "Just became one? I thought you all spawned as wandering traders."

I felt nauseous as I realized my error. If Oculus figured out that some wandering traders were made and not spawned, it would be my death sentence. "Of course we do. Poor choice of words on my part," I lied. "What I meant was that I recently passed my final examination to be allowed to wander by myself. We do have a brief period of training," I said.

This response seemed to satisfy Oculus. "That makes sense. We spiders also have training in how to attack and kill players."

I nodded my head. "Exactly. Um, anyway, I need to get going. I'm going to try to make it to Creeper Junction by nightfall."

Oculus shuddered at the mention of Creeper Junction. "Be careful. I have heard things are not right in Creeper Junction of late."

"What do you mean?"

"The city has always been strange, ever since it was founded by the acolytes of the Rainbow Creeper many generations ago. But, lately there is a *darkness* falling over the city. There are only rumors. I can't give you any facts. And I have not been there myself. So, I suppose I could be wrong."

"What sort of darkness?"

Oculus shook his head. "I do not know. Perhaps you will hear something when you are there. Perhaps not."

I nodded my head. "I'll keep my eyes and ears open," I said, not expecting to hear anything. Oculus's description of the so-called darkness was very vague and without any details, I had to assume it was just a made-up, misguided rumor.

Oculus scurried away without another word, opening the path for me to leave the cave and continue to Creeper Junction.

Chapter 7

I managed to arrive at Creeper Junction just before nightfall. I made about half a dozen trades along the way. I even traded some of the spider string to a player making a fishing rod.

After entering the city, I stopped one of the townsfolk and asked for the nearest hotel with a stable. I noticed a slight look of disgust on his face when he saw me, but he didn't say anything other than to tell me that I should try the Wandering Cow Inn and Stable located a few blocks from where we stood. I thanked the resident of Creeper Junction and turned in the direction indicated.

The Wandering Cow Inn was clean but spartan. After getting Slimy from his saddle and stabling my llamas, I went inside to the front desk in order to check in. As I walked up to the front desk, a grizzled old woman with frizzy gray hair and a bad attitude pointed at Slimy. "That thing's gonna have to stay in your room. And it will cost you an extra five emeralds per night."

"Why would you do that? Slimy is fine. He won't hurt anyone or anything."

The woman snorted and then coughed. "You keep him in your room or you find someplace else to bed down for the night."

Because night had fallen and zombies and skeletons were beginning to spawn in the streets of Creeper Junction, I had no choice but to follow her rules. "Fine then. I need one room for the night."

"Furnished or unfurnished?"

"Unfurnished. I brought my own beds."

The woman grunted. She wrote a few words down on a piece of paper and then handed it to me. "Sign this. It will be twenty emeralds for the night, including the ... ewww ... the slime."

Now I knew how some of the players felt being ripped off by some of my trades. *Twenty emeralds for one night?!? Ridiculous!*

Anyway, I had little choice, so I signed the piece of paper and found twenty emeralds in my inventory and handed them to the woman. She handed me a key to the room and said, "Put that green thing in there first before you go anywhere else. I don't want him scaring the customers away."

I gave the woman an angry look, but didn't say anything back. *What was the use?* I climbed one flight of stairs and went to the room. I quickly set up my bed and Slimy's crib. I put Slimy in his crib. "You are going to have to stay here, Slimy, while I go get some food. Are you going to be okay?"

"Beep. Boop," he said sadly. I was worried, but then he flopped down in his crib and almost immediately fell asleep. I assumed he would be okay while I was gone. The worst thing that might happen would be if he got out of his crib and started hopping around the room, disturbing the guests staying in the room below us. It was a risk I was willing to accept.

Before I went out for dinner, I took a quick bath in the attached bathroom to wash off the road grime. Then, I changed into a clean robe and set out in search of food.

I walked downstairs to the dining room. It was small and crowded. I looked around for a place to sit by myself but every table had at least one other person sitting at it. But then I noticed across the room with his back to me was another wandering trader! Since we were in the Guild together, I knew we would have something to talk about.

I made my way between the tables, deftly maneuvering between the closely packed chairs and tables in order to avoid bumping into anyone. When I arrived at the table of the wandering trader, I said to his back, "Hey brother, do you mind if I sit with you?"

The trader turned around and ... it was Wolf!

"Sure thing, kid," he said.

"Wolf! No way! Are you still on your mission?"

Wolf reached up and grabbed me by the throat and sat me down roughly into a chair. "***Never*** discuss that in public."

I realized my stupid mistake. "I'm sorry," I whispered. Then, in an attempt to make it clear to everyone that we were just discussing banal topics, I said more loudly, "What's good here?"

Wolf shrugged. "Mushroom stew's all right. They make something called a 'chicken pot pie' that looks pretty good too. Basically a hunk of bread with a bunch of chicken soup stuffed inside of it. Messy, but delicious."

At that moment the waiter came over and I ordered a chicken pot pie and a bottle of water. The waiter looked at Wolf and said, "Can I get you anything else?"

Wolf shook his head. "I'm full."

Since Wolf would not let me speak about his mission aloud, I reached into my inventory and pulled out a piece of paper. On the paper, I wrote: *Are you still working on your mission?* I handed the paper to Wolf. He read the question and then pulled a quill from his inventory. *No. It's done*, he wrote before handing the paper back to me.

I nodded and then wrote on the back of the piece of paper: *Can we discuss after dinner?* Wolf read the piece of paper, crumbled it, and ignited it with the flame from a wall torch. He looked at me and nodded his head in the affirmative.

After that, we didn't talk much. I told him about a couple of my trades while I was en route to Creeper Junction, but he just stared off into the distance.

After I finished my dinner and paid for it, I asked Wolf if he wanted to come up to my room to talk. He nodded his head and we went to my room. When we arrived, Slimy was still asleep. We sat in a corner away from his crib so as not to disturb him.

"So, what was your mission?"

Wolf took a deep breath and sighed. "Typical political assassination," he said.

Typical?

"How many of these have you done that they are now *typical?*"

Wolf shrugged. "I've lost count."

"So who did you ... assassinate?"

"Wickham wanted me to assassinate one of the husk princes in order to send a message to his father, the Husk King."

I was shocked. My eyes were as wide as a creeper spawn egg. "What message?"

Wolf shook his head. "I have no idea. I'm just a foot soldier. Whatever the message was, the Husk King now has it," he said grimly.

I put my hand over my mouth. "So you did it? You assassinated the husk prince?"

Wolf nodded. "It was easy. When your target is not expecting it, they don't ever even come close to stopping you."

"I wonder what the message could've been?" I said.

"Probably something to do with trade. The husks have been acting up lately, trying to disrupt wandering trader routes. Be my guess anyway."

I nodded my head. "I didn't realize the geopolitics of regional and inter-biome trade were so violent."

Wolf looked at me with an exasperated expression. "You've got a lot to learn, kid."

At that moment Slimy woke up and started crying. I could tell he was hungry. I walked to his crib and picked him up. I bounced him in an attempt to calm him down, but he kept crying.

Wolf stood up. "That's my cue. I'm going to get out of here. I don't like babies." Wolf took two-steps toward the door, opened it, and left.

I reached into my inventory and pulled out an apple and held it in front of Slimy. He absorbed the apple, stopped crying, and fell back to sleep.

Chapter 8

The next morning I woke up a little after dawn. Slimy was already awake, bouncing around in his crib. I took him out and played with them a little bit and gave him a few pieces of bread to eat.

After he ate them he said, "Beep. Boop. In-ston."

I snapped my head at him. "Did you just say Winston? Winston?"

Slimy giggled. "In-ston. In-ston."

I picked up Slimy and gave him a big hug. "You are learning to talk! Good for you."

Slimy laughed and then his eyelids became heavy and he fell asleep in my arms. I never knew how much slimes slept or how quickly they could fall asleep. I put Slimy back in his crib and then went downstairs to eat breakfast in the dining area.

When I arrived at the dining area, I looked around for Wolf, but he was nowhere to be seen. I sat down at a table by myself. When the waiter came over, I asked, "Have you seen any other wandering traders in here this morning?"

The waiter, who looked incredibly bored, shook his head. "No. In fact, you are only the fourth person to come in this morning. It is still pretty early."

"Okay, thanks for the information," I said. "Anyway, I'd like some fried eggs and steak with fried tomatoes on the side and a glass of milk."

The waiter wrote it down and nodded. "Should be ready in about five minutes."

* * *

After I ate my breakfast – which was quite tasty – I walked up to the front desk. The same annoying lady with the frizzy hair was working there. When I got to the desk, she said coarsely, "You ready to check out? Get that green thing out of my hotel?"

"What time is check out time? I thought I might look around the city for a while."

She inhaled a deep breath and then exhaled it slowly, making a deep sighing noise, to indicate her annoyance with me and Slimy. "You can stay until 10 o'clock. After that, you pay for another day."

I nodded my head. "Okay, then. I'll be back before ten."

The old lady didn't care. She flipped her hands at me to shoo me away. "Get. I've got other customers waiting."

I turned around and didn't see anyone. But, it was clear that she wanted me gone so I did not bother to correct her.

I left the Wandering Cow Inn and walked for about fifteen minutes until I arrived at the heart of old Creeper Junction. By now it was about 7 o'clock in the morning. I admired all of the great and historic architecture in the old quarter of the city. Large banks and vaults for emeralds dominated the skyline. The great Creeper Junction University grounds were also rather impressive. There were green lawns everywhere, architecturally and artistically designed streams flowed through the campus. There were statues created by the great artists of the past. The buildings were made mostly of cobblestone, but with obsidian accents here and there.

I wandered further along. It was still only 8 o'clock. I could easily sightsee for another hour and get back to the hotel in time.

I came to an even older neighborhood, probably built around the time of the city's founding. The streets were much more narrow and close together, likely built for protection and to keep the heat contained during winter storms.

The drawback to walking through narrow and winding pathways was that it was hard to see more than a few block-lengths ahead or behind you. Still, the quaint architecture and weathered stone lent a sophisticated patina to the otherwise plain streetscape. In addition, there were odd-looking door knockers on most doors, and many of the doors were painted different colors to stand out from the dull stone.

I was admiring a door knocker shaped like an Ender Dragon claw when suddenly a black hood was placed over my head. I fought back, but I was hit by something heavy and knocked unconscious.

Chapter 9

When I regained consciousness, the hood was still over my head. I could just see hints of light through the cloth bag. There must have been a window in the room where they – whoever they are – were holding me. My arms were tied behind my back around a chair so that I couldn't escape.

Although I could not see anything, I could smell **some**thing. And what I smelled was the distinct odor of desiccated corpses. I knew that I was in the presence of *at least* one husk.

Having regained consciousness, I now felt the sharp pain of my head wound and I moaned a few times. I heard someone stand up and take a few steps toward a door and open it.

"He's awake," said a raspy voice. I heard two or three others enter the room and stand near me. A few seconds later the hood was snatched from my head.

My suspicions were confirmed. Standing before me were four husks. They wore diamond armor and had diamond swords. They looked like soldiers.

Husk regular army? Special forces?

"What do you know about the assassination of our prince?" asked one of them.

I blinked my eyes as though I had no idea what they were talking about, trying to remember all of my training in spy and manipulation tradecraft. "I don't know what you're talking about. Why have you kidnapped me?"

One of the husks slapped me across the face with his leathery, desiccated hand. "You know something. We aren't stupid."

"How can I know *anything*? I've been wandering through the Overworld for the past two days. I just got into Creeper Junction last night."

The four husks looked at each other and considered my explanation. Finally, one of them said, "Be that as it may, you may know something even though you probably aren't the assassin."

"I'm a wandering trader. How would I know anything about assassins? They freak me out."

"Someone killed our prince yesterday. As he fled the room, he was seen wearing a wandering trader cloak."

Oh, no! How could Wolf be so careless and not change into different clothing?

I had to think fast. "So ... um ... maybe someone was using a disguise. Why would a wandering trader be involved? All we do is wander and trade. That's why we are called ... well, you know."

One of the husks leaned in at me. He stared at me with crazy, mad dog eyes. He grated his old, disgusting, rotten teeth together. I could smell the dust flaking off from his dry, rotted flesh. "But, what if it **were** a wandering trader? I'm sure you all know each other."

I shook my head. "We're loners. Sure, I have said 'hi' to a few wandering traders now and then, but it's not like we hang out together."

More and more lies. Must protect Wolf. He would do the same for me.

The four husks stood back and considered my words. "Let's step outside and discuss this," said one of them. Three of them left the room while one remained to keep me under guard.

I could hear muffled voices outside. I could not make out anything they were saying though occasionally they would have brief arguments about one thing or another. The entire time the guard just stared at me with his dead, dry eyes. I could hear his eyelids scrape them each time he blinked.

Disgusting.

After about five minutes, the three husks returned. "Okay, we have decided to let you go. But if we ever find out you were involved in this assassination or you knew something about it, we will find you and kill you."

A different husk ordered, "Untie him." The husk who had been guarding me went behind me and sliced the ropes from my wrists. I moved my hands in front of me and massaged my wrists until the blood returned to my hands. The husk reached down and cut the ropes around my ankles as well.

After I stood up, I looked at all four of the husks. "I had no involvement in any assassination of your prince. I don't even know who he is or what he looks like. I'm sorry for your loss."

The husks nodded in acknowledgment of my condolence. "You may leave, wandering trader."

I made a beeline for the door, not wanting to be around them anymore, but before I left the room, I asked them, "What time is it, by the way?"

One of the husks replied, "It should be about 11:30 by now."

"Netherrack!" I said as I rushed out the door to the room and back to the hotel.

* * *

By the time I got to the front desk it was nearly noon. The old lady was working there and smiled at me with a big, broad grin. "That'll be another night for the room and another night for the stable."

"Can't you prorate it or something? Just charge me for like a couple of hours?"

The old lady smirked and shook her head. She reached under her desk and pulled out a thick book labeled **Policies and Procedures**. She flipped to page 429. She spun the book around so that I could read it as she pointed to the words: "Any guest who stays even one second beyond check out time will be charged for another night. **No exceptions.**"

If it weren't for the fact that I had been suspected of assassinating a husk prince and had been recently kidnapped, I would've argued with her about this for hours, just to make her life miserable. I would've worn her down and gotten away without paying anything. But, the circumstances were not favorable at this time.

I reached into my inventory and pulled out enough emeralds to cover the additional charges and threw them at the woman.

Several bounced off of her stomach and fell to the floor. She didn't care. She greedily gathered the emeralds as I walked away to go up to my room and get Slimy and my belongings so that I could return to wandering trader headquarters as soon as possible and inform them about the husk search party.

Chapter 10

Even though I was traveling quickly, it still took me nearly two days to get back to headquarters. After all, llamas can only move so fast.

My trip was thankfully uneventful except for one player who went ballistic over a trade. He started shouting about how wandering traders are all thieves and deserve to die. He started swinging a sword at me, threatening to kill Slimy and me if I didn't back up. I backed up, but I guess it wasn't fast enough. He kept coming for me and almost hit Slimy with his sword. I wasn't going to stand for that! I pulled out a crossbow and shot him right through the heart, killing him instantly. I collected all his drops and inventory for resale at a later date.

When I got back to the headquarters, I quickly took my llamas to their corral and cleaned their hooves. Then, I rushed to Wolf's room and banged on the door. It took him nearly a minute to answer the door. He looked like he had just woken up.

"What do you want?" he said groggily.

"It's about that assassination," I said.

Wolf shook his head. "I don't want to tell war stories right now. I'm sleeping."

He tried to close the door, but I put out my hand to stop it. He looked at me angrily. I shook my head. "No, not war stories. They are after you."

Those words woke him up. His eyes got wide. He reached out and grabbed my robe and pulled me into his room and shut the door. "What are you talking about? Who is **they**?"

"The day after we had dinner together, I decided to do some sightseeing in Creeper Junction. When I was in the old part of town, I got jumped by four husks. They put a hood over my head and took me to a room where they tied me up and interrogated me. They wanted to know if I knew something about the assassination of their prince or if I were directly involved."

Wolf was surprised. "Why would they think that?"

"One of the husks told me they saw the assassin running away, and he was wearing a wandering trader cloak."

Wolf closed his eyes and grimaced as though he were in pain. He put his hand on his forehead and rubbed it like he had a strong headache. "This is bad. This is really bad." He then sat there for a moment rubbing his temples and breathing rhythmically. "I guess I'll have to inform Wickham."

"Yeah, if I hadn't found you first, I was going to tell him next," I said. "Not to be a tattle tale, but because ... well ... it is the Way."

Wolf took a deep breath and let out a long, slow sigh. "Let's go together. Give me a minute to put on a fresh robe."

* * *

About ten minutes later we were in Wickham's chambers telling him the bad news. Wickham shook his head and glared at Wolf. "How could you be so stupid? I thought you were better than that. That's why I gave you this assignment."

"I must've stepped wrong while I was sneaking, revealing my presence for a moment," said Wolf, shaking his head not comprehending how he could have been seen.

Wickham exploded with anger. "Oh, you think so? Could it be that you made a mistake? Of course, it's your fault! And, why weren't you wearing a disguise?"

Wolf's face turned red due to a combination of embarrassment and anger. "There was no reason for a disguise. Security was lax. It was an easy hit."

"Always! Follow! Procedure!" yelled Wickham, slamming his fist on the table.

I put my hands out. "Maybe we should all just calm down a little bit," I said, trying to restore some peace to the room.

Wickham looked at me with fierce anger in his eyes. "Get out! I don't need a noob in here right now."

Gee whiz, Wickham.

I wanted to yell at him. Slap him in the face. But I knew if I did that, I would surely suffer death. So I pretended I wasn't upset, backed away, walked out the door, and shut it behind me. I stood outside the chamber next to Wayne, who was on guard duty. We could hear yelling and heated words coming from inside but could not make any of them out. "How often does stuff like this happen?" I asked.

Wayne gave me the side-eye. "Why would I tell you that?"

I shrugged. "I don't know. Just to pass the time."

Wayne grunted. "You are kind of an idiot, Winston, but you've got moxie, I'll give you that. Anyway, I shouldn't tell you this, but Wickham has had more than his fair share of heated arguments in there."

I nodded my head. "I assumed as much."

As the argument continued inside Wickham's chamber, I saw Wynter coming up the stairs. He was slightly out of breath when he made it to the top. He waved at me and said, "Hey, Winston! You're back."

I nodded my head. "Yeah, I am. It was a pretty good wander overall." I assumed it wasn't my place to bring up the husk hunting party that was after Wolf. "What about you? How was your first wander?"

Wynter smiled. "Yeah, it went fairly well. I turned a pretty good profit and picked up some supplies from a wolf. He told me that it was part payment for some agreement between the Wolf King and Wickham. I didn't get any details."

"That's interesting. I picked up a bounty of spider strings for the same reason from a cave spider."

At that moment the door to Wickham's chamber slammed open and Wolf stormed out and began walking down the stairs without another word. Wickham stood in the doorway and yelled at him, "Don't let it happen again!"

Wickham stood staring daggers at Wolf as he continued down the stairs. But once Wolf was out of sight, Wickham's emotions completely changed and he became calm again. He looked at me and Wynter. "Perfect. The two of you may come in. I have an assignment for you."

We went into the chamber and sat down in its uncomfortable chairs. Wickham sat down opposite us. "Your assignment should be fairly straightforward, but I'm sending the two of you together because you are both new to this life. That way, you can help each other out or, if one of you is killed, the other one can complete the mission."

Intense.

"What is the mission, Wickham?" asked Wynter, his voice trembling slightly.

"We have received word that a griefer has built a walled village. He is keeping villagers inside as his slaves. He forces them to work and then he takes the product of their work without paying for it. He either keeps it for himself or sells it."

"That's terrible!" I said.

"That should be illegal!" said Wynter.

"Well, by the laws of Notch, players seem to be able to do whatever they want. Or, at least ... they think they can. The two of you are going to put a stop to it. Your assignment is to kill the griefer and tear down the wall. After that, the villagers can figure it out for themselves."

"That's it?" I asked. "We don't need to find anyone or locate anything?"

Wickham shook his head. "No, just a simple assassination and liberation."

"Is there any contact person inside the village?" asked Wynter.

Good thought.

"No, there is not. The request for liberation came from an uncle of one of the villagers trapped inside the walls of the griefer's village. He's paying handsomely for this mission too, so do not fail," said Wickham, an ominous tone in his voice.

We stood up and balled our right hands into a fist and then put our fist against our hearts. "We shall honor the Way. We shall honor you," Wynter and I said in unison before leaving Wickham's chamber to get ready for our first assignment.

When we exited Wickham's chamber, Wayne handed us each a map indicating the location of the enslaved village. I tucked my map into my inventory. Wynter and I saluted Wayne and began walking downstairs.

"This is exciting," said Wynter. "My first assassination. And it sounds like the guy deserves it too."

I nodded my head. "Yes, it does sound like a righteous kill, which is something I don't think most assassinations are."

"Maybe," said Wynter. "But I'll think about that later."

"When do you want to leave?" I asked.

"How about the first thing tomorrow morning? It's just about dinner time, and I don't like to travel at night."

I nodded my head. "It's agreed then. I will meet you at the stables at first light. But first, I have to find a babysitter for Slimy."

* * *

I stopped at Wolf's room and asked if he would watch Slimy while I was gone, but he just slammed the door in my face. I asked nearly a dozen wandering traders, who had similar reactions, before I realized what I had to do.

I found a young trainee wandering the halls. "You. What is your name?"

"Willmar, sir," he said with a cracking, nervous voice.

"How old are you?"

"Thirteen, sir."

"I've got a very important task for you. It is easy, but tiring."

Willmar saluted. "Sir. Yes, sir."

I smiled. It was fun ordering people around. "You will babysit my slime, Slimy, for the next few days while I am on a mission."

A look of disgust crossed Willmar's face. "But, aren't slimes kind of, you know, gross?"

"They are not!" I yelled. "Slimy is fun. Do you want to disobey my orders?"

Willmar looked terrified. "Oh, no, sir. I will babysit Slimy."

"Good," I said. "Follow me, and I will introduce the two of you."

Chapter 11

The next morning, Wynter and I met at the stables and checked our teams of llamas out. His llamas were named Bob and Mortimer. They were an older pair of llamas, but very well behaved. Fortunately, Wes was not working the check-out desk. Instead, it was a new trainee who looked like a player!

As I filled out the paperwork, I asked, "I didn't think players could become wandering traders."

The trainee shrugged. "I didn't either, but if we agree to follow the Way, we can. I mean, we all basically look like villagers and natural-born wandering traders except our noses are smaller."

I pondered his words. "I suppose so. Anyway, what is your name?"

"It was BRBasher, but Wickham renamed me Wenlan."

"Cool name, I guess," I said, handing him my completed paperwork. Wynter handed his paperwork over as well.

"Good luck out there," said Wenlan.

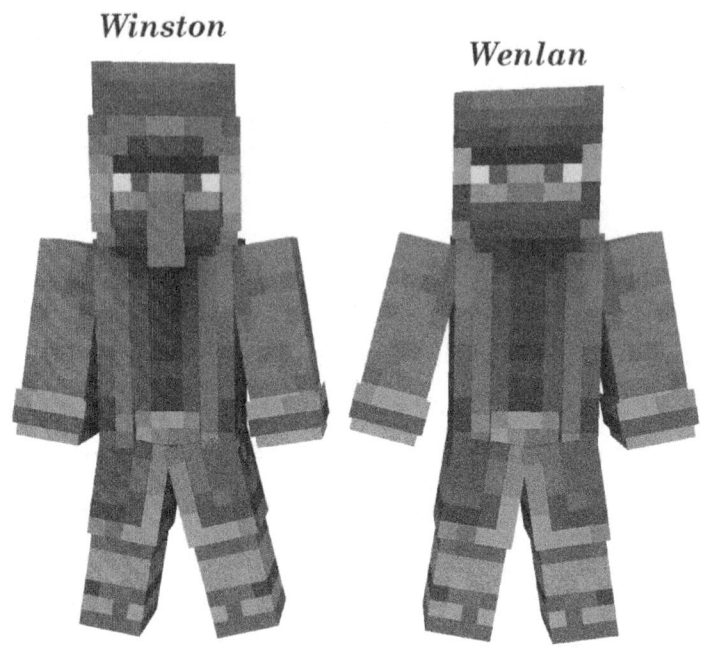

Winston   *Wenlan*

As Wynter and I walked up to the gate to leave the headquarters, the old guard Wenceslaus stopped us. "Where are you two going?"

"Secret mission. Can't discuss it," I said, feeling pretty important.

Wenceslaus blinked a couple of times and then smiled. "Your first mission, eh? Don't blow it."

"Whatever. You're just jealous you can't go," said Wynter.

Wenceslaus nodded his head. "Maybe I am. I'm just a broken down old man now, but I used to do some pretty noteworthy things back in my day."

"You will have to tell us about them sometime," I said. "But, we need to get going."

Wenceslaus smiled and said, "It'll take a while for me to tell my tales, but you'll be amazed." And then he reached over and flipped the lever to open the gate for us to exit the headquarters.

* * *

Wynter and I each had a map of the destination. Because it was virtually unheard of for two wandering traders and their llamas to be seen together, we wandered on separate paths, agreeing to meet at a rendezvous point about five hundred blocks away from the target village.

Along my way to the rendezvous point, I engaged in a few trades with players and was ridiculed and insulted by others. All in a day's work.

When I finally got to the rendezvous point, Wynter appeared to have been there for at least an hour. He had set up a small tent and put his bed inside it. His llamas were tied to a tree. He was standing next to a campfire.

"Hey there, Winston. I was just about to start cooking some dinner. What do you want?"

"How about a steak or a pork chop?"

Wynter smiled and reached into a chest on the ground next to him. He pulled out two steaks and two pork chops as well as some potatoes and carrots. "How about all of the above?"

I smiled and my stomach rumbled. I hadn't eaten in several hours. "Sounds great. Let me just set up my tent and get my llamas situated."

* * *

After we ate dinner, there was still enough sunlight for us to do a bit of reconnaissance. We climbed up a nearby hill and were able to see the village in the distance. I noticed a wall about ten blocks high and three blocks thick surrounded the entire village. No villagers could get in or out. There was a single entrance gate guarded by an iron golem and a couple of husks, who must have been servants of the griefer.

"Looks pretty well fortified," said Wynter.

I grunted. "It does. Our mission is to kill the griefer, so we need to figure out his routine. I don't see any player down there obviously in charge. My guess is the griefer is not on site."

Wynter nodded his head. "I agree. We will have to watch the village tomorrow and see if we can learn anything."

"Yep," I said. I looked at the darkening sky. "It's just about dark, so let's get inside our tents and get some sleep."

Chapter 12

The next day dawned cold and crisp. Our tents were in the shadow of a nearby hill blocking the sun, so the area did not warm up quickly.

For breakfast, I drank a glass of warm milk and ate a loaf of bread. Wynter had a similar breakfast, except in place of warm milk he just had water.

We walked up to the top of the nearby hill and looked down at the village. We saw the villagers actively engaged in their various tasks, making armaments, weapons, leather goods, etc. At around 9 o'clock in the morning, a player wearing all diamond armor and a flashy yellow cape rode toward the village on an armored horse. I tapped Wynter on the shoulder and said, "That's got to be the griefer."

We watched as the griefer rode up to the entrance gate and the two husks stepped aside. They knocked on the gate a couple times with their spears and the iron golem, who was standing inside the village, pushed a few dozen villagers away from the gate. The gate then swung open and the griefer trotted into the village.

The villagers who were close to the entrance cowered. Many of them took a knee and bowed their heads, waiting for whatever punishment the griefer might choose to dole out.

Sad.

I watched as the griefer rode silently through the mass of villagers when he suddenly pulled out a sword and chopped the head off of a librarian who was doing nothing other than standing there.

"That was horrible!" said Wynter, retching slightly.

"It was. I'll be happy to kill this guy," I said, cold determination in my voice.

We continued to watch as the griefer rode his horse around town and entered various shops and exited with goods or emeralds. He executed a couple more villagers for no reason we could discern from our vantage point. After about thirty minutes, the griefer left the village and rode back in the direction from which he had come.

"Do you think he does that every day?" I asked Wynter.

"Hard to tell. We've only been here for one day. But if he does keep that schedule, setting up the assassination will be easy."

"It would be really helpful if we had some insider information. Maybe we can sneak into the village later and try to talk to someone about that?"

Wynter thought about it for a moment and said, "Seems like a good idea though the villager might tell on us and blow our cover."

"If the villagers do, then they don't deserve to be freed. Can you imagine living under the yoke of a tyrannical griefer like this who just randomly kills people? I couldn't."

"Nor could I," said Wynter. "But you and I have lived different lives than these villagers, spawned behind the walls of slavery."

I nodded my head. "True. I am sure many of them have never known a life other than behind the wall, under the heel of a savage diamond boot."

"Why don't we sneak around to the side of the village opposite the gate? We can dig under the wall and see if we can find someone with knowledge of the griefer's schedule."

I smiled. "You read my mind."

Chapter 13

We walked around to the other side of the village. We went wide of the village so that we would not be spotted by any of the guards, or if we were spotted, they wouldn't think anything of it. We wandered separately, each of us leading our pair of llamas in order to appear as though we were just normal wandering traders.

Once we had arrived at the other side of the village, we tied our llamas to trees and regrouped. "So, tunnel under the wall and hope we pop up somewhere safe?" asked Wynter.

"We can either do that or we could wait until evening and climb up the wall," I said. "But then, we would have to contend with hostile nighttime mobs, so that may not be the best approach."

Wynter nodded. "It looks like there is a house of fairly large size adjacent to the wall straight ahead. Why don't we tunnel under the wall and try to pop up in that house? Worst case scenario, the villager living there screams and we have to gag him."

"Sounds like a good idea," I said. "Let's do it. But first, let's put on our ninja disguises." This was Wolf's mistake, failing to disguise himself. Had he done that, the husks would never have known a wandering trader was involved in the assassination of their prince.

After we changed into our ninja gear, we each reached into our inventories and pulled out a shovel to dig through the surface layer of dirt. Once we had dug through three blocks, we hit stone. We got our pickaxes and dug down a few more blocks. After that we went horizontal towards the wall. Based on our calculations, we needed to mine through about twenty-five blocks before we would be directly under the house. Once we had done that, we paused for a moment.

"Okay," I said. "Why don't you light a torch and I will mine vertically? When I come to the wooden floor of the house, I'll stop and then we will get ready to burst through."

Wynter nodded and pulled a torch out of his inventory and ignited it. I mined up about six blocks before I came to the wooden floor. I looked at Wynter and motioned, indicating that I would go on three. I then silently mouthed the words one, two, three, before smashing the floor and leaping up into the house.

When we popped up, we found a villager girl about the same age as me, sixteen or so, standing in a corner staring at us with shock on her face.

"Don't scream," I whispered. "We're here to help you."

The girl looked suspiciously at us but did not scream. "How can you help me?" she asked. "Two ninjas are usually up to no good."

"We're here to free your village from the griefer," said Wynter.

"How is that possible?" asked the girl, still in shock.

"Just trust us," I said. "We just need to know about the griefer's daily routine. Can you tell us about it?"

The girl was still in shock. She wasn't saying anything. It was time to try different tact.

"Look, my name is Winston. This here is Wynter, spelled with a 'y' instead of an 'i'. What's your name?"

The girl shook her head, brought back to reality by the simple question of her name. "Um, hurrr, my name is Penelope."

"That's a pretty name," I said. "Does anyone live here with you?"

She nodded her head. "My uncle lives here, but he's at work right now. He has to make ten saddles a day for the griefer or else the griefer will kill him." A tear came to her eyes.

"That's horrible!" said Wynter.

"It sure is," I said.

Penelope, the shock of our sudden appearance finally wearing off, sat down at the kitchen table. "You want to sit down?" she asked. We walked over to the table and sat down. "So what is this about freeing our town?"

"I can't give you all the details, but we've been sent here by a relative of someone in the village to free the village and make sure the griefer doesn't bother you – *or anyone else* – ever again," I said. "And to do that, we need to know his routine so we can find an opening to ... well, make sure he doesn't come back."

Penelope's eyes got wide. "Are you going to kill him?"

"Why would you think that?" asked Wynter.

"I don't know. The way Winston was talking, the fact you are ninjas, etc. Seems kind of obvious."

Wynter and I exchanged a glance. We both laughed. "I guess it is pretty obvious," I said.

Penelope smiled. "Anyway, sure, I know his routine. He comes every morning shortly after breakfast and goes through the town to check on the progress everyone is making towards crafting any items that he has ordered. He usually kills a few people just to keep us all scared," Penelope's voice trailed off. I could tell there was some pain behind it. "That is what happened to my aunt. She was just out delivering bread to some of the shops and the griefer chose her for his wrath that day."

"What about your parents? Where are they?" I asked.

"I barely knew them. They were killed by an illness when I was a little girl. My aunt and uncle adopted me after that."

"I'm sorry," I said, putting a comforting hand on Penelope's shoulder.

Penelope nodded her head and then pushed my hand away before wiping tears from her cheeks. "Anyway, his routine. So yeah, he comes a little after breakfast time, goes around the town for thirty or forty-five minutes, kills two or three villagers, and then leaves. No one knows where he goes. We've never been outside the walls of the village."

Wynter nodded his head. "What about the two husks and the iron golem by the entry gate?"

Penelope sighed. "The iron golem is named Evan. He used to be the village protector, but then the griefer kidnapped his son and now Evan does whatever the griefer says because he doesn't want his son to be hurt."

"Savage," I said.

Penelope nodded. "The husks arrived with the griefer. Once the griefer built the wall and enslaved all of us, they stayed to keep order in the town. That entry gate is the only weak spot in the wall, so as long as they can keep that secure, there's really no way for any of us to escape."

I nodded my head and looked at Wynter. "Any more information we need?" Wynter shook his head. I looked back at Penelope. "Thanks for the information. Can you promise me you won't tell anyone about this? Not even your uncle. We need to maintain the element of surprise."

She nodded her head. "As long as you can give me something I can use to fix the floor. I wouldn't be able to explain that giant hole very easily."

I chuckled. "Good thinking. I think I have a few boards in my inventory. Let me check." I reached in my inventory and found enough wood to repair the damage we had made. I stacked the boards on the floor next to the hole.

"Thanks for the information and the hospitality," said Wynter.

"Indeed," I said.

Penelope walked with us to the exit hole. "So, when are you going to free the village?" she asked, wringing her hands anxiously in front of her.

"Soon," I said. "Maybe tomorrow. We just need to come up with a plan."

Penelope smiled. "I can't wait."

Chapter 14

Wynter and I spent the rest of the day coming up with a plan. We thought of various options, all of which ended with the death of the griefer, as we'd been instructed to do. Once we decided on a plan that we thought would be effective, we had dinner and went to sleep.

* * *

The next day we woke up at dawn. Wynter had a small breakfast. I was too nervous to eat. We left our llamas tied to trees and readied our weapons. We changed into ninja suits specifically designed to blend in to a forest environment. Then we walked down the hill to implement our plan.

We snuck as close to the entry gate as we could without being seen, about ten blocks away. I was hiding behind a small pile of rocks while Wynter was some distance away on the opposite side of the traveling path that the griefer would use. Wynter was hiding behind a thick tree trunk.

The next step of our plan was simply to wait for the griefer's arrival. We waited for about an hour and a half until I heard the beat of hooves. I checked my position to make sure I was truly hidden and then watched as the griefer arrogantly trotted past my position, his diamond armor shining in the sunlight and his yellow cape flapping behind him.

What a prima donna!

The griefer rode up to the gate of the village and instructed the husks to open the gate. As they had done yesterday, they knocked on the gate. We could hear Evan the iron golem clearing the way for the griefer. The gates opened and the griefer trotted into the village.

Once the gate shut, Wynter and I both jumped out from our hiding place and, using bows and arrows, shot the husks in the chest. Our first shots hit home, surprising the husks. Before they could even react, we sent a second shot their way and then rushed toward them.

Wynter's second shot was a critical hit and one of the husks flashed red and disappeared into a puff of smoke. My second shot wasn't quite so good, but the second husk was severely injured. As I ran toward the husk, I removed a ninja throwing star from my inventory and threw it. Since I was only about three blocks away, the throwing star buried itself in the husk's chest, killing him.

We then jumped onto the wall of the village, using our climbing skills to scale the wall quickly, like spiders. When we got to the top of the wall, we pulled ourselves up and over slowly so as not to be seen by the iron golem. I reached into my inventory and grabbed a handful of poppies. Then, when the iron golem was close enough, I leapt onto his shoulders and held the poppies in front of his nose. He shrugged his shoulders and shook me to the ground. Then he looked at me angrily. He raised his massive foot in order to stomp on me, but I rolled away just in time to avoid being squished. I reached out and held the poppies in front of me as high in the air as I could. "Evan! These poppies are for you."

"They look nice, but I have to kill you," said Evan. "Otherwise the griefer will...." He then swung his huge arm at me and I ducked just in time to avoid having my head ripped off.

Wynter dashed over to my side. Fortunately, the griefer had gone further into the village and did not hear the ruckus by the front gate. "It's true, Evan. Penelope told us."

At the mention of Penelope's name, Evan's face softened. "I like Penelope. I've known her since she was quite young. But, I have to protect my family first." He then took a swipe at Wynter and caught him on the shoulder. Wynter screamed in pain, his shoulder dislocated. He slumped to the ground.

I put my hands up. "Stop! We are here to kill the griefer. Then your son can be free."

My words shocked Evan. For a brief moment, he didn't react.

"You are here to kill me?" said the griefer, who had returned, attracted by Wynter's screams. "Evan, I see that you have tried to defend the village from these foolhardy ninjas. I shall not kill your son."

The iron golem bowed to the griefer. "Thank you, sire. I am most appreciative."

"Sire?" I said derisively. "You're just an arrogant, mean, selfish, horrible person!"

The griefer smiled. "I certainly am. And I'm going to kill you and your friend right now just to prove how right you are." The griefer hopped off his horse and pulled out two enchanted diamond swords, one for each hand. "Evan, back away. You can clean up the mess when I'm through."

The griefer came toward us. "You think you can fight both of us at once?" I asked.

The griefer looked over at Wynter who was holding his shoulder and clearly in pain. "Looks like one against maybe one and a third. Your buddy is in no condition to defeat me."

Using the correct tactical approach, the griefer rushed toward me. If he could take me out, then he would have a much easier time with Wynter. But I don't think he realized the type of training the Guild had provided. Just as the griefer came within a sword length of me and began to slash his swords together like a pair of scissors, I ducked low and slid between his legs. Before he could turn around, I leapt to my feet and buried a dagger in his back.

He grunted and turned around. "How dare you? I am the great griefer Maximus."

I chuckled. "Never heard of you. Plus, that is a stupid name."

The griefer growled and rushed toward me again. Overcome with his own anger, he forgot about Wynter who had used his working arm to reach into his inventory and remove a crossbow. He shot the crossbow at the griefer and hit him in the leg. The griefer screamed in pain and rolled to the side. I was moving in to finish him off, when he pulled a crossbow out of his own inventory and shot at me. I just avoided being hit in the center of my chest by rolling onto the ground, the arrow whizzing past me.

As I rolled on the ground and stood up, I heard an agonizing scream and looked over and saw that Wynter had been shot dead center in his chest with the crossbow arrow meant for me.

He was flashing red.

"Wynter! I'll be right there," I shouted as I rushed toward him and pulled a potion of healing out of my inventory.

I knelt down and lifted his head. But, just as I was about to tilt the healing potion into his mouth, he flashed red and disappeared into a puff of smoke.

"No!" I screamed with rage and sorrow.

"Yes!" said Maximus the griefer. I turned and saw that he was drinking his own potion of healing. But I wouldn't let him heal.

I reached into my inventory and pulled out a trident. I threw it at the griefer, hitting him in his gut. He doubled over in pain, dropping the potion of healing and shattering the bottle in which it was contained.

I stood up and walked slowly to where the griefer lay on the ground writhing in pain. I wanted him to suffer, for what he did to Wynter. For what he had done to these villagers.

By now a crowd of stunned villagers had gathered. They watched me approach the griefer and yelled at me to finish him. I looked around at the crowd and saw several dozen villagers with anxious, imploring eyes. I knew what they wanted. They wanted vengeance. Like I had wanted and achieved against the pillagers who destroyed my village and killed my parents.

I turned around and looked at the villagers and said, "Have at it." Then I stepped aside as a mob of villagers rushed toward the griefer and beat him with sticks. It was not a pretty sight, but it didn't last long and the griefer soon vanished in a puff of smoke.

The villagers cheered and I felt happy for them, though I had lost Wynter. I pulled out a few bricks of TNT inventory from my and walked up to the wall and blew a gigantic hole in it. The villagers cheered more.

"You're free now," I shouted to the crowd. "Don't lose your freedom."

I was leaving the village to go back to the hill to find my llamas when Penelope rushed up to me. She grabbed hold of me and hugged me tight. There were tears in her eyes.

"You're welcome," I said, as I hugged her back.

"It's not that," she said. "Well, it is. But, when the griefer came in this morning, before he fought you ... hurrr ... he killed my uncle!" Penelope buried her face in my shoulder and sobbed uncontrollably. I held her there.

"Will you stay here then?" I asked.

She lifted her head from my shoulder and said, "I don't know what there is for me here anymore."

"I'm not supposed to tell you this, but I'm a wandering trader."

There was shock on her face. "That can't be. You're some sort of ninja, right?"

"No. It is a cover." I paused and thought for a moment. Even with all the hardship I've been through and all the strange politics circulating through the wandering trader Guild, I knew it was a good option for Penelope if she wanted it. "Would you like to become a wandering trader?"

She stopped crying and sniffed. "Would it mean I could kill other griefer's like you did?"

I shrugged. "Probably, sometimes. Other times, who knows. If you become a wandering trader you have to swear obedience to the leadership no matter what you think about what they have asked you to do. That is the Way. You must follow the Way or you will be expunged."

Penelope understood what I meant. She would be *killed* if she disobeyed. She stood there for a moment and then said, "Yes, I'd like to become a wandering trader."

I smiled. "Come with me then. But know this, there is no going back. You can think about while we travel. But once we get to a certain place, you have to make a forever decision."

Penelope nodded her head. "I understand."

We both walked back to the hill. I untied Wynter's llamas and set them free. They had to wander back to headquarters by themselves.

I went into my tent and changed into my wandering trader robes and then packed all my gear away onto my llamas.

"Let's get going. I think it's all right if you walk with me. There's probably nothing too unusual about a villager and a wandering trader being seen together."

Penelope nodded her head. "Thank you again, Winston. I wish you would have arrived a day earlier so that my uncle would still be alive, but then, I would not have the opportunity to become a wandering trader."

I nodded my head sadly. "I guess that is something at least."

Chapter 15

When we arrived at headquarters, Penelope faced the same challenges I had when I first entered. I explained her desire to become a wandering trader and that she understood the consequences of changing her mind. Once she had been allowed entry, we went to the llama stables and put away my team.

After that, we headed for Wickham's chambers. I told him the story of Wynter's death and Penelope's desire to become a wandering trader. Wickham nodded his head slowly the entire time I was speaking.

"She is a bit old to begin the training, but I can sense a fierce determination in her. What is your name, girl?"

"Penelope."

Wickham, as he had done when I had told him my birth name was Kevin, had a sour look on his face and shook his head sadly. "That will never do. You have to have a name that starts with a W. I will find one in the *Book of Names*."

"Wickham, sir," said Penelope. "I understand the other wandering trader who was killed was named Wynter. I would like to take that name to honor him ... if that is permitted."

Wickham stopped in his tracks and turned and looked at Penelope. "That is a very good idea. However, his name was spelled with a Y. We will spell your name Winter with an I. So let it be known throughout the Guild."

I bowed to Wickham. Penelope ... I mean ... Winter did the same.

"I will have trader Winona come and take you to the girls' dormitory. She will get you situated and you can begin your training tomorrow."

At that moment there was a knock on the door and Winona, a tall, fierce-looking woman of about thirty years, entered. "Come with me, Winter." Winter looked over her shoulder at me and smiled. "I hope we will see each other again."

I felt something stir in me, and I smiled back. "I hope so too."

Winter and Winona left the room and shut the door behind them.

After they left, Wickham looked at me silently for a few seconds and then shook his head. "I can't believe the griefer killed Wynter. It should have been an easy mission."

I nodded my head. "It seemed like it was going well. Somehow the iron golem landed a lucky blow on Wynter's shoulder and it gave the griefer an advantage. I apologize for the mishap."

"Do not apologize. Sometimes it happens. Death in battle is inevitable."

I nodded my head. "That is the Way."

"Victory breeds hatred, the defeated sleeps in misery," said Wickham. "That is why we must kill our enemies, so that they do not survive to hate us for our victories. That is the Way."

"That is the Way," I responded.

"You may leave now. I will not give you another assignment for at least one month. You may use that time to wander and to train."

I nodded my head. "Thank you. I will do so." Then I left the room and walked down the stairs, anxious to get back to Slimy.

* * *

I entered the trainee dormitory and found the room Willmar shared with two other trainees. I knocked on the door. A few seconds passed before Willmar, looking tired and bedraggled, answered the door. When he saw me, he smiled broadly. "Praise be to Notch! You have returned!"

I nodded my head and looked over his shoulder into the room. "Where is Slimy?"

"Sleeping. Finally."

"What do you mean?"

Willmar took a deep breath and then responded. "He was confused when you left. I think he thought maybe you had abandoned him. Until he fell asleep an hour ago, he hadn't slept at all since you left."

"I'm so sorry. I had no idea that would happen," I said. "Can you take me to him?"

Willmar led the way to a small bedroom which was made for another trainee, but which was empty except for Slimy's crib. I looked in and saw Slimy sleeping. He was even snoring a little.

"I'm not sure I should wake him up," I said.

Willmar glared at me. His eyes were bloodshot from lack of sleep. He looked like a crazy man. "I don't care what you do. Just get him out of here. I need some sleep."

I thought about scolding him for his tone with a superior, but I knew that he had been through a tough few days, so I let his insubordination pass without comment.

I reached into the crib and picked up Slimy. His eyes opened part way. He saw me. He muttered, "In-ston. Boop." Then, he fell asleep in my arms.

"Punch the crib and put it in my inventory for me," I said to Willmar. He did as asked.

I walked to the front door and stepped out into the hallway. I turned around to thank Willmar, but he slammed the door in my face. I chuckled.

I walked back through the halls of the trainee dormitory toward my own room. But, after a few seconds, I felt eyes watching me. I turned around and saw Wes standing in the doorway to his room and staring at me with a burning hatred.

"What?" I said.

Wes just smirked, walked back inside of his room, and slowly closed the door.

I would need to keep my eye on him, that was for certain.

End of Book 2 of
The Ballad of Winston, the Wandering Trader

Book 3

Chapter 1

After killing the griefer and liberating Penelope's village, I spent the next month training and occasionally wandering here and there. It was an uneventful month for the most part. As is typical for wandering traders, I ran into some angry and bitter players who insulted me, but nothing got out of hand and I didn't have to ... hurrr ... *neutralize* them.

My ward Slimy had continued to increase his vocabulary. Now he could say my name clearly and even ask for a few items. Usually, he would ask for food or to play with my action figure, Creepy.

"Creepy! Give. Pwease," he would say.

At first, I resisted giving Creepy to him to play with. After all, Creepy was *my* doll ... hurrr ... I mean *action figure*. It was my one memory of my childhood and my parents. But, I also realized that Slimy was still a child, and he needed to have some good memories, so I eventually let him play with Creepy.

"You need to be really careful with Creepy," I said as I held the action figure just out of Slimy's reach. He bounced up and down excitedly. "Creepy is very important to me. As long as you don't hurt Creepy, I will let you play with him from time to time."

Slimy bounced up and down even faster. "Creepy! Creepy!"

I handed Creepy to Slimy and he absorbed Creepy into his body cube. He spun Creepy around inside of his cube and giggled. I assumed they were having some sort of imaginary conversation and going on all sorts of adventures. It's what I would've done if I were still a child.

But Slimy was very considerate. Whenever he was done playing with Creepy, he would spit Creepy out from his slime cube so that Creepy would land at my feet and then I could clean any excess slime off of Creepy and tuck him safely back into my inventory.

During my wanders over the past month, I took Slimy with me every time. Wickham had forbade me using any of the trainees as babysitters and none of the full-fledged wandering traders had the time or inclination to babysit a slime.

As I traveled with Slimy, I got weird looks from some of the players. Some of them even asked me how much I would trade the slime for, but I always told them he wasn't for sale. I had to pretend he was my pet or that I was transporting him to another buyer. The real story was far too complicated and, honestly, most players just didn't care.

One morning while I was at wandering trader HQ, I left Slimy in my room playing with Creepy and went down to the weapons room to train. When I walked into the room, I saw Winter training with her trainer, Trader

Winona. They were practicing sword fighting. Each of them held a simple iron sword.

"It is important to train with a basic iron sword," instructed Winona. "If you can fight well with the most basic of weapons, you can fight even better with swords made of upgraded materials and with enchantments."

Winter nodded her head. "I understand."

"In that case, let us proceed," said Winona.

I watched as she and Winter practiced their fighting exercises. They started in slow-motion, the way you would practice with a brand-new trainee. But soon, Winter seemed to be going at a pace much quicker than I would've expected because she had only been training for one month. I watched in awe as she and Winona slowly brought their sword practice up to full speed. In fact, several other wandering traders who were in the room began to watch with excitement.

I could see sweat forming on Winona's brow while Winter seemed to look calm and cool, like there wasn't a problem at all performing the complex skills that she was being required to employ. The two of them continued fighting faster and faster and using more and more skilled maneuvers until finally Winona said, "Halt!"

Winter immediately pulled her sword away from Winona and tucked it back into her inventory. Then she went down to the floor on one knee and bowed her head to Winona, as a sign of respect.

Winona tucked her sword away and looked at Winter with a strange expression. "Arise, Winter." Winter stood up and maintained a neutral expression as she looked at Winona. Winona continued. "I've never seen a trainee advance so quickly in sword fighting skills. I have to say that you have reached the maximum of my ability to train you with the sword."

As Winter smiled, the rest of us gasped. The quickest I had ever heard of anyone advancing through the sword fighting practicum was two months. It had taken me four months, but of course I was several years younger than Winter at the time I endured my training.

Winter bowed her head slightly and said, "Thank you for the compliment, Trader Winona. I appreciate it greatly."

Winona smiled. "Well, you've earned it. Why don't you take the rest of the day off? Tomorrow, we will begin with archery instruction."

Winter smiled and bowed to Winona again and then began to leave the room.

As she was walking toward the door, she saw me and came over. "Hi, Winston. Haven't seen you in a couple weeks."

I nodded my head. "Slimy and I just got back from an extended wander. We went down to Zombie Bane and then continued out into the wilderness of the jungle and swamplands. I didn't make very many trades, but it was nice to be alone for a while."

Winter smiled. "I can't wait until I get to go on my own wanders."

I smiled back. "Judging by the way you're picking up the skills, it might not be too long."

"How long did it take you to become a wandering trader?" she asked.

"Gosh, almost five years," I said. "But I started when I was only ten years old. I could barely hold up a sword."

Winter smiled. "Well, I hope it doesn't take me that long. Winona seems to think that I might be ready sooner rather than later."

I smiled again. "I hope so."

Winter took a deep breath and then sighed. "Well, I'm pretty tired after that sword fighting practice. I'm going to go back to my room and relax."

"Okay then, see you later," I said.

I watched as Winter walked away and then I walked to the weapons stand and selected a trident. I did not normally use a trident, so I wanted to practice with it a few times just in case I was ever called upon to use one. After I picked up the trident, I walked over to the ranged weapons target area. After I had thrown the trident about a dozen times, hitting the target each time, but not always near the center, I saw Wes walk into the room.

Our eyes met and he scowled at me. I scowled back. I was about to walk over and put him in his place, but then I noticed something terrible. *He was wearing official wandering trader robes!* He had passed his test and was now a full-fledged member of the Guild.

Wes strutted across the room and walked right up to me. With an arrogant voice, he said, "Notice anything different?"

"Looks like you passed the test," I said bitterly.

Wes smiled with a sly grin like a fox. "Of course I did. It was easy." I didn't say anything in response. "And now, you can't pull rank on me anymore. You have to respect me."

I laughed. "I may not be able to pull rank on you, but I don't have to respect you. ***Ever.***"

Wes reached into his inventory and began to draw a sword. I stood there unmoving, waiting for this coward to strike me. But then Wes thought better of his anger and tucked his sword back into his inventory and pulled his hand out empty.

"You'll get yours one of these days, Winston," he said as he turned his back on me and walked away.

I looked back at the target at which I had been throwing the trident. I imagined Wes's face was right in the center of it. I cocked my hand and then threw the trident as hard as I could, burying its three points right in the center of the bulls eye.

Chapter 2

I spent another hour in the training room. After I finished with my trident, I practiced with my other ranged weapons including my bow and my crossbow. Finally, I also spent about ten minutes practicing fighting with an axe, which was probably my weakest weapon. There was a wooden target we could throw the axe at and a couple of upright logs we could practice chopping as though we were fighting a mob or player.

When I finished my practicing, I left the training area and went down to the stable to check on my llamas. Even though walking to the stables was not on the path back to my room, I felt it was important to check on my llamas at least once a day, to pet them, brush their hair, and just let them know that I cared. Most wandering traders did the same.

When I entered the stable, there was a new trainee working at the front desk. I had never seen him before. I walked up to him and said, "What's your name?"

The trainee, who was a villager of about thirteen years of age, stood at attention and said, "My name's Kyle ... hurrr ... I mean, Wally."

I chuckled. "You must be new here if you still accidentally use your birth name."

Wally nodded his head. "Just got here a couple days ago. And, I wanted to be named Walter, but Wickham told me that Walter was the name of the founder of the Guild of the wandering traders. He would not name me Walter, so he compromised and named me Wally."

"Do you like that name?" I asked.

Wally shrugged. "I mean, it's okay. I really did like Walter though."

I nodded my head. "So, what made you decide to become a wandering trader?"

A sad look crossed Wally's face. "It's just that ... hurrr ... well, I mean,...." I saw tears forming in Wally's eyes. "I'm not ready to tell you. Is that all right?"

I reached out and put my hand on his shoulder. "You never have to tell me if you don't want to. I was just making conversation." Wally wiped a tear from his eyes and nodded his head. "Anyway, I'm going to go check on my llamas. It'll just take a few minutes."

I left Wally and walked to the corral where Sunny and Pippa were housed. I saw that they had been recently fed their lunch, probably thanks to Wally or another one of the trainees who worked in the stables. When I opened the gate to the corral, I could see them both get excited. Sunny started acting like a total freak, jumping up and down and scratching her feet in the dirt.

"Calm down. I don't want you to get me dirty," I said.

Each of them nuzzled me with their faces, expecting a snack. I didn't disappoint them. Every time I visited, I gave them either a carrot or an apple. Today, it was a carrot. They both greedily chewed the carrots and swallowed them. They nuzzled me again, hoping for more snacks, but I never had more than one thing for them. I didn't want them getting fat and lethargic and slowing down my wandering. I spent a few minutes scratching their fur and saying nice things to them before leaving and returning to my room.

When I got back to my room, I found Slimy asleep on the floor. Creepy was still inside of his slime cube. I shuddered at the thought of being trapped inside a slime cube. As much as I liked Slimy and felt responsible for his welfare, I had to admit, if I were being perfectly honest, that slimes did feel kind of gross.

I picked up Slimy and put him into his crib which now had one of the railings removed. I wasn't any longer concerned he would fall out and hurt himself. He had been growing in size slightly, but the main difference was that he now seemed to have more control over his bodily movements as he got older.

I wonder when he will become a medium-sized slime?

I went to the small kitchen in my room and quickly roasted a pork chop. Then, I shoved it between two pieces of bread and drizzled it with some chorus fruit jam. I sat at the table and ate my sandwich. I had just finished my final bite of my sandwich when there was an official-sounding knock on the door. I sighed and shook my head. I really just wanted to take a nap. But, duty called.

I stood up from the table and wiped my mouth on a napkin. I walked over to the door and opened it. Wayne, Wickham's head guard, stood in front of me.

Before he had a chance to speak, I said, "Let me guess. Wickham wants to talk to me?"

Wayne nodded his head. "I wouldn't be here otherwise. I don't like you very much."

"Thank you for your honesty," I said sarcastically. "Give me a minute to change my robe. I was training this morning and I'm still kind of stinky."

"Hurry up then," said Wayne.

I shut the door and quickly changed into a new robe. I washed my face and my hands and then slicked my hair back before putting my wandering trader hood over my head. Then I went back to the door and opened it. "Let's go."

Chapter 3

Wayne walked behind me as I climbed the stairs to Wickham's chamber. I had to admit that even though I had only been required to walk to Wickham's chamber a handful of times, climbing the hundreds of stairs was getting old ... *really* old. I looked over my shoulder at Wayne and said, "Hasn't anyone ever thought about putting in some sort of lift system? Maybe a series of pistons you could just stand on and be lifted up to the chamber?"

Wayne guffawed. "That's the dumbest thing I've ever heard of. Wickham would never allow that. He likes people to have to work to see him."

"A power-play, eh?"

"Maybe he just wants all the wandering traders to stay in shape," said Wayne as he shrugged his shoulders and pointed up the stairs. "Get moving. I don't want to talk about this anymore."

About a minute later, we came to the platform just outside of the front door of Wickham's chamber. Another guard named Wiggoly, stood there. He put out his hand and said, "Wickham is not to be disturbed. I'll let you know when he is ready for you."

Inwardly, I rolled my eyes. I wasn't stupid enough to roll them outwardly where my disgust could be observed by one of Wickham's guards. I turned around and stood on the edge of the platform and looked back down the stairs. The stairs were carved into a rough rocky slope. Here and there throughout the slope and adjacent to the stairs were gaps which fell into an abyss of unknown depth. Those seemingly bottomless pits always gave me the creeps when I walked by them on the way up and the way down.

I looked back at Wiggoly after about five minutes and asked, "Any idea how long he'll be in there?"

The guard shook his head. "Shut up and wait."

Rude.

As I stood glancing around at the scenery outside of the chamber, I began to feel a strange presence. I couldn't quite explain it at first but then I began to focus on this feeling. It began to feel almost like something evil. I had never felt anything like it in my life, not even when that horrible pillager killed my parents. The hair on the back of my neck stood on its end and I shivered involuntarily. I suddenly felt like I was being watched ... no, there is a more precise word. I felt like I was being *studied*.

Wayne looked over at me and laughed. "What are you cold? You some kind of baby?"

I shook my head. "Who is Wickham meeting with, anyway?" I was beginning to suspect it was not a typical guest.

At that moment though, the feeling of evil suddenly vanished and the door to Wickham's chamber opened. "Ah, Winston. Just the trader I've been wanting to see. Please come in."

I looked at Wickham and tilted my head sideways. "Weren't you meeting with someone? Do they need to leave?"

Wickham scowled at Wiggoly. Then, he looked back at me. "Oh I wasn't ... hurrr ... meeting with anyone. Wiggoly was mistaken. I was just preparing for the meeting with you."

I didn't believe him for a second, but I kept my feelings to myself and said, "Oh. That makes sense." I walked up the stairs and into Wickham's chamber. He shut the door behind me.

"Please have a seat, Winston."

I sat down in one of the cushioned chairs that were in the room. Previously the chairs had been uncomfortable wooden chairs but for some reason he had his nice furniture out. As I got comfortable in the chair, I said, "Nice chairs. Where did you get them?"

Wickham shrugged. "They were here when I moved in. But, never mind that. We're not here to talk about furniture."

"I didn't think we were. Just curious."

"Anyway, I've been thinking about you and your role as a wandering trader. What you accomplished last month against the griefer was noteworthy. And, your bringing that villager girl who is now named Winter into the fold turned out to be a good decision. When you first arrived with her, I thought it was another boondoggle like your adopting that slime."

Boondoggle? He was saying Slimy was a boondoggle! I was furious, but kept it to myself.

"But, Winter has turned out to be quite a find. She's a prodigy even. It wouldn't surprise me if she's a full-fledged wandering trader within the next six months."

I smiled. "She'll be happy to know that."

Wickham shook his head. "Don't tell her. We can't give anyone false or even legitimate hope. She must focus on her training."

"Understood."

Wickham took a deep breath and scratched his cheek before continuing. "But that's not the reason I called you here either. I want to give you a task."

"Another assassination?" I wasn't sure I wanted to know the answer.

Wickham shook his head. "No, no violence required, at least none is planned. I need you to deliver a chest to one of my contacts in Capitol City."

Capitol City! I was excited. I had never been to Capitol City. It was at least a four-day wander, so I would get to see all kinds of sights that I had yet to see in the Overworld.

"That sounds great," I said. "I've always wanted to go to Capitol City."

Wickham smiled. "Excellent. And, I want you to take Winter with you. But take her in her villager clothes so that it is not suspicious that two wandering traders are traveling together. She can learn some of the basics of how to wander properly from you while you complete this mission. You know, kill two birds with one stone."

"That's great. I will let her know," I said. "I assume I should call her Penelope for the duration of that trip."

Wickham scrunched up his face and shrugged his shoulders up to his ears as though he were hearing fingers being scratched on a chalkboard. "Ugh. Names that do not begin with 'W' are so horrid. But, yes. You should use her villager name while you are out in the Overworld this time."

"So who is this contact? I guess I need to know where to deliver this chest."

Wickham nodded his head. "The contact will meet you. Go to the Golden Watermelon Hotel in Capitol City. On the day you check-in, be sure to have dinner in the hotel's restaurant and order an extra-large bowl of mushroom stew, a loaf of bread, half a watermelon, and a glass of milk. The contact will know it's you and identify him or herself."

I nodded my understanding. "Is there a password or secret handshake or something?"

Wickham chuckled. "I was just getting to that. The contact will approach you and will ask you what your favorite mob is. Your response is to say 'I haven't thought about that much, but I'd have to say my favorite mob is the silverfish'."

"Well, that's not true at all," I said, disgusted by the thought of anyone who would say a silverfish was their favorite mob!

Wickham slapped his forehead. "It doesn't matter if it's true, you idiot. It's the *password*. Now, repeat it to me."

I repeated the ungainly and stupid password response several times until Wickham was satisfied that I understood it. "Excellent. It's just after lunchtime right now, so go tell Winter the plan. The two of you are to leave first thing in the morning. I will have Wayne deliver the chest to you at the exit to headquarters. *Do not tell anyone else about this mission.* Tell Winter that she is not to tell anyone else. If I learn that either one of you has discussed this mission with anyone else, the penalty will be ... severe."

Chapter 4

After I left Wickham's chamber, I found Trader Winona and asked her if I could speak with Winter about a mission from Wickham.

"Why would you want to talk to her about it? And, why would Wickham want you to take a trainee on a mission?" asked Winona with a disbelieving voice.

"Wickham wants me to take her with me in her villager garb so that she can see what being a wandering trader is like."

Winona screwed up her eyes and looked at me with suspicion. "Why wouldn't he just want me to keep training her? I mean I've been a wandering trader for over ten years. You've just passed the final examination a few months ago."

I shrugged. "I have no idea. But Wickham told me what he wanted me to do and I must obey. That is the Way."

Winona, still wearing a perplexed expression, sighed and then said, "Indeed. That is the Way. I will tell Winter to come to your quarters presently."

* * *

About ten minutes later, Winter arrived at my room and knocked on the door. I opened the door and she came in. Slimy hopped over to her and said excitedly, "Inter. Inter."

She smiled at him and picked him up. "Hi, Slimy, you weird little cube of goo."

Slimy giggled. "Inter. Inter."

"I'll play with you in a minute. I need to talk to Winston first," she said as she put Slimy back on the ground. Slimy hopped around the room excitedly, waiting for the moment when Winter would play with him.

Winter looked at me and said, "What is it? Trader Winona said something about a request from Wickham?"

I told her about what Wickham wanted us to do and that she would need to wear her villager clothing and go by her villager name while we were on the mission. "But," I cautioned, "you cannot tell anyone about the true purpose of the mission ... ***ever.*** If anyone asks, it is just a training mission."

Winter smiled broadly. "This is amazing! I didn't think I would be able to leave headquarters for quite some time. It'll be good to see the outside world again."

I nodded my head and then looked at Winter seriously. "Anytime Wickham himself asks a wandering trader to do a mission, it is serious. This mission sounds simple, but I expect we may encounter some difficulties. I'm sure something very important is inside the chest he wants us to deliver."

"What? What do you think is there?"

I shook my head. "I have no idea. It could be emeralds, a book or a map, or something that I couldn't even dream of."

"Do you think it's some sort of ... contraband?" Winter asked conspiratorially.

"I *really* don't know. All I know is that I'm supposed to meet a contact at a restaurant in Capitol City and once I am sure it is my contact using some passwords, I'm supposed to give him or her the chest. That's all I know."

Winter looked disappointed at the lack of information, but she had better get used to it when dealing with Wickham. "Okay, then. When do we leave?"

"Wickham's personal guard is going to deliver the chest to me first thing in the morning at the exit to headquarters. So, meet me at the stable at dawn. I don't think that the trainee cafeteria will be open at that time, so if you're hungry in the morning make sure you eat something in your room."

"Okay," said Winter. "Do you mind if I play with Slimy for a bit?"

I smiled. "Of course not." I reached in my inventory and pulled out Creepy. "And ... hurrr ... he likes to play with this."

Winter grabbed Creepy and said, "This looks like an action figure that one of the little boys who lived next to me in the village used to play with."

I blushed, embarrassed that as a sixteen-year-old *official* wandering trader I still had the action figure. "Yeah ... hurrr ... it was my action figure when I was a boy. I kept it for ... sentimental value. My parents were.... Well, you know."

Winter looked sad for a moment. She *did* know. She knew what it was like to be orphaned at a young age. After a few seconds, she shook her head and looked happy again. "At least someone gets to play with it," she said as she turned around to play with Slimy.

Chapter 5

The next morning dawned and I quickly got dressed before eating a loaf of bread and drinking a glass of water in my room. I lifted Slimy, who was still asleep, from his crib and carried him down to the stables. Winter was already there, speaking with a wandering trader trainee I had never seen before who was working at the llama checkout desk. I motioned for Winter to follow me to the corral where Sunny and Pippa were waiting.

"Can I hold Slimy?" she asked.

"Sure," I said, handing her the little cube of goo.

"Inter. Inter," he babbled.

"Oh no, Slimy. Call me Penelope now. I have to pretend I am still a villager for the next few days."

Slimy looked confused and said, "Inter? Inter?"

Penelope shook her head. "No, no. Penelope. Pen. L. O. Pea. Penelope."

Slimy stared at her for a moment and then said, "LOP. LOP."

Penelope and I both laughed.

"Nice job, Slimy," I said. "Close enough, I think."

"Yes, it's perfect," said Penelope with a smile.

We arrived at the corral and I affixed the slime saddle on Pippa's back. I placed Slimy into the saddle and as I led the llamas out of the corral, Slimy quickly fell back to sleep even before we got to the checkout counter.

We arrived at the checkout location and I spoke with the unknown trainee, who appeared to be a villager in his early twenties.

"Who are you?" I asked.

"Weston's the name, Sir," he said.

"And, what were you before you came to the Guild."

Weston laughed like a madman. "Well, Sir, I was a nitwit. I didn't do much but walk around in circles, but then one day the wind blew me off course, and I walked and walked and walked and...."

"I get the idea," I said.

"Yeah, so anyway, when I finished walking, I found myself in front of a door. Then, the door opened and I thought maybe some zombie was going to come out and eat me, but it was a wandering trader. He grabbed me and said that since I had discovered their headquarters, I could either join the Guild or die."

"Intense," I said.

"Yep. So, I thought about it for a minute and, well, I may be a nitwit, but I ain't stupid. So, I joined the wandering traders."

"How goes your training?" I asked.

"They say I am destined to be a stable clerk for the rest of my days," he said.

I rolled my eyes and laughed. "Well, I guess it is better than being dead."

"Yep."

"By the way, have you seen Wayne this morning?" I asked.

Weston nodded his head. "He said he was going to go talk to Wit who is on guard duty at the exit gate."

"Thanks," I said.

"By the way, that girl with you is wearing villager clothes? Is that allowed?" asked Weston.

"Yes," I said. "We are on a secret mission. The clothes are camouflage."

Weston laughed. "No, really. I may be a nitwit, but that was a serious question."

I glared at him. "And, I gave you a serious answer. I'm not kidding. We are on a secret mission. Wickham himself will punish you ... hurrr ... probably *kill* you if you tell anyone about this."

Even after these words, I could tell Weston still did not believe me, but when I didn't crack a smile or change my expression, he realized I was telling the truth. Terror filled his eyes and he whispered, "I promise. I won't tell a soul."

I nodded. "That is the Way."

Weston stood at attention. "Yes, Sir, that is the Way."

Penelope and I walked to the exit and found Wayne speaking with Wit. Wit's single tooth still holding on inside his mouth by some miracle.

When Wayne saw us approaching, he looked at Wit and said, "Get lost by order of Wickham."

Wit had an offended expression but knew better than to question orders from Wayne. He stood up and saluted and said, "Wit obeys Wickham. That is the Way." And then he tottered off back toward the checkout desk, scowling at us as we walked past.

"Good morning, Wayne," I said.

Wayne grunted. "What's good about it? I'm usually sleeping at this time of day, but Wickham wanted me to come down here and do this, and I won't disobey him. That is the Way."

Penelope and I both spoke in unison, "That is the Way."

"Here it is," said Wayne, digging into his inventory and then thrusting a small chest at me. "Don't lose it. If you do, I suggest you hide, because I'll be coming for you to kill you."

Penelope gasped but said nothing.

"That is the Way," I said rather than responding with my true feelings of anger and disgust.

Wayne nodded his head. "That is the Way. Now get lost," he said as he flipped the lever to open the door to headquarters.

As the doors opened, the dim light of the new breaking dawn filtered into the dark and dusty entry corridor. Penelope and I looked at each other with a wordless understanding of the gravity of our mission. I gripped the leads on my llamas. I looked back at Slimy who snored asleep in his saddle without a care in the world. And then, we set off for Capitol City on our mysterious mission.

Chapter 6

The first day of Penelope's and my travels toward Capitol City were rather uneventful. We saw various mob wildlife, including some feral cows and rabbits. We passed through the edge of a jungle biome and saw a few dozen parrots and a couple of ocelots.

"I've always wanted a pet ocelot," said Penelope wistfully.

"Once you are a wandering trader, you can probably tame one when you're out on your wanders," I said.

"I suppose," she said. "Still, it would be nice to have one now. At least you have Slimy as a companion on your wanders."

I looked over at Slimy who was asleep in his saddle. "Yeah, life of the party," I said sarcastically.

Penelope giggled. "I guess he is a little boring sometimes."

We encountered a handful of players, all of whom were generally nice. A couple of them waved me away with a look of disgust, but none of them tried anything violent.

As the sun was beginning to set on the first day of our journey, we arrived at the cave where I had stayed a month ago on my way to Creeper Junction. I warned Penelope about the spiders in the cave but assured her that they were allies of Wickham and would not harm her as long as she was with me.

"Why do the spiders have an alliance with Wickham?" Penelope asked.

"I really have no idea. Wickham does a lot of things that we normal traders don't know about. It is all way above our pay grade ... hurrr ... even though we don't get paid. We have to live off our trades."

Derp.

Penelope nodded her head but said nothing. I led my llamas into the cave and we found the same alcove that I had slept in during my last journey. It was large enough for two beds and a crib as well as the llamas. But just. I bricked off the entrance to the alcove and hung some torches on the walls to prevent mobs from spawning. Then, I lifted Slimy out of his saddle and placed him on the ground.

"Cozy room," said Penelope sarcastically.

"LOP. LOP," said Slimy as he was hopping towards Penelope to see if she wanted to play.

I smiled. "Why don't you play with Slimy for a while and I will prepare dinner?"

"Okay."

The rest of the evening went as one would expect. We ate dinner, played with Slimy a little bit, and then we all went to sleep.

* * *

The next morning, we had a light breakfast of half a loaf of bread each and a couple of fried eggs. Slimy absorbed an entire apple for breakfast.

I smiled at him. "You must be having a growth spurt! I've never seen you absorb an entire apple that fast."

"I grow," said Slimy.

"Yeah, when are you going to become a medium-sized slime?" asked Penelope.

"E dee um," said Slimy.

I chuckled as I fed the llamas some carrots and wheat. Then, I unsealed the entrance to the alcove and was slightly disappointed that I didn't see Oculus or another spider there waiting to talk. Penelope could sense my disappointment.

"What's wrong?"

"Oh, nothing, I guess. I was just kind of hoping one of the spiders would be there to chat with. It's pretty cool talking to a spider."

Penelope looked a little concerned. "I suppose. But, I think I could live the rest of my days without speaking with a spider."

I chuckled. "Maybe you should reconsider becoming a wandering trader then." I did not wait for Penelope to respond. Instead, I plopped Slimy into his saddle on Pippa and led my two llamas out of the cave, followed by Penelope.

We continued on our way to Creeper Junction. The plan was to spend tonight in Creeper Junction, and then head out on the two-day journey to Capitol City tomorrow morning. I had been informed by other wandering traders that there was a small village about halfway between Capitol City and Creeper Junction called Del Mar, located on the shores of an inland sea. The village supposedly had some hotels and good food from what I was told.

Around midday, after not encountering any players, we stopped at the top of a small hill to have lunch. Slimy and Penelope were about twenty blocks away, playing, as I prepared lunch. Just then, two players were walking below the hill when they looked up and saw me. They recognized that I was a wandering trader and sprinted up the hill. I sighed and stood up.

"Judging by your excitement, it would appear you wish to trade?" I said.

One of the players shook his head and said, "No, we don't want to trade, we just want to talk to you. We think wandering traders are awesome."

"Totally," said the other.

"I fear you are a member of a tiny minority of players," I said.

The first player spoke again. "My name is Tantancrafter and this here is DJ. We've been traveling the Overworld for a few months, becoming richer and richer, and acquiring more powerful weapons."

"Totally," said DJ. "When you work with a partner, you can increase your wealth much more quickly than when you work by yourself."

I rolled my eyes. "Good for you. If you don't want to trade, can you move along? I'm preparing lunch for my guests over there," I said as I nodded in the direction of Penelope and Slimy who were now observing my interaction with the two players.

"Whoa! I didn't know wandering traders and villagers ever traveled together," said Tantancrafter.

"Totally," said DJ. "I thought villagers hated wandering traders."

I shook my head. "Not always." I paused, hoping they might get the hint. They didn't. "As I was saying, if you don't want to trade, do you mind getting lost?"

"Hold on a second," said Tantancrafter. "DJ and I were talking the other day and we were thinking that it would be awesome to be a wandering trader. Any chance we can join you?"

"Totally," said DJ.

I suddenly became concerned. Have they somehow heard that it was possible for a player to become a wandering trader? This was not information we could afford to have leak into the world at large. I might have to kill them....

"Why would you think you could *become* a wandering trader? All mobs and NPCs just spawn into their role in Minecraft, right? The same way you have no choice except to be a player."

Tantancrafter shrugged. "I mean, that's what everybody says. But, I just thought maybe...." His voice trailed off with a tone of sadness.

"Totally," said DJ sadly. "I mean, we could craft a wandering trader robe or something and pretend, but it would be cool to be part of the group."

"Be careful what you wish for," I said ominously. "Anyway, no, you cannot join the wandering traders. But, I appreciate the kind words. If you wouldn't mind telling all the other players that wandering traders are cool and that they should stop yelling at us, I and my fellow wandering traders would appreciate it."

Tantancrafter and DJ both laughed. "Okay, I suppose it's the least we can do," said Tantancrafter.

"Totally," said DJ. "We could do that at least."

I waved goodbye as the two exuberant fanboys left. *Who knows*, I thought to myself, *maybe they **could** join someday? Maybe I'd need their help at some point?*

Penelope came back carrying Slimy. "I overheard your conversation with those players. That was kind of weird," she said.

I nodded my head. "Yeah. I've never had a player ask that straight out. I mean there is that one player wandering trader, Wenlan, but I can't imagine he's been going around telling other players they can become wandering traders."

Penelope shrugged. "Probably not. But I mean, you told me I could become a wandering trader when perhaps you should have kept it to yourself. Maybe more of you are spilling the beans, as they say."

"Maybe. But, let's not think about that now. Here, have some lunch," I said as I handed Penelope a roasted chicken leg and a bowl of warm mushroom stew.

Chapter 7

It was late afternoon when we entered the gates of Creeper Junction and we began looking for a hotel. Within a few moments, Penelope spotted the Wandering Cow Inn and said, "Why don't we stay there?"

I shivered and shook my head. "No way. Too expensive and they are prejudiced against slimes. Let's find a different place. In fact, you are wearing your villager clothes, so why don't you ask around for a good place to stay?"

Penelope smiled. "My first real mission as a wandering trader trainee," she said quietly as she wandered off to find a good hotel.

I stood near a street corner holding the leads to my llamas. Dozens of villagers passed by. Some of them gave me dirty looks or stared in disgust at Slimy in his saddle. But most ignored me. A couple of players approached and asked for some trades. By the time Penelope returned, I had traded away two blaze rods, four potions of various types, and a set of golden armor. *Why anyone would want golden armor, I had no idea.*

"I found a place," said Penelope when she returned. "It's called the Mooshroom Motel."

I slapped my head. "Seriously? What a stupid name!"

Penelope chuckled. "I agree about the name, but two different villagers recommended it. They said it is situated on a quiet back street with a view of one of the town's parks. The motel has a stable and everything."

"Okay, sounds good, I guess. Let's go check it out."

* * *

Half an hour later, my two llamas were safe and secure in the stable. Penelope and I had rented adjoining rooms with a connecting door. I had set up Slimy's crib in my room, and Penelope was there playing with Slimy.

"By the way, Penelope, I forgot to tell you something. The last time I was in the cave where we spent last night, Oculus, a spider, told me without any details that things had been 'weird' in Creeper Junction lately. I didn't notice anything last time I was here, but stay alert. I know we are only going to be here for one night, but you never know what you might observe." *I thought it was wise to leave out the part about being kidnapped by husk soldiers.*

Penelope nodded her head seriously. "Interesting you say that. The villagers don't seem very friendly here. A couple of them shook their heads and walked away when I was asking them for a recommendation for a place to stay for the night. In my experience, villagers never do that to fellow villagers."

"Maybe they were just rude?"

She shook her head. "It seemed like they were ... what is the right word? ... *afraid* to talk to me."

"Well, I don't know if that has anything to do with what Oculus told me, but those are the sorts of observations we need to make."

Penelope smiled as she poked Slimy's cube. Slimy giggled every time she poked him on the sides.

Are slimes ticklish?

After about thirty minutes of playing, Slimy yawned and fell asleep almost instantly. I put him in his crib, and then Penelope and I went down to the Mooshroom Motel restaurant to get something to eat.

Once we were seated at a table, the waiter came over and said, "Welcome to the Mooshroom Motel restaurant. Our specials today are warm mooshroom milk and mushroom stew made with mushrooms harvested from the many mooshrooms which live in the stable just over yonder." The waiter pointed toward a window through which we could see the stable where my llamas were boarded for the night.

"As ... um ... *interesting* as your specials sound, I think I'll just have a steak with a fried egg on top of it, a carrot, a slice of watermelon, and a glass of water," said Penelope. The waiter wrote it down and looked at me expectantly.

"I will try the warm mooshroom milk, a pumpkin pie, two roasted chicken legs, and a carrot."

The waiter wrote that down and then said, "Very good. Your food should be out in about five minutes."

As the waiter walked away, I looked at Penelope and said, "Wow! Only five minutes? Quick service."

"I suppose," she said as she nodded her head before her expression turned serious. She leaned in and whispered. "Don't look, but there's a strange man sitting by the window. He looks like a ... hurrr ... a pirate."

I nodded my head and leaned back. I waited about thirty seconds before I glanced toward the window as though I were looking out of it. I saw the person to whom she had been referring. I saw a man, probably in his early twenties, wearing an all-black outfit with a thick yellow sash across it. He also wore a wide brimmed black hat with a skull and crossbones.

"What's a pirate doing here so far from the ocean?" I asked. "That seems a little weird." *Could this be evidence of what Oculus had told me?*

Penelope nodded. "I've never seen a pirate before."

The waiter returned with our food and, after he had placed it on the table, I asked, "So, do you get pirates in here very often?" I nodded my head in the direction of the peculiar young man sitting on the other side of the restaurant.

The waiter looked in the direction indicated before looking back at me and laughing. "Oh, that's no pirate. That's just Ebenezer. He's a little ... different. He likes to dress up in costumes. Yesterday, he dressed up like an evoker."

I let out a sigh of relief. "So every day is like a costume party in here?"

The waiter chuckled. "He comes in about three days a week. He comes from a very wealthy and eccentric family. Maybe you have heard of them, the Dretsky clan?"

I shook my head. "Can't say that I have. What about you, Penelope?"

Penelope sat there for a moment tapping her lips with her finger. "The name sounds vaguely familiar, but I can't place it."

"Big-time trading family. Lots of natural resources," said the waiter. "The family helped bring all the goods into Creeper Junction to help build the expansion about twenty years ago. Ebenezer's grandfather, Franklin, is the patriarch of the family. Very wealthy."

Penelope snapped her fingers. "That's right. I can remember my uncle, Notch rest his soul, would buy raw materials from someone who said he represented the Dretsky Commodities Company."

I looked back at the waiter. "So is this Ebenezer dude a little crazy?"

The waiter shrugged. "I'm no psychologist. All I know is that he likes to wear costumes for some reason. But, he always pays his bill, never makes trouble. Perfect customer."

"So is the Dretsky family living in Creeper Junction?"

The waiter shook his head. "Just Ebenezer. The rest of them live in Capitol City. He oversees the business here though. Sometimes his dad or even grandfather stops in. Once or twice a year. They never eat here though. They don't think the food is good enough for their sophisticated palates."

"Well, thanks for the information," I said to the waiter.

The waiter got the hint and walked away. "Enjoy your dinner."

Chapter 8

The next morning I woke up and played with Slimy for a few minutes. Then, I washed my face and put on a fresh robe. Once I was dressed, I knocked on the adjoining door separating my room from Penelope's.

"I'm almost ready," she said through the door.

"Great. Meet me in the hallway," I said. I turned around and punched Slimy's crib and put it back in my inventory. I picked up Slimy and did a quick once over of the room to make sure I had not forgotten anything. I checked my inventory to make sure the chest I was transporting was still there.

I opened my door and took a few steps down the hallway. I stood in front of Penelope's door for about ten seconds until she opened it. "I'm ready to go," she said cheerfully.

"Do you want to get some breakfast at the restaurant or should we just eat on the road?"

Penelope tapped her nose and pursed her lips while she thought about my question. "Maybe on the road. This village of Del Mar you told me about sounds pretty nice. I'd like to get there with some daylight left."

I smiled. "That's a good idea."

"LOP idea," said Slimy. Penelope and I laughed.

"He's trying so hard," I said like a proud father.

"It's cute," said Penelope as she pinched Slimy's cheek.

We walked down the hallway and took the stairs to the first floor, Slimy bouncing along behind us. I paid for the rooms and the stable and then we walked out to get my llamas. After I got the llamas, I led them back to the entrance to the stable and gave the stable hand the ticket I had received from the front desk indicating that I paid for the lodging for the night.

The stable hand, a grizzled old villager man, took the ticket then recognizing the llamas said, "You know someone was by here early this morning asking about the owner of those llamas, which I assume is you."

I tensed. *Could someone be following us trying to get the chest?* "Really? What, exactly, did this person say?"

The stable hand shrugged. "Not much, just asked if I knew where you were. I told him you were probably staying at the hotel if your llamas were here."

I nodded my head and then asked, "Can you tell me anything about this person? Anything distinctive?"

"Well, he had covered his head and face with a scarf. I could barely see anything other than two beady eyes. It was pretty obvious he was trying to disguise himself."

Netherrack. Of course a spy following me would disguise himself. "Anything else?"

The old man thought for a moment and said, "Actually, yes. This character didn't smell very good. Kind of like he was dusty and dry. Like he could use a bath or maybe some high-quality moisturizer."

A husk. It had to be.

"Okay, well, thank you," I said as I reached into my inventory for an emerald to tip the stable hand.

I handed him the gem and he smiled. "Thanks, mister."

"I'm only sixteen! Don't call me mister, just Trader Winston."

"Okay TW," he said with a smirk as he turned and walked back into the stable to clean some corrals.

As Penelope and I walked away from the stable, Penelope leaned over and whispered, "Why do you think someone was looking for you?"

I couldn't tell her that I knew I was being followed by a husk spy, who was following me because he thought I had something to do with the assassination of one of their princes. That was all top secret information. "Um, I don't know. Maybe just a thief looking to steal my inventory or ... perhaps someone who knows about the chest is trying to get it."

Penelope, who was holding Slimy, shivered a little. The force of her shiver sent waves through Slimy who quivered like a bowl of chorus fruit jelly. "Do you think we'll have to defend ourselves?"

"Maybe. I know you're not a full-fledged wandering trader yet but you seemed pretty handy with a sword the other day."

Penelope blushed. "I'll admit it, weapons come easy to me ... especially bladed weapons."

I smiled. "Good. We may need that skill. Why don't you put Slimy in his saddle, just in case our mysterious pursuer decides to confront us on our way out of town?" Penelope nodded, put Slimy on Pippa's back, and then reached into her inventory to make sure her best sword was at the ready.

We walked down the sleepy alleyway where the stable was located and then turned onto a main street. The street was surprisingly busy considering it was still the breakfast hour. I saw students rushing to and from school, business people trotting along to their stores and jobs, and dozens of delivery wagons depositing goods at various shops.

After we had passed a couple of side streets, I noticed someone ahead standing on a corner who was nearly completely bundled up with a thick scarf wrapped around his face, only the eyes showing through. I did not want to alert this person that I had spotted him so I didn't immediately mention my observation to Penelope. Instead, I led the llamas on a slight course change so we would run directly into the person on the corner. If he was friendly, he would just stand there. If he was following us, he would move away.

When we were about ten blocks away from the person who I was convinced was a husk spy, he slowly turned and walked around the corner.

I knew it!

I then redirected the llamas away from the corner and back toward the center of the street. I wanted to get out of Creeper Junction as quickly as possible.

"Boy, when they call you wandering traders, they sure mean it," said Penelope with a giggle. "You're wandering all over the road. Can't you keep a straight line?"

I chuckled. "Yeah, I try to stick to this wandering stuff literally."

We kept walking toward the gate in the wall around Creeper Junction. I looked behind me a couple times but did not spot the husk spy. Either he had given up or he was going to try to reacquire us later.

When we got outside of the gates and had been moving away from Creeper Junction for about five minutes, I told Penelope what I'd seen back there and why I had wandered in a weaving path as we left the town.

She looked very disappointed in herself. "I can't believe I didn't spot him myself."

"Don't be too hard on yourself. You haven't had your spy craft training yet. I'm not surprised you didn't see him."

"Well, whatever he wants, he sure is going to a lot of trouble to get it."

"I suppose," I said as I reached inside my inventory to double-check that I still had the chest. While my hand was in there, I gave Creepy a squeeze for good luck. "Just keep an eye out for anyone following us. Since we are traveling during the day, I think we should be safe. But ... you never know."

Chapter 9

Fortunately, the journey to the small picturesque seaside village of Del Mar was without incident. Neither one of us spotted anyone following us, whether they were wrapped in cloaks and scarves or otherwise. We ran into a few players along the way, making some valuable trades and only being insulted by one of them.

It was midafternoon and the sky was a cloudless bright blue when we first saw the village of Del Mar in the distance.

"We've made really good time," I said.

Penelope smiled. "Good. We can get some rooms in a hotel and then look at the beach. I heard it's all white sand. Very cute."

Cute?

I nodded my head. "Sounds good. I don't think I've ever walked along a beach before."

We were still about thirty minutes away from the village, which was still just a speck in the distance. After we had walked for another ten minutes, we heard rustling in the forest near the path where we were walking.

"Think it's that spy?" asked Penelope, with an edge of fear in her voice.

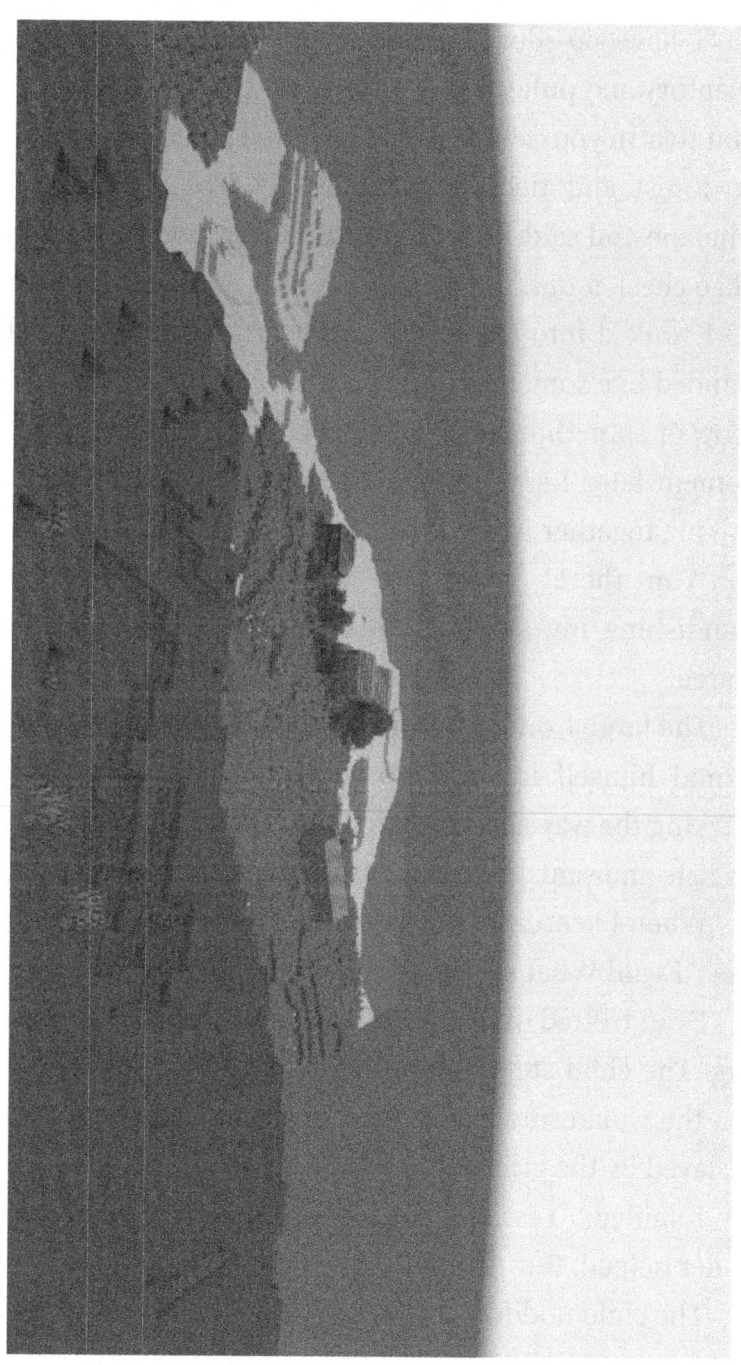

"I have no idea," I said calmly. I reached into my inventory and pulled out a sword. "By the way, you might want to arm yourself, just in case." I walked to the edge of the forest and tied the llamas to a tree. I turned to Penelope and said, "Stay here with Slimy and the llamas. I'll go check it out."

I walked into the forest and heard more rustling. It sounded like something big. Had to be at least the size of a cow or something or even bigger. I kept walking until a moment later I saw an iron golem and child iron golem walking together in the forest.

"You there! What are you up to?" I shouted, brandishing my sword to make it clear that I was in charge.

The large iron golem quickly pushed the child golem behind himself in order to protect it. He stood there blocking the way and ready to fight. But then, he lowered his fists and said, "Winston? Is that you?"

When I heard his voice, I realized immediately who it was. "Evan! What are you doing here?"

Evan trotted over and gave me a surprisingly delicate hug. The child stepped around his father and said, "Are you the wandering trader who freed my dad from being enslaved by the griefer?"

I smiled. "Yes, but not just me. Another wandering trader helped. But ... hurrr ... the griefer killed him."

The child nodded his head. "Yeah, I heard about that. Sad."

I fought back a tear of grief for the loss of young Wynter before looking at Evan. "You probably won't believe this, but Penelope is with me. She's waiting just beyond the tree line at the edge of the road."

A giant smile crossed Evan's face as he picked up his son and rushed to the edge of the forest. As I followed along behind Evan and his son, I could hear the joyful reunion between Evan and Penelope.

When I got to the edge of the forest, Evan and Penelope were just finishing their hug. "I thought you'd moved away from the village forever," said Evan.

Penelope smiled. "Actually, I have."

Evan looked sad. "Oh. Sometimes it's not good to be correct."

Penelope reached out a hand and gave a comforting pat to Evan's gigantic fist. "It's okay. I can stop by the village from time to time ... once I'm a wandering trader."

No! Don't reveal that!

As I stood behind Evan, I caught Penelope's eyes, shook my head, and put my finger to my lips to indicate that she needed to be quiet.

"You are going to be a wandering trader?" said Evan, confused. "I thought they all spawned as traders."

Penelope, realizing her mistake, immediately began backpedaling. "Oh, yeah. They do. I'm just trying to get a job as an assistant to the wandering traders. Trader Winston said I could do that for a while to earn some money and then I can go to college or something."

This ridiculous explanation seemed to satisfy Evan. Iron golems are not known for their intelligence, after all, and his inborn loyalty to villagers made him trust her even though she was speaking nonsense.

Evan nodded his head. "That makes perfect sense." He paused for a moment to think and then said, "Since you're in the area, I think I should tell you something. About an hour ago, my son and I were traveling through the forest looking at all the different animal mobs. It was our first father-son outing since I was enslaved by the griefer. Anyway, I saw two evokers and a husk gathered underneath a tree chatting. When they saw us coming through the woods, they scattered, like they didn't want me to know what they were doing. I just thought you might want to be on the lookout for them. It seemed like they were up to no good."

I nodded my head. "What did the husk look like?"

Evan thought for a moment and then said, "Kind of weird. He wasn't wearing normal husk clothing. He had on a thick cloak. The only reason I could tell it was a husk was he removed his hood. Otherwise, I might've thought it was just an old villager."

I looked at Penelope with a knowing gaze. *The same husk who had been spying on us?* She returned my glance with one of her own, but wisely she said nothing.

"Thanks for the information, Evan," said Penelope. "But, I think we need to get going."

Evan nodded his head. "That's fine. My son and I still have some forest to explore."

Penelope and I watched as Evan and his son returned to the forest, making a noisy racket as they did. Once they were out of earshot, I turned to Penelope and said, "So, it seems like that same husk who was spying on us is working with evokers. That can't be good."

Penelope nodded her head. "Indeed. They must be after the chest."

That could be *one* explanation. Or maybe the husks had just decided to kill all the wandering traders in revenge for the death of their prince. The evokers could just be hired assassins. But I didn't want Penelope to know about that ... or Wolf's involvement.

"Could be. Or, maybe they are up to something else," I said as I untied my llamas from the tree trunk. Slimy giggled as the llamas began to move. "Anyway, let's just stay alert and get into town as quickly as we can. I want to go on that beach walk."

Chapter 10

Once we arrived in the quaint seaside village of Del Mar, we checked into a hotel called the Sunset Inn. The inn had a small stable with room for six animals. Fortunately, there was space for my two llamas. I noticed there were two horses in the stable as well.

After we deposited our things in our separate rooms, Penelope, Slimy and I went down to the beach. It was fun to walk along the beach and watch Slimy play on the sand and in the water. The flat oceans of the Overworld were always impressive. Smooth as glass, like a gigantic lake stretching to the horizon.

I pulled a piece of cobblestone out of my inventory and punched it into little, flat pieces about as wide as a chorus fruit. I threw the pieces across the water, skipping them, leaving a series of round ripples in their wake.

"I've never seen anyone do that!" said Penelope. "Let me try." I gave her a few pieces of rock and she tried to skip them. Her initial attempts were laughable failures, but eventually she got the hang of it. We even had a contest to see who could skip a single rock the most times. I thought I had won the contest when I got one of the rocks to bounce twelve times across the water, but Penelope topped me with fourteen bounces.

"I don't believe it! I've never seen anyone skip a rock that many times. Even my twelve-bouncer was my personal record."

"I told you I was a natural with weapons," said Penelope with a smile.

Not sure a tiny rock is a weapon, but ... okay.

"Skipping," said Slimy as he bounced in the sand. "Me try. Me try."

I laughed. "How can you throw a rock without any arms?" I said handing Slimy a piece of rock. He absorbed it and then spit it out of his mouth, skipping it twice!

Whoa!

"Good job, Slimy," said Penelope, bending down and patting him on the top of his cube.

We spent the next hour walking along the beach, chatting, playing with Slimy, and skipping more rocks. I really enjoyed Penelope's company. I never really had any friends my own age, well, not since my village was destroyed when I was ten. And, I certainly had never had a girlfriend. But, I thought Penelope was pretty great. Of course, I wasn't going to ask her on a date right now. That would be improper for me as a full-fledged wandering trader to go on a date with a trainee. But maybe once she passed her test and we were equals, I'd see if she wanted to get dinner or something.

* * *

In the evening, I put Slimy in his crib to sleep and then Penelope and I went down to the restaurant. About ten minutes into our meal, a player approached our table. "Can I talk to you Mr. Wandering Trader?" he asked shyly.

I shook my head and waved him away. "Store's closed. I'm having dinner."

"Oh, it's nothing like that," said the player pulling out a chair from under the table and sitting down without being invited. "It's just…. Let me explain. My name is Glitchmaster. I am a sociologist studying the different mobs and characters in the Overworld. I've been trying to find a wandering trader who is willing to tell me all about his or her life."

"What do you mean? Like all the biographical details?" I asked.

"That's part of it," said Glitchmaster. "But there's more to it. As a sociologist, I'd want to know about your interactions with other wandering traders and whether you ever spend any time with other mobs." He looked over at Penelope. "It looks like you hang out with villagers. I'll make a note of that." He pulled out a notebook and jotted something down.

"Look, hurrr, Glitchmaster, was it? I don't feel like talking about my life or my work, with you or anybody else." I said these words with a hint of anger and menace which I hoped Glitchmaster would understand.

Glitchmaster looked disappointed. "Well, can you at least tell me your name? Maybe we will run into each other again and you will have changed your mind."

"I doubt that. But the name's Winston, Trader Winston."

Glitchmaster jotted my name down in his notebook. "Thank you. I'm always traveling between Capitol City, Creeper Junction, and Zombie Bane, checking up on the villagers that I am profiling for my sociological studies. I'm sure we will run into each other again."

"I suppose so," I said without any enthusiasm. Glitchmaster smiled and then got up and left the dining area.

I looked at Penelope. "Obviously we can't be telling players about our ... hierarchy or our Guild. We need to keep that to ourselves."

Penelope nodded her head as she took a bite of a roasted chicken leg. "Gotcha."

After we finished our main course, we ended the evening with a slice of pumpkin pie and then returned to our rooms where I said goodnight to Penelope. When I entered my room, I found that Slimy was still asleep. And if past performance was any indication of the future results, he would sleep through the night. I took a quick bath, put on some pajamas, and went to sleep.

Chapter 11

The next day dawned with gloomy, foreboding clouds in the sky. As I looked out the window of my room, I wondered if it would rain. I hated traveling in the rain.

After I finished packing my things, I woke up Slimy and then knocked on the door to Penelope's room. She opened the door immediately. "Good morning," she said.

"Good morning. We should get going. If we leave now, we should arrive in Capitol City by early afternoon. Then I can make the exchange in the evening. Plus, I think it might rain, so the sooner we get to Capitol City, the better."

"Sounds good to me," said Penelope as she followed me down the hallway to the front desk. We paid our charges, grabbed my llamas from the stable, and began wandering toward Capitol City.

On the way to Capitol City, we only encountered one player. We were walking along and I saw him in the distance. I tried to avoid him, but he saw me and made a beeline for me, obviously wanting to trade.

As he got closer I noticed that he was wearing a mismatched set of armor. He had leather boots, an iron chest plate and a golden helmet. He still wore his original pants that he had spawned with.

I leaned over to Penelope and whispered, "What a ragamuffin."

She looked at me with a confused expression on her face. "What are you, ninety years old? Who says ragamuffin?"

I grunted because I was offended. "I guess I do."

The player was now within speaking range and said, "Hold up a minute. I need to trade."

I put on my best singsong-y wandering trader voice and said, "In that case, my dear player, Trader Winston is at your service. What can I offer you?"

"I need a full set of diamond armor. I've been mining for nearly a week and all I can find is emerald ore. Do you have something like that?"

I smiled. "Of course, Trader Winston has what you seek. And it will cost you a mere ... fifty emeralds."

The player looked slightly upset at my price but to his credit, he simply dug into his inventory and pulled out the fifty emeralds without attempting to negotiate. After I pocketed the emeralds I reached into a carry bag on Sunny's back and pulled out the armor and handed it to the player.

"Cool. Um, do you think you two could turn around? You know, so I can change into my armor in private?" Penelope laughed as she turned around. I rolled my eyes and did the same.

About five seconds later the player said, "Okay. How do I look?"

"Well, you look like just about every other player I've ever seen," said Penelope.

"Yeah, you guys all look the same to me," I said.

The player became red-faced with anger. He flexed his muscles and said, "Look again. Behold my diamond armor. I ask once more, how do I look?"

These players always let the diamonds go to their heads....

"No change," said Penelope.

"Agreed. You look the same to me," I said.

Without warning, the player reached into his inventory and pulled out an enchanted iron sword and slashed at me. I just had enough time to bend backwards. The blade of the sword passed barely a hair's width above my nose. I did a somersault backwards and was reaching into my inventory to pull out my sword and take care of this player when, quick as a flash, Penelope pulled out her sword and slashed the player, severely wounding him.

The player collapsed on the ground and looked at Penelope with angry, confused eyes. "What are you doing?" he coughed. "Villagers don't attack players. That's illegal."

"Then you can call me an outlaw," said Penelope as she slashed the player once more, finishing him off.

After the player disappeared into a puff of smoke, I quickly grabbed all of his inventory and tucked it into one of Sunny's carry bags. I looked up at Slimy on the back of Pippa. "You okay, Slimy?"

"LOP kill you. Kill."

Yikes! I hoped we weren't breeding a monster.

I really wished Slimy hadn't seen that. Penelope walked up the Slimy and said, "Only in self-defense though."

"Fence. Fence," said Slimy.

"Come on, Penelope," I said. "Let's get moving. If that player respawns anywhere nearby, he's going to come running to find his dropped inventory. We don't want to be here when he shows up again."

Penelope shrugged. "I'm pretty sure we could take care of him again."

"Probably, but discretion is the better part of valor."

"Right," she said with a confused look on her face. "You know, you talk a little weird sometimes, Winston."

"Whatever, let's get going. We should be in Capitol City in about an hour."

As we resumed our wandering, I felt the first drops of a cold rain begin to fall.

Chapter 12

Besides enduring the cold, misty rain, the remainder of our trip to Capitol City was the easiest leg of the journey. In fact, a couple of kind players approached us and asked for trades. Simple trades, inexpensive. Those were the kinds of trades I liked, even if it was raining.

We arrived in Capitol City a little after noon. Miraculously, the rain stopped just as we were entering the main gate of the city.

Penelope noticed the timing of the end of the rain too. "We are favored by Notch," she said.

"Then, why did it rain for the entire last hour of our journey?" I said. Penelope rolled her eyes.

I told Penelope to approach one of the villager residents of Capitol City and ask where the Golden Watermelon Hotel was located. After she got directions, we went further into the city and located the hotel. It was situated immediately adjacent to a giant watermelon patch. The front desk clerk told us that the hotel had purchased that land many years ago and grew watermelons on it for use in their signature "watermelon water" drink.

"So, it's just watermelon juice, right?" I asked, not impressed by the clerk's hard sell of the drink.

The front desk clerk looked at me with a sly grin. "I can't give away the recipe. You'll just have to try one."

I shrugged. "Maybe later. By the way, you have a restaurant in here, right?"

The front desk clerk smiled. "Of course we do. Just go down the hall to my left and then turn right at the first doorway. Seating for seventy-five."

"Perfect," I said.

The front desk clerk handed Penelope a key to her room and me a key to mine. "As you requested, your rooms are next to each other. I've given you rooms on the third floor, overlooking the watermelon patch."

"Thanks. See you later," I said.

After we checked into the rooms, Penelope told me that she was going to do some sightseeing. I was jealous, having never been to Capitol City before, but I had to do the exchange in a couple of hours and did not want to risk being delayed.

"Okay, have fun," I said. "Do you want to take Slimy with you?"

"Not right now," said Penelope. "But, if I can find a place where he can play, I will come back and get him. Just leave the adjoining door between our rooms unlocked if you leave."

"Sounds like a good plan. See you later."

After Penelope left, I went back into my room. I played with Slimy for about twenty minutes before he fell asleep. Then I removed the mysterious chest from my inventory. It was locked with a lock made of a combination of diamond and enchanted iron. I probably could have eventually broken it open, but I wasn't supposed to know what was in the chest. So, my curiosity would likely never be satisfied about the contents of the chest.

Since there was still time before the dinner hour, I lay down and took a nap. When I woke up I saw that the sun was setting. I jumped out of bed and splashed some water on my face. I needed to get down to the restaurant and try to make contact with the person who would pick up the chest.

I knocked on the adjoining door to Penelope's room and when I didn't hear any response, I opened it. There was no indication Penelope had returned at any point during my nap. I left the door open in case she returned and Slimy wanted to play. I pulled Creepy out of my inventory and put it on the floor next to Slimy's crib. That way, if he woke up alone, he would have something to do.

* * *

About ten minutes later I was sitting at a table by myself in the Golden Watermelon restaurant. When the waiter approached to take my order I ordered an extra large bowl of mushroom stew, a loaf of bread, half a watermelon, and a glass of milk, just as I had been instructed by Wickham. The waiter dutifully wrote down my order and left.

I looked around the dining room and saw that there were ten other diners. Four groups of two and two people eating alone. One of the people eating alone was a female player. The other person eating alone was some sort of villager. The dining room was rather dark. I couldn't tell the villager's profession. I could tell however that it was a male villager.

A few minutes later the waiter brought me the food and I sat there for a moment, hoping my contact was in the restaurant and he or she would see what I had ordered. After a minute passed and no one in the restaurant had approached me, I decided to start eating.

I was about halfway through my bowl of mushroom stew when a middle-aged villager man approached my table. He had not been eating in the restaurant, so it was unclear how he had seen me order my meal. His robe was tattered and had been repaired many times. It looked like he had been a librarian at some point, but his clothes were in such bad condition that I didn't think he could possibly be employed right now.

Could this ... hurrr ... ragamuffin be my contact?

"Hello, you young whippersnapper," said the old villager.

I put my soup spoon down and looked at him. "Hello, you old whippersnapper," I said.

The old man laughed and started coughing like his lungs hadn't had that much exercise in years. "You're funny. I like that."

I rolled my eyes. "Can't you see I'm eating here? What do you want?"

Suddenly the old man became very serious and leaned in and whispered to me. "What's your favorite mob?"

*He **was** my contact!*

"I haven't thought about that much, but I'd have to say my favorite mob is the silverfish," I said, repeating the password verbatim and feeling like an idiot as such a stupid sentence was emitted from my mouth.

The old man nodded his head and looked over both shoulders. Satisfied that we weren't being watched too closely he whispered again, "Give me the chest."

I reached into my inventory and pulled the chest out, careful to conceal it as much as possible, using the old man's body to block anyone else seeing it. The old man's eyes got wide at the sight of the chest as he grabbed it and quickly tucked it into his inventory.

"Say, do you mind me asking what was in that chest?" I whispered.

The old man scowled at me. "You're just the messenger. Don't forget that." He turned and walked quickly out of the restaurant.

What a jerk.

My mission complete, I tossed a few emeralds on the table and got up and left. I didn't really want to eat the rest of my dinner, especially not the rest of an extra large bowl of mushroom stew.

Chapter 13

As I was walking out of the restaurant, I noticed a door at the end of the hallway was just closing. I hadn't noticed that door before. Instead of turning left and walking back to my room I decided to go right. I walked up to the door and pushed it open.

The door opened onto a narrow alleyway. Although it was nearly dark outside, the remaining sunlight and the flames of several torches on the walls allowed me to see well enough. I saw the old man to whom I had just given the chest already at the end of the alley. He turned right on the street.

Even though I knew that it was probably a bad idea, I decided to follow him. I slowly walked down the alleyway until I got to the intersection of the alley and the street. As I peeked my head around the corner to make sure the old man wasn't too close to me, I saw that he was being attacked by someone wearing wandering trader robes!!!

I rushed toward the fray as I watched in horror as the wandering trader stabbed the old man to death and stole the chest. The thief began to run from the scene. I shouted, "Hey you! Stop!"

The other wandering trader recognized my robes and an expression of surprise crossed his face. He ran faster. I wasn't sure I would be able to close the distance between him and me; he was running very fast. But then, out of nowhere, Penelope darted from a side street and tripped the wandering trader thief. She rushed to attack him, but he was quicker. He grabbed her by the neck and put a knife to her throat just as I got to where they were standing.

I put my hands out to calm the situation. "Don't do anything you're going to regret," I said menacingly.

"Don't worry," said the wandering trader. "I can kill her and then I will kill you. No problem. **No regrets**."

Now that I was closer to this wandering trader, I realized that I had never seen him before. I knew all the official wandering traders at HQ, at least by sight if not by name. He clearly wasn't a trainee; he was far too skilled.

"Say, what's your name anyway? I don't recognize you."

The wandering trader laughed. "That's because I don't belong to your stupid Guild anymore, you bunch of mindless sheep."

Bro.

"What do you mean? What guild *do* you belong to?" As I was talking, I was trying to find an opening to kill him and rescue Penelope, but he was too good. I knew that if I made a move, Penelope would lose her life.

"I belong to no guild. I serve no one. I only serve money and power."

"I suppose that makes you the same as most villagers," I said attempting a joke.

The wandering villager shook his head. "Winston, you're an idiot."

Gasp.

"How do you know my name?"

"I've got my ways," he said. "If anyone asks who stole your precious chest, you can tell them it was Wex. They'll know who I am."

And then, Wex shoved Penelope at me, knocking us both to the ground as he dashed down a side street. It took us a few seconds to get back to our feet and we rushed after him, but he was gone. But, through the dim evening light I noticed two evokers and a husk, disguised as villagers, standing at a distant intersection, waiting for us to try something.

"Stop, Penelope," I said. "Wex is gone, and it looks like he left a small gang up ahead to stop us from following him."

Penelope looked down the street and saw the three toughs standing on the distant corner. She grunted. "Was that all about?" said Penelope. "I heard you yelling and saw you chasing him and just figured I would try to stop him."

"I have no idea. I mean, he murdered my contact and stole the chest, but I have no idea *why*. I don't even know what was in the chest." I shook my head and sighed. "I do know that Wickham is going to be very disappointed. But it's not my fault. I completed my mission."

"Indeed," said Penelope. "I guess it was a good thing I happened to be walking down the street."

I nodded my head. "Well, it's about to pitch black out here so we can't leave until tomorrow morning. But we need to be out of here at first light. And then, we need to travel like the wind."

Chapter 14

We traveled as quickly as we could during the daylight and even into the early hours of night until the hordes of monsters became too thick to travel safely. We made it back to wandering trader headquarters in just two days.

Penelope and I quickly put the llamas back into their corral, and I told her to come with me. She held Slimy in her arms as I rushed to Wolf's room.

"Shouldn't we tell Wickham?" she asked.

I nodded my head. "We will. I just need to ask Wolf about something."

When we arrived at Wolf's door, I banged on it as hard as I could. Finally, he opened it and shouted, "What?"

I pushed in and Penelope followed me shutting the door behind us.

"You better have a good reason for this intrusion," said Wolf, his face red with anger.

"I do. I was on a mission for Wickham to Capitol City. I was delivering a chest. Mission accomplished and then ... hurrr ... a few minutes later, the person to whom I had given the chest was murdered.... He was murdered by someone wearing wandering trader clothes!"

Wolf was shocked. "What do you mean? An imposter? What did he look like?"

"He looks like all of us. But, he did give me his name. Wex."

A sick look clouded Wolf's face. It looked as though he had been punched in the gut. "Wex. I haven't heard that name in years. Not since he went rogue."

"What do you mean?"

Wolf shook his head. "Occasionally, some of the traders get fed up with following the Way. They go rogue. We always hunt them down and kill them. But Wex has managed to evade us."

"This could be worse than I thought," I said.

Wolf nodded his head. "What was in the chest?"

I shook my head. "I have no idea. Wickham just told me to deliver it."

"Then, you had better go tell him what happened," said Wolf.

* * *

Penelope and I stopped by my room to deposit Slimy. I tossed Creepy to him and he happily played with it. "Creepy. Creepy."

Penelope and I rushed up the stairs toward Wickham's chamber. When Wayne saw us rushing up the stairs, he put his spear across our path as we approached and said, "What do you want?"

"There was a problem with delivering the chest," I said breathlessly. "Wickham needs to know about it. Now!"

Wayne, even though he was usually an angry idiot, sensed the urgency and truth in my voice. He rushed up to the door to Wickham's chamber and banged on it. Wickham opened the door, a scowl on his face. "What is it? I am talking to Wes right now."

Wes?

I stepped forward and said, "I delivered the chest. But a few minutes later, the recipient was murdered ... hurrr ... by someone wearing wandering trader robes! He called himself Wex."

Wickham slumped slightly in the doorway. "Did Wex take the chest?"

I nodded my head. "He murdered the old man who collected the chest. I wouldn't have even known it happened if I hadn't been ... well, following the recipient to see where he was going."

Wickham took a deep breath and then exhaled slowly. He turned around and looked at Wes, who was standing behind him. "Run along. We will continue this conversation later."

Wes walked out of Wickham's chamber and smirked at me, like he and Wickham were best buddies and I was just a piece of trash he saw blowing in the wind. He walked past me without saying a word and then walked downstairs.

Wickham rubbed his wrinkled forehead. "Did Wex say anything that would give any indication about where he was taking the chest?"

I shook my head. "He called all of the wandering traders in the Guild 'mindless sheep'. I have no idea what he was going to do with the chest." I paused for a moment and then remembered. "But, there were two evokers and one husk working with him. Penelope ... I mean *Winter* and I saw them in the distance, waiting to attack us if we pursued Wex."

A look of deep consternation passed across Wickham's face. Something was truly amiss. Wickham snapped his fingers and turned to Wayne. "Alert the five best assassins in the Guild. Order them to come to my chambers. Immediately!"

Wayne saluted and dashed down the stairs.

"You can go now," said Wickham.

Winter had already turned and was walking down the stairs but I stood there for a moment and asked, "What was in the chest that this Wex person would want enough to commit murder?"

Wickham's face turned red with anger and he pointed down the stairs. "Out of my sight! Now!"

I knew I couldn't push it anymore. I turned around and followed Winter down the stairs.

Chapter 15

When Winter and I reached the bottom of the staircase, I told her that she should go back to her trainee quarters. "I'm not sure if we'll get to work together again before you become an official wandering trader, but I'm sure I'll see you in the weapons training room."

Winter nodded. "Thank you, Trader Winston. I ... well, this has been an enlightening experience." I nodded solemnly as she walked away and back to the trainee area of headquarters.

When I got back to my room, Wes was standing there leaning against the door. "Stand aside," I said.

Wes chuckled and then said with a growl, "Make me."

I walked up to Wes and punched him in the face. He bent over and rubbed his jaw for a few seconds before leaping up and trying to punch me back. But I was waiting for it. I moved to the side and his fist went past me, punching only air. I punched him in his stomach while his punching arm was still extended and he collapsed with a groan.

I stood over him and said, "What's your problem?"

"You're my problem," he said as he kicked me in the knee. I fell backwards and rolled on the ground. I was going to come back after him but he pulled a sword. "If you come at me again, you're dead."

"What were you doing in there talking to Wickham anyway?"

Wes smiled. "Wickham and I are best buddies now. You'll see one day. You'll see what I mean."

That sounded rather ominous to me. "What do you mean by that? What have you got planned?"

"You'll never see it coming. It'll just happen one day. And then…." His voice trailed off. I was pretty sure he was going to say that I'd be dead. But he didn't. He had probably already said too much.

Wes backed away, still holding a sword in front of himself. When he got to the end of the corridor, he tucked his sword back into his inventory and saluted me sarcastically and said, "See you around, Winston."

I grunted, allowing my pent-up rage an escape. I pushed open the door to my room. **What I saw inside angered me more than I had ever been angered before!** At that moment, I swore I would get revenge on Wes some way or another. *He* wouldn't see *that* coming.

Slimy was in his crib crying hysterically. Someone, obviously Wes, had crafted a fence and put it on top of the crib and then put several cobblestones on top of the fence so that Slimy couldn't get out.

In front of the crib was my action figure, Creepy. It had been stomped on and destroyed by someone's foot. Obviously, Wes's foot.

I rushed over to the crib and removed the blocks on the fence and lifted Slimy out of the crib to comfort him.

As I was doing that, there was a knocking on my door. I turned around and saw that it was Wolf. "What happened in here?"

"I can't prove it, but I'm sure Wes broke in, tortured Slimy, and destroyed my one memory of my childhood."

Wolf shook his head. "If you can prove that, Wes would be expelled from the Guild. You know as well as I that wandering traders are not supposed to damage another trader's property."

"Well, I *can't* prove it. Wes was standing outside my room when I got here. I suppose it could've been someone else."

Wolf rubbed his chin and nodded his head. "You're probably right ... about not being able to prove it, I mean." He paused for a moment and said, "Did you talk to Wickham yet about Wex?"

"Yes. He was shocked when I told him. He is going to send some assassins after him."

"Of course, he is. At least he didn't ask me this time," said Wolf.

Slimy had finally calmed down, and I returned him to his crib where he fell asleep again. Wolf and I sat down at my small table to talk.

"So, how many wandering traders have you known to go rogue?"

Wolf shrugged. "Five or six over the past decade. But Wex was a different case. He was always pushing the envelope. Angry all the time. The weird thing is ... he spawned as a wandering trader. He didn't join the Guild from the outside. As far as I know, he was the first and only original wandering trader who has left the Guild in its history."

"Wickham must hate him then," I said.

Wolf nodded. "Wickham was Wex's training trader. Wickham feels personal responsibility for Wex's betrayal. The fact that Wickham hasn't been able to kill him yet is a black stain on his reputation."

I would never say it aloud, but part of me was almost glad about what Wex did, if it made Wickham uncomfortable. "I wonder what was in that chest? When I told Wickham that Wex had taken it, he looked very worried."

"Wex might not even care what was in there. He probably just wanted to ruin Wickham's plans."

I scratched my hair. "Yeah, about that. How would Wex have known that I was transporting a chest on behalf of Wickham? As far as I knew, the only people who knew about it before Winter and I left were Wickham, Wayne, maybe Wiggoly, Winter, and me. And, I can't imagine any of them is a traitor."

Wolf bit his lip. "I've been thinking about that ever since you told me what happened. I agree with you. There is a traitor in our midst. And, the sooner we can find the traitor the better."

End of Book 3 of
The Ballad of Winston the Wandering Trader

Book 4

Chapter 1

Wolf and I, investigating separately, spent the next three days trying to determine who within the wandering trader HQ had betrayed the purpose of my mission. Who among us would have been willing to betray The Way and tip off Wex about the delivery in Capitol City? I interviewed everyone I had spoken to from the moment Wickham gave me my assignment to deliver the chest until I departed HQ with Winter the next morning.

Of course, I couldn't come right out and ask them if they were a traitor, but I asked them if they told anyone about my mission. They all denied any such discussions. The strange part was, no one even seemed remotely nervous when I was talking to them. Perhaps this was because they didn't suspect why I was asking these questions. Or, perhaps, none of these people was the traitor. If that were true, then how could Wex have known about the meeting in Capitol City?

Actually, there was one wandering trader who seemed somewhat nervous when I spoke with him: Weston, the former village nitwit. But, the longer I spoke with him, what had initially appeared to be nervousness looked more like confusion.

"I can't remember who I talked to after you," he said. "That was, like, a week ago, right? I can't even remember what I had for breakfast. I mean, it was food. But, I can't remember what kind of food. It might have been bread or chicken or mushrooms or kelp or ... I mean, I can't remember!!!"

"Chill, Weston. I can't always remember what I had for breakfast either, but that doesn't mean I don't know who I talked to a few days ago."

The nitwit shook his head rapidly. "I can't remember *anything*, really. That is what happens when you spawn as a nitwit. Or at least, I think that's what happens. I never really understood how spawning works."

I wasn't getting anywhere with Weston. He was too clueless to be a traitor. If he did betray the secret, he would never even realize it.

Although Wolf and I were having no luck finding the traitor in our midst, Wickham was having no better luck capturing Wex. Although more than three days had passed since he sent his assassins to track Wex, there was no news that Wex had been spotted, much less apprehended and executed.

On the evening of the third day after I had returned with the news of Wex's treachery, I was sitting in Wolf's room chatting with him. "Either the traitor is far too smart to get tripped up by a few questions or we are asking the wrong people," I said with a sigh.

Wolf pursed his lips and scratched his chin. "I agree. It's hard to investigate a crime which *may* or *may not* have been committed when you have no strong suspects and no evidence."

"Maybe it was just luck? I mean, Wex and his thugs might've been in Capitol City for some other purpose and when they saw me they could've guessed something was afoot."

Wolf cocked an eyebrow. "Afoot? Kickin' it old school with your word choices today?"

"Dude, gimme a break. People say 'afoot' sometimes."

Wolf laughed. "Anyway, I suppose you could be correct. It could be as simple as dumb luck. But, in my experience, there's no such thing as luck."

I shrugged. "Well, there's certainly something known as *randomness*, if not luck. I mean, look at the random places that mobs will spawn. Sometimes it feels like all of Minecraft is based on a random-number generator or something like that."

Wolf chuckled. "You are weird, Winston. How do you come up with this stuff?"

"Whatever. Say, do you think the assassins will find Wex?"

Wolf shook his head. "I doubt it. When he first went rogue, the then leader of the wandering traders, Willow, sent a dozen of the top assassins after him. They even were following his fresh trail at the time, but somehow he managed to escape. I don't think they'll be able to catch him now when he has a multi-day head start."

"Did you say Willow?"

Wolf nodded. "She was the first female leader of the Guild. In fact, she was the first and only leader who did not spawn as a wandering trader. She spawned as a villager named Evie."

"So, how'd she end up here and why haven't I heard of her?"

Wolf took a deep breath and a sip of water from the glass resting on the table in front of him. "She ran away from home when she was a teenager. No one ever found out why. Anyway, she was a wandering trader for about twenty years, when the prior leader of the Guild died of old age. Two male traders were the main contenders for the leadership position, but they ended up killing each other in a duel to decide who would rule."

"Whoa! Is there always a duel to determine the leader?"

"No. Only when there is disagreement as to who the leader should be. Anyway, after the duel, there was unrest among the traders in HQ. It was eventually decided that new blood was needed for the leadership position, so Willow was selected."

"Was she a good leader?"

Wolf nodded. "I thought so. She was fair and honest. She only assassinated the truly evil mobs who deserved it as a punishment. Not like Wickham who uses murder as a political tool."

"So, what happened to her? Die of old age too?"

Wolf shook his head. "After she ruled for about five years, Wickham and his faction became impatient with the slow growth of the Guild Empire. They urged her to form alliances and increase the Guild's wealth. But she refused. She said that the Guild was made to protect wandering traders from attacks by villagers, like the Great Walter intended, not to make some of the traders obscenely wealthy."

"So, she was deposed?"

"No. Soon after her disputes with Wickham's faction became publicly known, she contracted a mysterious illness and died within one week."

I was shocked. "Wickham killed her?"

Wolf leaned forward in his chair quickly. "Never suggest that again or Wickham will have you ... silenced. But, it was suggested at the time. Nothing was ever proven ... or investigated."

"Dang. That's crazy," I said, shifting in my chair. "Anyway, I hope Wex does get caught and punished. It was horrible what he did to that old man to get the chest."

A strange expression passed over Wolf's face. "Maybe. Or maybe the old man deserved it. Maybe Wex knew something you didn't."

"Are you saying that you support Wex?"

Was Wolf the traitor?!?

Wolf shook his head slowly. "*Support* is not the right word. But, he has a point: the Guild is very controlling and increasingly based upon the greed of its leaders while the rest of us follow them blindly. That is The Way, right?"

I could not believe I was hearing Wolf, a dedicated wandering trader and for years a top assassin, say such things. *What did he know that I didn't?*

"Is there something you should tell me about Wex? Is there something Wickham is hiding from me?"

Wolf burst out laughing. "Of course he's hiding something from you. He's hiding things *from all of us*. What was in the chest Wex stole? No one knows. Why is Wickham allied with the Wolf King and the Spider Queen? No one knows. And yet we do whatever he says."

Wolf was right. It was strange that so many of us followed so blindly. But, that *was* The Way, devised by the Great Walter to keep us safe. *Who were we to question it?* The Great Walter founded this organization as a self-preservation society. As long as the group worked together, it would be preserved.

At least, that was what they told us during training. Or was it ... *indoctrination?*

"But, if Wex went rogue while Willow was the leader, why do you think she is better than Wickham?" I asked.

"I don't think he went rogue because of her. He would have gone rogue no matter who was in charge."

"So, you think Willow was a better leader than Wickham, right?"

Wolf nodded his head. "My first handful of years as a wandering trader, she was in charge. She definitely was hiding things from us as well ... I mean, all leaders do ... but they didn't seem sinister. The number of assassinations carried out since Wickham took over has jumped *tenfold* from Willow's regime. Before, we would usually just kill evil griefers and villagers who didn't play nice with wandering traders. Once Wickham took over ... *everyone* became a potential target."

"I see. But, maybe that's a good thing? I mean, you see these players rampaging through Minecraft all time, indiscriminately killing mobs and villagers and even wandering traders. It's a deadly world out there." I paused as emotions suddenly welled up in me. "Just ask my parents."

Wolf nodded solemnly. "That's a true statement, but it would be nice to know what the killings are for, beyond mere obedience."

At that moment there was a loud, stern knock on the door. Wolf stood up, walked to the door, and opened it. Wayne stood in the doorway, his face red from exertion. He glared at me. "Why aren't you in your own room?"

I shrugged. "Is there a rule against hanging out with your fellow traders?"

"No, but there should be. I've been running around headquarters for the last fifteen minutes looking for you."

I chuckled. "Maybe you need to exercise more? You should go on a few wanders yourself."

"How dare you?!? I serve only Wickham and there is no need for me to wander around the Overworld like a ... foundling."

I stood up and pushed my chair behind me, its feet scratching against the floor. "What did you call me?"

"You heard me, Foundling. You're not a pure wandering trader and you never will be."

Wolf stood in front of me and put his hand against my chest to keep me from rushing Wayne. "What's gotten into you, Wayne? Once someone joins the Guild, they *are* a wandering trader, regardless where they spawned. That is the Way."

Wayne stared angrily at Wolf but knew that Wolf spoke the words of part of our creed. Wayne took a couple of deep breaths, calmed himself, and responded, "That is the Way."

We stood in silence for a few seconds before Wolf said, "Why were you looking for Winston?"

"Why else? He's been summoned by Wickham."

Chapter 2

When Wayne and I arrived at the top of the staircase leading to Wickham's chambers, the door was wide open. Wickham's other guard, Wiggoly, stood at attention but nevertheless appeared relaxed. He nodded at us but said nothing. I continued walking up the stairs until I stood in front of the open door. Wickham looked up from where he was sitting and smiled. "Winston. Do come in and have a seat."

He seems awfully nice. What's up with him?

I walked in and sat down. He still had the comfortable chairs out, the same chairs that had been out when I was in his office just before leaving to deliver the chest to Capitol City.

Wickham looked at Wayne who was still standing in the doorway. "You may go. Please shut the door behind you." Wayne bowed slightly and then shut the door.

"Why did you want to see me?"

Wickham steepled his hands in front of his face and then tapped his fingertips together. He did this for a few seconds. I'm not sure if he was trying to build tension or think of the right words to say or if he was just enjoying the feeling of his fingertips touching each other.

Finally, he spoke. "A couple of reasons. The first one is to ask you a little bit more about what happened a few days ago in Capitol City."

I shifted in my chair. "Okay. I think I told you everything, but feel free to ask."

"When you initially informed me about Wex having stolen the chest, did you say there were two evokers and a husk that you thought were his thugs?"

I nodded my head. "Definitely. Winter and I saw a suspicious husk in Creeper Junction as well. Then, we ran into the iron golem, Evan, from that village the other Wynter and I saved from the griefer. Evan mentioned having seen two evokers and a husk conspiring in the forest."

Wickham continued to tap his fingertips together. "Interesting. I've never known Wex to work with the evokers and husks before."

"Who does he normally work with?"

Wickham squinted his eyes at me suspiciously. "That's none of your concern."

"If you say so."

"Did your contact in Capitol City say anything to you when you gave him the chest?"

"Not much," I said, remembering how rude the old man had been to me. "I just asked him what was in the chest and he told me to mind my own business."

"And indeed you *should* mind your own business. But, are you certain he said nothing else?"

I shrugged. "Nothing else to me. The next sound I heard was him screaming in agony right before he died."

Wickham nodded his head. He sat there breathing slowly. His breaths were loud and sounded slightly labored. I wondered if he was fighting a cold. "And he called the Guild a bunch of mindless sheep? Those were his *actual* words?"

"Verbatim. He obviously doesn't like the Guild."

"*Obviously*. Now, tell me again where Winter was during all this."

What was he getting at? Did he suspect Winter of something?!?

"Well, she went out to do some sightseeing while I stayed at the hotel and met with the contact. The next time I saw her was a couple hours later when she tripped Wex when he was fleeing with the stolen chest."

"And that's when Wex grabbed her and threatened to kill her?"

"Exactly. I really thought he was going to do it too."

Wickham stared at the ceiling and thought for a few seconds. Then, he lowered his gaze and looked me directly in the eyes. "Is there any chance that Winter is working with Wex?"

I gasped. "How could she be? She was by my side the entire time we were away, except when she was sleeping in her own hotel room and those couple hours when she was sightseeing."

"So, she could've told Wex what you are doing, right?"

I could not believe he was suggesting this. There's *no way* Winter was on Wex's side. She had been a villager until a few months ago. And if I hadn't told her about the wandering trader Guild, she would not know anything about it. There isn't any way she could've been helping Wex. *Was there?*

"I don't think that's true. I think she was sightseeing."

"Did she ever tell you what she looked at while she was sightseeing for those handful of hours in Capitol City?"

I realized then that she never did. She never brought it up. I could feel the blood draining from my face. *Could*

Winter really be allied with Wex? Was she hiding something?

"I guess ... hurrr ... she never did."

Wickham nodded his head as though he had just solved a great mystery. "Interesting."

"You don't think she is a traitor to the Guild, do you?"

"Silence!" ordered Wickham. "What I think is none of your concern. That is the Way."

I was very, *very* upset at Wickham right then. He was treating me like a little baby. But, I knew my place. I had to know it ... or else. That's how the Guild operated – on hierarchical principles, like a giant disciplinary pyramid scheme. "That is the Way," I responded obediently.

Wickham smiled patronizingly at me. "Excellent. And now for the second thing. I need you to go find the Wolf King and take a package to him."

"But I just got back from delivering a package to Capitol City a few days ago. And that didn't work out so well."

"No whining. You will do as I say. This mission is *not* top-secret but you do need to deliver a chest again and you are not allowed to know the contents."

"I'm detecting a pattern here," I said, attempting to make a joke. But Wickham didn't laugh.

"Here's the chest," said Wickham after reaching into his inventory and removing it. "You must find the Wolf King and give this directly to him, not to any of his pack or any of his servants. Only to him."

I reached out and took the chest. It was a little larger than the one I had delivered to Capitol City, but it wasn't particularly heavy. Whatever was in it was not dense. I tucked the chest into my inventory. "Got it."

"There is one more thing," added Wickham. "The Wolf King will give you a package which you are to deliver directly to me. You are not to tell anyone about this package or your mission to retrieve it. Understand?"

I nodded. "Understood." I paused for a moment and felt Wickham's eyes boring into me. "Um, how do I find the Wolf King?"

Wickham blinked very deliberately, twice, before responding. "He lives in the giant tree taiga. It is a wander of about a day and a half to get there. The wolves in that area all obey the Wolf King and tolerate wandering traders. Once you encounter a wolf in the giant tree taiga, ask to be taken to their leader and they should comply."

"Can I ask you something else about Wex?"

Wickham turned red with anger and shook his head as he pointed at the door. "Our conversation is over. Leave at first light tomorrow."

Again, I was very upset, but I simply stood up, said, "That is the Way," and then left without another word.

Chapter 3

The next morning I woke up at dawn and gathered my supplies. I woke up Slimy and said, "It's time to go."

Slimy groaned and jiggled a little bit. "Tired. More sweep."

I shook my head and picked him up. "Sorry, buddy. I've got another mission and I'm not allowed to leave you here by yourself. Remember?"

Slimy sniffed and nodded his head. "Still baby. Baby. Baby."

I smiled. "I wouldn't call you baby, but you're not a big kid either. When are you going to become a medium-sized slime?"

"Medium. Yay."

I chuckled as I glanced around my room one more time to make sure I had remembered everything. I quickly checked my inventory to ensure that the chest Wickham had given me was still there. Instinctively, I reached for Creepy, but then I remembered what Wes had done to him. I looked over at the bookshelf where I kept Creepy's remains, the pieces of his torn cloth body. I had thought about having him repaired, but I wanted the visual reminder of his dismemberment so that I would never forget. I would get my revenge on Wes ... eventually.

I carried Slimy with one arm as I walked to the llama stable. After I situated him in his saddle on Pippa's back, I started to lead my llama team toward the checkout station.

Suddenly, Wes stepped out from behind a post and stood in my path. "Move," I growled.

Wes yawned. "I was here first. You can go around."

"You stood there on purpose. To make a scene."

"Purpose. Purpose," said Slimy.

Wes sneered at Slimy. "You better learn to control that giant booger. I might have to put him down."

That was it! I dropped the llama leash and launched myself at Wes. He was too surprised to avoid me. My right shoulder connected with his stomach and I knocked him back into a pile of mud. When he hit the ground, I could hear the wind get knocked out of him. As he lay on his back gasping for air, I started to pummel him with punches.

I went insane. I don't know how long I was punching Wes or how many times I hit him. It wasn't until a rough hand grabbed my shoulder, pulled me off of Wes, and tossed me against the wall that I stopped punching him. It was Wayne. He glared at me and then began tending to Wes.

I moved forward, intent on returning to my rage-fueled violence, when I heard a girl's voice. "Winston. Stop it." I looked toward the voice and saw Winter. Her eyes betrayed her concern and her fear. "You hit him a lot. He's really hurt."

"Good," I snorted.

Winter shook her head. "You know that you will be punished if he ... well, if he dies."

She was right. Mutual combat was one thing, but my rage had taken it too far. If I murdered Wes without justification, I would be executed. *That is the Way.*

At that moment, Wickham rushed into the stable and assessed the situation. "What is the meaning of this?"

"I found Winston pummeling Wes," said Wayne.

Wickham turned toward me. "How dare you?!?"

"He insulted Slimy!" I said.

Wickham and Wayne both laughed, expressing their derision for my explanation. I heard sniggers from some of the others in the room. Slimy sat in his saddle looking sad.

Wickham approached me and grabbed my arm. Everyone in the crowd gasped. Wickham dragged me away from the crowd that had gathered and into a corral. "You will complete the mission I gave you yesterday," he whispered with a hiss. "But you will pay for this after you return."

I nodded my head. The consequences of my actions were just beginning to set in. "I understand. That is the Way."

Wickham released my arm and nodded his head. "That is the Way. Now, get out of my sight!"

I walked back to where my llamas and Slimy were waiting. I avoided looking at anyone. I grabbed the llama leash and walked toward the checkout counter. Winter tried to talk to me, but I ignored her and she left the stable.

I saw Wes' bruised and cut face as I walked past where a wandering trader doctor was working on him. Wes looked terrible. *Why did I have to react like that? Stupid.*

Behind the desk at the checkout counter was yet another young villager who was now a wandering trader trainee. I had noticed him a few days earlier cleaning up a llama corral but I didn't speak with him at that time.

As he handed me the checkout paperwork, I could tell he was afraid of me. I ignored him and quickly completed the paperwork before handing it back. He took the papers with trembling hands and then read through them.

"Going to the giant tree taiga? That sounds cool. I don't think I've ever checked out llamas for someone who was going there."

"Yeah, I heard a lot of wolves live up there. My guess is there are a lot of noob players trying to tame them for pets. I plan on selling lots of bones to them to try to profit from that," I lied.

The trainee nodded his head. "That's smart. I can't wait until I am a wandering trader and can profit off of noobs."

"What's your name anyway, kid?"

"I'm not a kid. I'm fourteen years old."

I smiled. "I didn't mean any offense. I am older than you, after all."

The trainee shrugged. "It's all right. My name is Oliver ... hurrr ... I mean William."

I reached out my hand and we shook. "Nice to meet you. How far along are you in your training?"

"About six months. I've seen you around in the weapons training area a couple of times."

"I'm surprised I hadn't noticed you until a couple days ago. But, I've been on a lot of wanders and missions lately so I guess that would explain it."

"I suppose."

"Anyway, William, it was nice to meet you. Good luck with your training."

"Good luck out there, Winston." He glanced at Wes getting medical treatment. "I guess you can handle yourself."

I grunted before leading my llamas to the exit of HQ. Old man Wenceslaus was manning the exit this time. "Where are you heading, Winston?"

"I thought I'd wander up to the giant tree taiga and see if I could sell some bones to some players taming wolves."

Wenceslaus chuckled. "Good idea. When I was your age, I used to sell bones and fish to the noobs who were looking for pets."

"I've been starting to read more business development books in the wandering trader library at night. It's really all about giving the customer what they need. I'd rather be selling cool stuff like weapons and armor all the time, but it seems like players are fairly proficient at getting those things."

Wenceslaus nodded. "If you can find a way to supply them with items from the Nether, that's how you can *really* make some money."

I rubbed my chin. "That's a good idea. Maybe I should try to give them the components to build a nether portal or something. Like an all-in-one building kit."

Wenceslaus smiled. "That sounds perfect. The only problem is we have to *wander*. So you can't just set up a store with a big sign that says *Nether Portal Kits for Sale*. Know what I mean?"

I nodded. "That is the problem with being a wandering trader. I still haven't figured out how to pick the right customers or find a way for them to pick me."

Wenceslaus laughed. "I don't think you'll ever solve that problem."

"Maybe not. Can you open the door now?"

Wenceslaus nodded and pulled the lever to open the door and I left headquarters.

Chapter 4

Because my journey to the giant tree taiga would take about a day and a half, I would have to spend the night somewhere. Unfortunately, there weren't any well-known caves or friendly villages along my route in which to spend the night. That would mean I'd have to build my own shelter. Consequently, I made sure to pack materials to build a shelter large enough to house my two llamas safely as well as my bed and Slimy's bed.

When we were less than fifteen minutes from HQ, I saw one of Wickham's assassins who had been dispatched a few days earlier to find Wex was returning to headquarters. "Oi, Wind? Any luck finding Wex?"

Wind shook his head. "No clue where he went. I found a few villagers who seemed to know something, but no matter what I did to them, they wouldn't talk."

"What did you do to them?"

Wind shook his head. "It doesn't matter anymore. They're dead," he said flatly.

I wasn't sure if Wind liked his job as an assassin or if it just didn't bother him. Some people are like that. I wasn't. I didn't like killing. I did it when I had to, but I would prefer to live in a world where it wasn't necessary.

"Do you have any ideas about where Wex might be?"

Wind shrugged his shoulders. "He probably lives among villagers. Maybe he disguises himself as one of them. Or maybe he doesn't. Most players think villagers and wandering traders look alike, except for their clothing. Wex probably uses that to his advantage as camouflage."

I nodded my head. "So, what now? Are you going back out there to search for him some more?"

"If Wickham orders it. That is the Way."

I nodded my head. "That is the Way."

"Good talking to you, Winston, but I need to get back to HQ and give my llamas a rest. Good luck on your wanders."

"Thanks. See ya," I said as I pulled on my llamas' leashes.

"Bye-bye," said Slimy.

Wind rolled his eyes. I don't think he liked Slimy very much, but he was too polite to say anything to me about it.

* * *

The first day of the wander was rather enjoyable. I only traded with a couple of players who were polite and respectful. I netted only about thirty emeralds from those trades, but at least it was easy money.

At one point, we wandered through a meadow filled with many different types of flowers. Slimy got excited. "Flower! Flower!"

I looked up at Slimy in the saddle. "You like flowers?"

Slimy jiggled an affirmative response. "Play in flower."

I laughed. "All right. We don't have a set schedule. I guess we can play for a while." I reached up and lifted Slimy out of his saddle and put him on the ground in the meadow. He hopped around amongst the flowers. He was having a lot of fun. He would hop on top of a flower and absorb it into his cube. Then he would shake it back and forth inside his gelatinous mass before releasing it, miraculously undamaged.

"Are you, like, smelling them that way or something?"

Slimy didn't answer me. He was too busy giggling and hopping on top of flowers.

"Don't go out of my sight," I said. "I'm gonna prepare some lunch."

I sat down and sliced a watermelon and made a couple of pork chop sandwiches. When lunch was ready I called Slimy. "Slimy! Come get some food."

As I sat down and began eating my sandwich, I could hear the jiggling of Slimy's cube as he hopped toward me from behind. I was just about to take another bite of my sandwich when Slimy hopped in front of me. I almost choked with surprise.

"You ... you grew!"

"Yes, I did, Winston. I am medium-sized now."

I nearly dropped my sandwich when I heard him speak with complete sentences and proper pronunciation. "And you can talk!"

Slimy smiled. "Yes. We slimes get the full ability to speak once we become medium-sized."

I started feeling a little dizzy from the surprise of it all. "Well, that's great! Um, do you want a sandwich?"

"Of course I do. You make great sandwiches." I handed Slimy the pork chop sandwich and he immediately absorbed it into his cube and digested it.

"What about some watermelon?" I asked, holding up a slice.

Slimy nodded his head and I tossed a couple slices into his cube. After he dissolved the two watermelon slices, he burped. "Oops. Sorry about that."

I laughed. "It's okay when you're out here in the wilderness. Just try to avoid that back at wandering trader headquarters. Burps and farts are not part of the Way."

Slimy giggled but then became serious. "Now that I can speak properly, I wanted to thank you for saving me from those players who killed my family. I wish I had a family so I could go live with them. Not that I haven't enjoyed living with you. It's just that ... well, I'm a slime and you're not."

I felt sad but I knew what he meant. "That's okay. Maybe we can find a slime family for you eventually."

Slimy looked down at the ground with a forlorn expression on his face. "I don't know. I'll probably just stay with you for a while if that's okay?"

I reached out and patted Slimy's cube. "Of course it's okay. You can stay with me as long as you want. And, if you ever decide to move out, I can help you find a place to live."

Slimy smiled and looked at the saddle on Pippa's back. "I think I'm too big for that saddle now."

"I guess you're right about that. Do you mind hopping alongside?"

"Of course not."

I put away all the lunch supplies, and I removed Slimy's saddle from Pippa. I packed it away in one of her carry bags.

"Guess we had better get going. I'd like to get as close to the giant tree taiga as possible before nightfall."

"Let's do it!"

Chapter 5

Shortly before nightfall, we found a secluded patch of ground surrounded by trees on which to build our shelter for the night. I centered my llamas in the middle of the patch and told them to "Stay." Then, I quickly erected four walls using cobblestones and wood blocks. I put a small window on one side and a door on the other. I put the window at the height of my llamas' heads so that they could look out the window and not feel claustrophobic.

Once the shelter was built, I started a campfire outside and roasted some chicken legs and boiled some carrots for dinner. I also gave each of my llamas some wheat. After Slimy and I had finished dinner, I pulled two cookies out of my inventory. "Dessert?"

Slimy smiled. "Of course. Thanks!" I tossed a cookie into his cube and he quickly dissolved it. I ate my cookie a little slower, enjoying the delicious crunchy texture.

By now, it was dark enough that the night mobs had begun to spawn. I could hear the nearby moaning of zombies and clicking of skeleton bones. I looked at Slimy and said, "We had better get inside and go to sleep." Slimy went into the shelter while I doused the campfire. Then, I trotted to the shelter and shut the door, just in time to avoid a wandering zombie. I was asleep in less than five minutes.

* * *

The next morning, I was awakened by an insistent knocking on the front door. I looked out the window and saw that the sun had just come up in the east. I rubbed my head as I sat up in bed. "What moron is banging on my door this early?" I mumbled.

"I don't know, but it's annoying," said Slimy. "Probably some noob player who wants to make a trade."

"How would a player know there's a wandering trader in the shelter? We built it when no one was around."

The knocking continued. I knew it wouldn't stop until I opened the door. Just to be safe, I removed a sword from my inventory and held it behind my back as I walked up to the front door and opened it.

Standing in front of me was a player. He was wearing full diamond armor and had a cocky expression on his face. "It's about time you opened the door. I've been knocking for a few minutes."

"Seriously? You knock on a stranger's door *first thing* in the morning?"

"I saw you building this shelter last night from that hilltop over there," he said as he pointed. "But I didn't come talk to you then. I wanted you to be well rested before I made this proposition to you."

I rolled my eyes. "What do you want? I'll trade with you after I eat some breakfast."

The player laughed. "I don't want to trade for anything. I want to *challenge* you ... to a duel."

I stepped back, put my sword in front of me, and took a defensive stance. "Why would you want to fight me?"

The player smiled and clapped his hands when he saw the sword. "I knew it! I knew the rumors were true."

"What rumors?"

"I was in a restaurant the other day and I heard some players saying that they'd seen wandering traders fight back against mean players and even kill some of them. One of the players said wandering traders even had very impressive fighting skills."

I suppose it would be hard to deny this to his face given that I was holding a sword in front of him. "So? What does that matter?"

"I want to challenge you to a duel to see if you can best my fighting skills. I've been traveling through Minecraft in hardcore mode, so I am pretty dominant."

Hardcore mode? What was this narcissist talking about?

"Don't duels usually end with someone dead?" I asked, still ready to kill the player if I had to.

The player shook his head. "That's not necessary. We'll just agree that the first person who lands a blow with a weapon wins. That way, the worst thing that will happen is you lose a heart or two from your health bar. That will regenerate pretty quick."

"What's in it for me? I'm a wandering trader after all. I have to get something out of this other than a little exercise."

The player nodded his head. "I understand. What about this? If I win, you will give me one of your wandering trader robes as a souvenir. And if you win, I'll give you my diamond armor that you can sell to someone else. Deal?"

I thought about it for a moment. Having a free set of diamond armor would be nice. I didn't think the player could defeat me but I said, "I'll give you a wandering trader *robe* but not a *hood*. I can't have anyone going around pretending to be a wandering trader who isn't one."

The player looked disappointed but nodded his head. "I understand. A robe would be fine."

"I get to choose the weapon too," I said.

"Fine by me."

"Also, what's your name? I want to know who I'm dueling."

"My name is DoomBoyPro. I used to be called DoomBoyAmateur, but that was when I was a noob. That was a long time ago."

I laughed. "Nice joke. Anyway, let's use axes." Initially, I had considered choosing a sword as the weapon, but most players are very proficient with swords. However, when it comes to fighting with an axe, a lot of them are below average. I hoped that was the case here.

DoomBoyPro nodded his head. "Are you positive you want to choose that weapon?"

"Of course."

"Fire. Should we duel now?" asked DoomBoyPro.

I shook my head. "I need to eat breakfast and stretch a little bit. Why don't you go wait by the stream to the north of here? I'll be down in about fifteen minutes."

The player nodded his head and walked away. I went back inside the shelter and told Slimy what was happening.

"You don't think it's a trick, do you? Like, he's actually going to try to kill you or something?"

I shrugged. "It could be a trick, but I doubt it. Even if it were, there's no way he could defeat me. Not with the training I've had."

"Never say never. I thought I would always have my parents around...."

With those sad words ringing in my ears, I ate a quick breakfast of two slices of bread and one roasted potato. I shared it with Slimy.

"You want to watch the duel?" I asked.

Slimy shook his cube. "No. I'm still tired from hopping all day yesterday. I haven't hopped that much in ... well, ever! I want to relax."

I smiled. "Makes sense. I'll see you in a few minutes with a new set of diamond armor."

I walked to the stream where I saw DoomBoyPro was sitting on a boulder. When he saw me, he smiled. He stood up and spun his axe around on his fingertips.

Whoa. Maybe he's better than most players with an axe?

"Did you have a good breakfast?"

I nodded my head as I pulled my axe out of my inventory. "Let's get this duel over with. I got stuff I need to do today."

DoomBoyPro shrugged. "Let's get it on."

We rushed toward each other with our axes held tightly. Both of us took ready positions and circled each other, looking for an opening to attack. I held my axe in my right hand and DoomBoyPro held his in his left. I didn't have as much experience fighting against lefties, so I had to be careful.

DoomBoyPro leaned to one side and slashed at me but I easily avoided his attempted attack. As he followed through with his axe, I slashed at his arm with mine, but he was able to bend his body in an almost unbelievable angle in order to avoid the blade of the axe.

He is really good. Uh-oh.

We began circling each other again, waiting for the next attempt to win the duel. After we'd circled for about twenty seconds, I saw an opening. I dropped onto one knee and slashed at DoomBoyPro's stomach, but he leaned back just in time and my axe missed him by the narrowest of margins.

Unfortunately, that attempt left me in an exposed position. I had gambled that I would easily hit him and the duel would be over. DoomBoyPro quickly slashed at my shoulder. I leaned to one side and raised my axe to block the blow. But I was too late. The blade of his axe cut into my shoulder, and I screamed in pain.

DoomBoyPro , true to his word, backed away and then pumped his fist in the air. "Yes! I defeated a wandering trader."

I held my shoulder to stop the bleeding. "Nice move, kid. I guess I should've chosen swords."

"Maybe. But I'm pretty good with a sword too. Here," he said as he reached into his inventory. "Drink this potion of healing."

I reached out and grabbed the potion. I guzzled it and my shoulder was good as new in no time. I gave the empty bottle back to him. "Thanks. I guess I owe you a robe now?"

DoomBoyPro smiled. "Yeah. I'm gonna hang it up on my wall in my mansion. It's going to be my most prized possession."

I chuckled. "You players and your mansions. Why can't any of you be happy with a humble little house?"

The player shrugged. "Why settle? Minecraft is a world of unlimited resources. Why not take advantage of it?"

I suppose that was a fair response. I reached into my inventory and removed a robe and tossed it to the player. He unfolded it and held it out in front of himself inspecting it. "So awesome! Thanks for agreeing to the duel."

I nodded my head. "Yeah, sure. Next time though, don't knock on my door first thing in the morning."

DoomBoyPro nodded his head. "Sorry about that. I was just excited."

"All right, kid, I need to go wandering now."

DoomBoyPro tucked the robe into his inventory and nodded. "See you around, maybe."

"Maybe."

Chapter 6

I returned to my shelter and told Slimy what happened with the player.

"That's strange," he said. "Have you ever heard of a player challenging a wandering trader to a duel?"

I shook my head. "Nope," I said, as I knocked down a wall to let my llamas out. I took them to a nearby tree and tied their leashes to it. After that, I returned and punched the remaining walls and the two beds into pieces and put everything back into my inventory.

"I'm still hungry," whined Slimy. "I burned a lot of calories yesterday hopping so far."

"Okay. Here." I tossed a loaf of bread and two apples to Slimy. He absorbed everything into his cube and digested it. I was still a little hungry as well, so I ate a couple of roasted chicken legs. Then, I made sure my llamas got their fill of wheat.

After we had all finished eating, we set off for the giant tree taiga.

* * *

About ten minutes later, we entered a standard taiga biome. I admired the spruce trees and harvested wild sweet berries. I gave some to Slimy.

"These are delicious," he said. "Much better than farmed berries."

I smiled. "I agree."

As we made our way through the taiga toward the giant tree taiga, we spotted a taiga village in the distance. "I don't want to deal with those guys today," I said. "They are usually pretty hostile to wandering traders."

"I'll activate stealth mode," said Slimy.

I chuckled. "Me too."

About ten minutes later, we encountered our first giant spruce tree. The ground changed from the grass and dirt of the normal taiga to podzol and coarse dirt. Occasionally, we passed cobblestones covered with moss in the shade of the large trees.

"Looks like we are in the giant tree taiga," I said.

"How do we find the Wolf King?" asked Slimy.

I shrugged. "I've a feeling he will find us."

A few minutes later a rabbit dashed across our path. Slimy laughed at it. But then a fox, who was in hot pursuit of the rabbit, ran in front of us.

Slimy looked concerned. "Do you think the fox is going to eat that rabbit?"

"Yes, if he can catch it."

Slimy nodded his head sadly. "Is the entire world like this? Kill or be killed?"

"I can see how you might think that. But look at the beautiful environment we're walking through. These trees are amazing."

Slimy glanced up at the trees. "I suppose you're right. Still, it seems like every time we leave headquarters, we have to worry about someone trying to kill us."

"I can't say that you're wrong," I said. "But, no one has killed us yet. Sometimes, we just have to find the joy in still breathing." I'm not sure I believed my own words; I was just trying to cheer up Slimy.

"I guess."

I pointed to the highest hill in the biome. "Let's head to the top of that. My guess is the Wolf King lives somewhere near the top where he would have a good vantage over his realm."

"Ugh. You mean I have to hop all the way up there?!?"

"Well, you're too big to ride on the llamas and I am not strong enough to carry you."

"Lame."

About fifteen minutes later, despite Slimy's constant complaints, we were nearing the summit of the large hill when suddenly two wolves jumped from behind bushes and growled at us. One of them spoke haltingly. "What. Do you. Want?"

Slimy was scared and hopped behind me for protection. I held out my hands to show the wolves I had no weapons and meant them no harm. "I've been sent to deliver a chest to your king."

One of the wolves approached and sniffed me. He turned back to the other wolf and said, "Truth, he tells."

The other wolf nodded his head and said, "Follow." I walked behind the wolves as they led me, Slimy, and my two llamas along an increasingly narrow path. Eventually, as rock walls closed in upon us, the path became too narrow for the llamas.

"I need to leave my llamas here. Can you promise you won't eat them?"

The wolves glared at me with fire in their eyes. "We no eat. You are guest." I tied my llamas to a small bush growing out of a crack in one of the rock walls and hoped for the best.

Slimy and I continued to follow the wolves until we came to a narrow crack in the mountain. "I'm not sure I can fit through that," I said.

"Use pickaxe," said one of the wolves.

I pulled a pickaxe out of my inventory and mined one block out of the rock surface. That opened the crack just wide enough for me. The wolves led the way while Slimy and I followed. We entered what appeared to be the beginning of a large cave system. The interior of the cave was dimly lit with a few torches at distant intervals. It was extremely warm compared to the outside air. I could smell wolves, probably hundreds of them.

"This is just like our headquarters," said Slimy. I shot him a look and put my index finger over my lips to indicate he should be quiet. Slimy's face registered surprise and then he nodded his head, understanding what I meant.

The wolves led us through a maze of corridors. It was so confusing that I didn't think I'd be able to get out of this cave without them showing me the way unless I just mined horizontally through a wall. We passed multiple dens where wolf families lived. They regarded us with suspicion, their keen eyes measuring us to determine how they would kill us if the need arose.

Eventually, about five minutes later, we arrived in front of a large opening at the terminus of the corridor. Two of the largest wolves I'd ever seen were sitting in front of the opening. The four wolves barked and growled at each other and finally the two guard wolves who had been sitting in front of the passageway stood up.

One of them looked at me and said, "Wolf King will see you. Only you. Slime stays here."

"You aren't going to hurt him, are you?" I asked.

The wolf shook his head. "You guest. Plus, slime taste disgusting."

I looked over at Slimy. I could tell he was relieved for once in his life that people thought he was gross. "Don't worry, Winston. I'll be fine."

I looked at the guard wolf who had been speaking to me. "Okay. Lead the way."

Chapter 7

I followed the wolf guard into the large chamber. The chamber was very dimly lit and it took a moment for my eyes to adjust to the darkness. The wolves, of course, had no problem seeing in the low light.

Even though I couldn't see the Wolf King at first, I could hear him. His breathing was loud and deep. There was a background hint of a growl with every breath. The wolf guard held up his hand indicating that I should stop. I did.

The wolf guard walked forward. As he did, I could begin to see the outline of the Wolf King, his back turned toward me. He was lounging on the ground, but I wasn't prepared for how large he was.

I've heard it said that wolves in packs are led by an alpha male. The alpha male is the strongest and bravest of the male wolves, earning his title by defeating all challengers. Judging by the size of the Wolf King, I knew that he was *unquestionably* the alpha. He was at least twice as large as any wolf I had ever seen. His fur was thick and bristly. I noticed a scar along his ribs where I assumed another wolf had clawed him. But the scar had healed a long time ago.

When the guard got close enough to the Wolf King, he barked and growled a few times. The Wolf King raised his head and turned around. His dark, steel eyes pierced into mine. It was like he was looking into my very soul.

The Wolf King barked a couple of times at the guard who barked back. The Wolf King, apparently not liking what the guard had said, roared and growled. The guard then tucked his tail between his legs and slinked out of the chamber leaving me alone with the Wolf King.

"I understand you have brought something from Wickham," the Wolf King said. I noticed that the Wolf King had no trouble speaking my language. There was no halting speech or broken grammar like the other wolves I had heard speak.

"Yes, Your Highness. Would you like it now?"

"Yes."

I reached into my inventory and removed the small chest. I approached the Wolf King and set the chest on the ground near his massive paws. Then, I backed away.

The Wolf King tapped the box a couple of times with his paw. Then, he opened the lid. He examined its contents. Then a sly smile curled his lips. He shut the chest. Then he looked up at me. "Please be sure to thank Wickham for the chest ... and its contents."

I nodded my head. "Of course. By the way ... hurrr ... what was in the chest?"

The Wolf King growled. "I'm sure if Wickham wanted you to know, he would've told you." Obviously, that was the end of the discussion.

I rubbed my neck nervously and began to feel itchy all over for some reason. "Sure, you're right about that, I guess. Um, Wickham said something about you having a chest for me to take back to him?"

The Wolf King nodded his head. "Yes. And I will not tell you what's in that chest either. Don't open it until you get back to Wickham." The Wolf King reached behind a large rock next to him and removed a small chest. It was secured with several locking mechanisms. The King put the box down in front of him. "Come get it."

I approached and picked up the chest and examined the locks. "Will Wickham be able to open this?"

The Wolf King nodded his head. "He knows the secrets for opening these chests."

I tucked the chest into my inventory. I wished I knew what was in these chests, but I guess that was not a secret these leaders wanted revealed.

"I guess that's everything then. Should I go now?" I asked.

The Wolf King shook his enormous cubic head. "I have one question for you. Is it true that Wex stole a chest recently?"

"How do you know about Wex?!?"

The Wolf King roared. "I'm asking the questions here. You either give me the answer or tell me you don't know."

I involuntarily shivered with fear. I could tell the Wolf King was getting truly upset. And, I didn't think I would like him very much when he was truly upset.

"Yes, Wex did that. In fact, I saw it happen. I tried to capture him, but he got away."

The Wolf King looked concerned. "Yes, he tends to do that." He paused for a moment and took a couple breaths, the scratchy rumbling in his chest echoed in the room. "Do you see the scar on my ribs?"

I nodded my head. "I saw it when I came in. Hard to miss."

The Wolf King sighed. "It is. Wex did this to me. I was trying to help wandering trader assassins track him down after he went rogue. I cornered him and thought I had the upper hand ... but he managed to escape."

"I thought that might've been from a battle against a wolf challenger for your position as alpha."

The Wolf King laughed. "No one has challenged me for the last twenty years. And no one will. When I die, the males will fight each other for supremacy. They will not fight me."

This Wolf King was truly the definition of *dominant*.

"Well, Wickham has sent assassins after Wex again. I'm sure they will catch him eventually."

The Wolf King scratched behind his right ear with his rear paw. "Somehow, I doubt that. Wex is ... elusive."

"I guess you're right. Um, do you have any more questions, or should I go?"

The Wolf King bared his teeth and smiled. At least, I think he was smiling. "Yes. Be careful on your journey back to Wickham. I'm sure Wex and many others would kill for what's in the box."

That really made me feel great. Just what I needed, a box that Wex was interested in.

"Well, it was ... um ... nice to meet you, Your Highness," I said, before bowing and walking out of the chamber. After I had emerged, the two wolf guards quickly took up their positions in front of the opening in order to block the entrance.

"Can one of you take me and Slimy to the exit? I'm sure I would get lost without a guide."

The wolf guards both chuckled. "Of course. Lost you would be," said one of them.

The other wolf guard howled and soon a smaller, younger male wolf arrived. "Yes, sir?"

"Korosense1, take wandering trader and slime to exit. Take trader out of giant tree taiga safely before return."

Korosense1 barked twice and then looked at me and Slimy. "Follow."

Chapter 8

The young wolf led us back outside the wolf den and to our llamas who were being watched by another wolf. It looked like he had been drooling, but somehow managed not to kill and eat the llamas. The two wolves barked and growled at each other and then the second wolf departed for the wolf den.

When I approached my llamas, they seemed very nervous and anxious, but other than that they appeared to be in good health. I gave each of them an apple and they seemed very happy afterward.

"Is everything all right with Sunny and Pippa?" asked Slimy.

"Seems to be. I'm sure they were nervous being left alone. Normally, they are either with a trader or in a stable at all times."

"At least they have each other," said Slimy optimistically.

I chuckled. "I suppose you're right." I looked at Korosensei and said, "Let's go."

Korosensei walked alongside of us without saying much, constantly scanning the landscape of the giant tree taiga for any threats. I doubted there would be any. The place seemed overrun with his fellow wolves. I saw several prowling around, probably wishing they could eat my llamas.

"Say, Korosense1, if you don't mind me asking, do all wolves have names with letters and numbers?"

The wolf shook his head. "No. Parents name babies what they want. I named after player who fed them bones."

"Did they become his pet dogs?" asked Slimy.

Korosense1 growled. "My parents never dogs! Always true to wolf strength!"

Slimy quivered and looked at me with fear in his eyes. "I'm sorry. I didn't mean to say something stupid."

The wolf calmed down and shook his head. "That ok. Some wolves weak; become dogs. But true wolves wild forever."

"What's your King's name?" I asked.

Korosense1 shook his head. "No name. Call him Highness, King, or Alpha."

"I guess that makes sense. By the way, is there a Wolf Queen?"

The young wolf suddenly became sad. "Used to be. She was in forest and three players killed her. When King found out, he raged. Sent entire pack to find and kill players."

"Did ... did they find them?" asked Slimy with a quiver in his voice.

The wolf nodded his head. "Found them and killed all."

"So, the King hasn't remarried?"

The wolf shook his head. "Not permitted in wolf culture. If he remarry, he have to renounce Alpha status. Of course, he never do that."

We continued walking for another fifteen minutes, mainly in silence. Slimy asked a couple questions about trees and podzol, which the wolf answered to the best of his ability. Eventually though we crossed beyond the boundary of the great tree taiga biome.

Korosense1 looked at us and said, "I go no farther. Hope you have safe journey."

I nodded my head. "Thank you for your help. I wish I could have a wolf with me always." Korosense1 narrowed his eyes and growled. "No. No. You misunderstand me. Not as a pet dog, but as a true wolf. It would be nice to be able to have a wolf as a warrior companion."

"What about me?" asked Slimy, feeling slighted.

The wolf laughed at the thought of Slimy as a great warrior and then howled before turning around and trotting back up the mountain to his den.

I looked at Slimy. "Don't worry. You are a good companion too. I'm just not sure how good you would be in a fight."

Slimy looked upset. "I *can* fight. Now that I'm a medium-sized slime, I can jump on players and mobs and inflict damage."

"I suppose so. But, let's hope we don't have to fight anyone before we get back to headquarters."

* * *

Slimy and I led the llamas through the normal taiga and then into a forest biome. We stopped for lunch and then continued on. As we walked through the dappled sunlight filtering through the majestic oak trees in the forest, I took a deep breath and sighed. "What a nice day."

"Yes, it is," said Slimy. The two llamas grunted their agreement as well.

"I think we should set up our shelter earlier today. Maybe we can find a nice meadow in the forest. We won't get back to headquarters until tomorrow no matter what we do, so we might as well enjoy the journey."

Slimy smiled. "That sounds great! I can hop around the meadow and absorb some flowers."

"Sure. Maybe the llamas can enjoy eating some fresh grass?"

We continued walking through the forest, admiring the beauty of the biome surrounding us. Our idyll was soon disturbed, though, when I heard a whooshing sound like something passing through the air. It didn't sound like an arrow or trident or anything like that. It didn't sound like wings either, so I knew it wasn't a bird or a bat.

"Slimy? Do you hear that noise?"

It was then that I heard a ***thump*** to my side. I looked over and saw that a large rope net had fallen on top of Slimy! He was struggling against it, trying to free himself. I looked up in the trees to see who might have dropped the net on him but could not see anything. I pulled a sword from my inventory and rushed toward Slimy. "Don't worry, I'll cut you free."

As I began to cut the ropes forming the net, I noticed Slimy's expression become extremely scared. "Winston! Behind you!"

I turned to see what had scared him so much, but the only thing I saw was the back of a shovel as it moved rapidly toward my face and then smashed it.

And then, everything went black.

Chapter 9

When I regained consciousness, my hands were tied around a slender tree trunk against which my body had been placed. I blinked my eyes and shook my head, and the world slowly came into focus.

I looked around the area. I began to panic when I realized I couldn't see Slimy anywhere. My llamas were gone too! As I became more panicked and my adrenalin began to surge, I struggled against the ropes binding me. But, it was futile. I wasn't going to get free without something to cut the ropes. Still, I kept pulling at the ropes again and again, refusing to give up. I *had to* find Slimy. I *had to* find my llamas.

After about a minute struggling against the ropes, I heard a chuckling sound coming from above me. I looked up and saw movement. "Who's up there? What have you done?"

And then, as if by magic, the chuckling was coming from directly in front of me. I swiveled my head down from looking at the treetops and saw an enderman standing in front of me. He was pointing at me and laughing.

"It's about time you woke up! You've been unconscious since yesterday. I had to kill nearly a dozen zombies and skeletons last night."

It had already been a day since I was ambushed?!?

"Who are you? What have you done with Slimy and my llamas?"

The enderman continued to laugh for a few more seconds and then said, "Look at yourself. Pathetic."

"Why don't you untie these ropes and then we'll see how pathetic I am?"

The enderman smiled and shook his head. "Oh, I know all about you wandering traders. Vipers in disguise. I know how good you are with weapons."

"What are you going to do to me then?"

The enderman stood in front of me and tapped his chin with his left index finger. "Oh, I'm not going to do anything to you. I wish I could. But, I am under strict instructions to give you only a message."

"What would that be?"

"I was told to tell you that you need to stop searching for the traitor at headquarters. If you continue to look for the traitor, you'll never see Slimy ever again. Not alive, anyway."

I erupted with anger. I pulled against the ropes and yelled at the enderman. "Who sent you? Was it Wes? Was it Wex? Was it Wickham?"

"You traders and your W names. *So stupid*. My name is Dan. Dan the enderman. See how it rhymes? Now, *that* is cool. Your name should be something like Vader the wandering trader. Then your name would rhyme and be cool too."

"Shut up, Dan! Who sent you?"

"Oh, Dan the enderman may not be the smartest mob to have ever spawned, but Dan is not an idiot. I'm not gonna tell you who sent me."

"Where's Slimy?" I demanded.

"Oh, he's in a safe place ... for now. I've been told that if you cease your search for the traitor, Slimy eventually will be released."

I didn't believe that for a second. If his captors released Slimy, he would know who they were and then he would tell me. I knew they were going to kill him. I had to get out of this mess and then find him and save him.

"Okay, then. I promise to stop investigating. You can untie me and return Slimy to me now."

Dan chuckled and shook his head. "You don't give up, do you? At least you have tenacity. I can appreciate that. No. My employer will need to see ample proof that you have stopped the investigation before the slime is released."

"So you're saying your employer is at headquarters, aren't you?"

Big brain!

The confused and angry look on Dan's face told me I was correct. "I said nothing like that. You just *inferred* that. I have no idea where my employer is."

"I can tell you're lying. Now, let me go and I promise not to kill you if you take me to the location where Slimy is being held."

Dan laughed. "Oh, no. That's *not* going to happen. You'll just have to find a way to free yourself. I'm sure you can do it. It might take a day or two, assuming none of the nighttime mobs kill you before then, of course."

"How can I stop the investigation if you don't free me?"

"Well, if you're dead, you'll have to stop investigating, right?"

"Why don't you just kill me now and get it over with?"

"I wasn't told to *kill* anyone, just capture the slime and give you the message."

"Fine then, I guess we are at a stalemate. Get lost."

Dan gasped. "No one tells Dan the enderman to 'get lost'. Dan gets lost when he feels like it." And with that, Dan snapped his fingers and teleported away, leaving me in my predicament.

I looked at the sun and saw that I had about an hour of sunlight remaining. But, if I didn't get free soon, I would probably be eaten by a zombie or shot dead by a skeleton. Too bad we were so far away from the giant tree taiga. I could call for help from the wolves. Actually, I could call for help from anybody. It was my only chance.

"Help! Help!" I shouted. I continued calling for help off and on for another fifteen minutes before I heard footsteps. I looked around but didn't see who it was. The footsteps sounded like they were coming from all directions.

Was this an ambush? Had an illusioner cast a spell to create multiple copies of himself to distract me and so he could approach and murder me?

I kept yelling for help, hoping that if it were an illusioner coming to end my life, someone noble and good would stop him in the nick of time.

Suddenly, I felt a hand grasp my hand behind the tree to which it was tied. "Quit your sniveling," said the masculine voice.

"What are you going to do to me?"

There was no verbal response. Instead, I heard a sword being removed from the inventory of the thing standing behind me. And then, I heard the sword slash through the air. *Were my hands about to be cut off?!?* And then ... the sword cut through the ropes, freeing me.

I pulled my arms in front of me and rubbed my wrists as I stood up to see who had set me free. To my surprise, it *was* an illusioner. "Thanks," I said.

The illusioner shrugged. "Don't mention it. Your shouts for help were bothering me and ruining my concentration. I have been trying to learn a new spell."

"Sorry to interrupt you, but an enderman waylaid me and I thought he was about to kill me. Then, he disappeared and left me here to be killed by the mobs of the night."

"Whatever. Can't say I've never heard a sob story like that before."

Dang. Harsh.

Suddenly I had a shocking thought. *Did Dan steal the chest I had been given by the Wolf King? Would this be the second time in as many missions that a chest had gone missing?* I reached in my inventory and breathed a sigh of relief when I found that it was still there.

The illusioner noticed my concern. "Lose anything?"

I shook my head. "Nope. I guess Dan the enderman didn't want to rob me."

"I suppose not." The illusioner looked up at the sky and saw the sun was beginning to set. "Look, buddy, it's about to be dark. I have a spare room in my cabin if you want to use it for the night. I could use the company."

Although I would normally not trust an illusioner, he had every opportunity to kill me and he didn't do it. Plus, if there really were a separate room, I could put something in front of the door so that he couldn't murder me in my sleep. I really wanted to get home to headquarters and form a search party for Slimy, but I knew I wouldn't be able to travel safely through the night.

"I suppose so. Thank you. Are you close by?"

The illusioner nodded his head. "About a five-minute walk."

I brushed some of the dirt off the back of my robe from where I'd been sitting tied to the tree. "Let's go."

Chapter 10

I followed the illusioner through the darkening forest to his cabin. It was a cozy affair, but well-built.

"How long have you lived here?" I asked.

"About five years. I used to live in a woodland mansion with some vindicators and evokers, but they were annoying so I decided that I preferred living by myself."

"I get it. Sometimes living with people isn't any fun."

The illusioner opened the door to the cabin and walked inside. I followed him. Inside the cabin was a compact kitchen next to a cozy seating area with a small table and four chairs. On the far wall were two doors. The illusioner pointed at one of them. "That's the guest room. Make yourself comfortable and I will cook some dinner. Do you like chicken?"

I smiled. "I love roasted chicken. I'll be right back."

I walked into the guest room and saw that it was lightly furnished. There was a bed and one chest. There was also a mirror and a wardrobe in which to hang clothing. I changed out of the robe I had been wearing and pulled a clean one out of my inventory to put on. I hung the dirty robe in the wardrobe and went back to the living area.

The illusioner was busy making dinner. "By the way, my name's Winston. What's yours?"

"My name's xXShadowXx."

"Why so many Xs?"

"My given name is Shadow. But when I became an adult I added the Xs because I thought it was more dominant. It's a little mysterious too, don't you agree?"

I shrugged. "I suppose. It just doesn't really roll off the tongue does it?"

"I don't mind. It's better than being called Shadow. I mean, come on, xXShadowXx is memorable, don't you agree?"

I nodded my head. "I *will* agree with that."

"Why don't you sit down at the table and I will bring your plate to you in a minute?"

I sat down at the small table and thought about Slimy. I hoped he was still alive. I didn't trust anything Dan the enderman had said. "Say, xXShadowXx, do you remember hearing anything yesterday a little after midday in the forest? That's when I was attacked."

xXShadowXx thought about it for a moment and then said, "I don't recall anything unusual. Just the sound of birds and bats and ocelots. I usually take my nap right after lunch, so I might've been asleep at the time. Plus, I found you pretty far from my cabin. I'm not sure I could've heard it."

"But you heard me yelling for help?"

"I was out practicing a new spell and looking for medicinal herbs to use in some potions I'm working on."

"I thought witches were the only mobs who made potions?"

The illusioner shook his head. "Anyone can make potions. Players do it all the time. I'm trying to develop some new potions that have – um, how shall I put this? – *special* applications."

I raised an eyebrow. "Like what?"

The illusioner shook his head. "I'm not telling anyone until I've investigated it fully myself. I'm not going to let anyone steal my ideas."

"I'm not gonna make any potions. But I understand the need for protecting your own intellectual property."

Now it was the illusioner's turn to raise an eyebrow. "You do?"

I laughed. "You caught me. I have no idea about intellectual property one way or the other."

The illusioner finished cooking the chicken and he brought me a plate with two chicken legs, a slice of watermelon, a loaf of bread, and a glass of milk. "I hope you like the food."

"I'm sure I will," I said. I lifted a chicken leg to my mouth and was about to bite into it when a wave of grief passed through me. I put the leg back on the plate and looked at xXShadowXx.

"Did you see a medium-sized slime yesterday or today? Or someone with a slime?"

The illusioner shook his head. "I don't usually see slimes in this part of the forest. I think it's too dry here. Or something. I really don't understand slimes."

I nodded my head. "It's just that the slime was my friend and I want to go find him. I was hoping maybe you had seen him and would give me a clue as to his location."

"Maybe tomorrow morning you can find his trail or the trail of his kidnappers?"

I nodded my head. "Maybe." I picked up the chicken leg again and bit into it. It was juicy and delicious. Slimy would've loved it.

* * *

After dinner, the illusioner made each of us a cup of hot chocolate. It was quite tasty. I hadn't had a good cup of hot chocolate since before my parents were killed. It made me nostalgic for them. The layer of nostalgia added to the foundation of grief over the loss of Slimy was too much for me to take. "I'm really tired. I think I'll go to sleep early. I'm going to leave at first light to look for Slimy, so if you are not awake when I leave, I just wanted to say thank you for your hospitality."

The illusioner smiled. "Don't mention it. We mobs need to stick together."

"I suppose. If I'm ever by this way in the future, I will stop at your cabin and give you a good deal on anything in my inventory."

The illusioner smiled. "I'd like that. Goodnight, Winston."

I went into the guest room, lay down on the bed, and fell asleep almost instantly.

* * *

I woke up in the middle of the night feeling very strange. I felt like I was floating. I tried to reach up to scratch an itch on my nose but I couldn't move my arms. I looked down and saw that I was tied to the bed!

"What's going on?!? Help! xXShadowXx, where are you?"

At that moment the illusioner stepped out from a dark corner of the room. "I'm right here, Winston."

"What are you doing to me? I thought you were helping me."

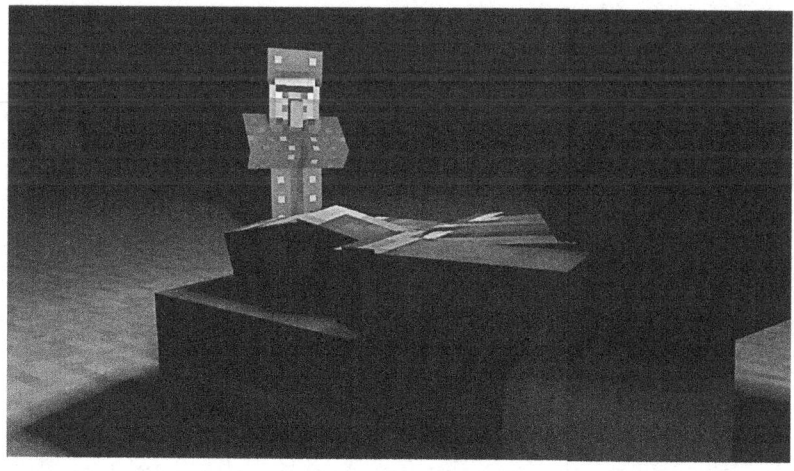

The illusioner grinned at me like an evil cat. "I *did* help you out. But not because I'm a kind-hearted soul. I needed to get you in here so I could run some experiments on you."

I pulled at the restraints but to no avail. "Don't do this. You'll regret it."

"I doubt that. Once I'm done with my experiments, I'm going to kill you and then I won't have to worry about you seeking revenge on me. That's what I did all my prior subjects."

"How many mobs have you betrayed?!?"

xXShadowXx shrugged. "I lost count years ago."

This guy was a homicidal maniac in addition to being an illusioner. I knew I shouldn't have trusted him. "Did you put something in my hot chocolate?"

"Do you feel like you're floating right now?"

"You drugged me?!?"

xXShadowXx looked upset. "I don't *drug* people. I experiment on them by giving them potions which have certain *effects*. What I put into the hot chocolate is a delayed levitation potion. If you weren't tied to that bed right now, you would float away."

"What are you talking about?"

"You know how shulkers can shoot bullets at things and make them levitate? I wanted to bottle that power. And ... it looks like I've succeeded."

"You're mad!"

"I'm not mad. I'm a *genius*. And besides, that was the easy potion. I tried it myself already. I just wanted to make sure it would work on anyone. This next potion however...."

xXShadowXx reached into his inventory and pulled out a dark purple potion. It was bubbling inside of its container, as though it were alive. I recoiled in horror. "What is that?"

"Oh. This is my zombie potion. I've been trying to develop an easy way to turn players and mobs into zombies. So far the test results have been ... well, not very promising. But I've re-formulated the ingredients and added a little additional rotten flesh. I think this might work."

"You can't make me take it. I won't drink it."

"I knew you'd say that. They *all* do. It's easy to fix. See?" He reached into his inventory, removed a splash potion, and threw it at me. It was a potion of weakness. I suddenly felt my strength disappear and my muscles go slack.

The illusioner grinned as he approached me. He reached for my mouth and pried it open with a small metal rod. I tried to resist, but I was too weak.

He took the stopper out of the zombie potion bottle with his teeth and spit on the floor. "Open wide!"

He brought the bottle to my lips and began to tilt it. I tried to resist, but was too weak. The illusioner was just a moment away from pouring the foul-smelling potion into my mouth when suddenly the door burst open and Wolf, Winona, and Winter stood there with their swords drawn.

"Release him! Now!" yelled Wolf.

The terrified illusioner dropped the potion on the floor. The bottle shattered, spilling the vile liquid harmlessly on the ground.

"I'll never surrender." Suddenly xXShadowXx cast a spell, turning himself invisible and making four copies of himself. Wolf, Winona, and Winter fought against the copies. I saw the window in the room push open and then slam shut, as the invisible illusioner escaped.

As the window slammed shut, Wolf yelled at Winter. "You stay with Winston. Winona and I will go after the illusioner." Wolf and Winona each pulled a torch from their respective inventories and leapt through the window in pursuit of the illusioner.

By now, the illusioner copies had vanished. Winter cut me free of my restraints, and I sat up in the bed. The potion of weakness was beginning to wear off and I could feel my strength returning.

"Winston? Are you all right?"

"I think so."

Winter looked around the room. "Where is Slimy? I thought he'd be here."

I shook my head. "Gone. Captured."

Winter gasped. "How? Why?"

I shook my head sadly. I was about to tell her my tale of woe when Wolf and Winona walked back into the room. "We couldn't follow him. It was too dark and he was casting all kinds of spells and trying to hit us with dozens of splash potions. We will get him eventually."

I nodded my head. "How did you guys find me? I thought I was done for."

"You have Wickham to thank for that," said Wolf. "When your llamas wandered back to HQ without you, we all assumed you were dead. Wickham wasn't really worried about you but he was worried about some package he said the Wolf King had given you. We were supposed to find that. We followed the tracks of your llamas back to this area and were just approaching this cabin to speak to its inhabitants when we heard you yelling at the illusioner."

I opened my eyes wide in shock. "That's got to be the best coincidence of my entire life."

Wolf laughed. "I suppose. By the way, do you have the item from the Wolf King?"

"I should." I reached into my inventory and checked. It was still there. The illusioner didn't have any interest in my stuff, just using me as a lab rat. "It's still here."

"All right then. Let's get you back to HQ."

I shook my head. "You can take the box back. I have to go find Slimy."

"What do you mean?" asked Wolf.

I told him, Winona, and Winter about everything that had happened. I told them about the ambush. I told them about the threat about the investigation. I told them that Slimy was the bargaining chip.

"Here's what we're going to do," said Wolf. "We will spend the remainder of this night in this cabin. Winter, Winona, and I will take turns on guard duty. In the morning, Winona can take the Wolf King's box to Wickham, and the rest of us will search for Slimy. With any luck, we will find the illusioner too."

"Shouldn't I stay? Winter can take the box back," said Winona.

Wolf shook his head. "If we give the box to a trainee and she loses it, Wickham will have our heads."

Winona nodded. "I guess you are right. Okay, I agree with your plan."

"Yeah," I said, "your plan sounds great, except you left out one thing."

"What's that?" asked Wolf.

"First thing in the morning, we burn this cabin to the ground."

Chapter 11

Wolf shook me awake at first light. "Let's do this."

I nodded my head. I was wide-awake instantaneously. I was ready for some revenge ... or at least to destroy the property of a madman.

Trader Winona was already waiting outside with her team of llamas. I handed her the box I had acquired from the Wolf King. "I have no idea what's in this thing, but it's obviously very important."

She nodded. "I'll take it directly to Wickham. I'll let him know what you guys decided to do."

"Thank you, Trader Winona. And thank you for letting Winter accompany us."

"Of course. She's basically ready to be an official wandering trader. I just haven't had time to take her on her first solo wander for the final examination."

I looked over at Winter who was blushing from the praise. "Congratulations."

"Thank you."

"Now, if you all will stand back, I'm going to burn this evil place to ashes." I reached into my inventory and pulled out a bow enchanted with flame and several arrows. I shot them into the wooden structure and watched with satisfaction as it caught fire. I hoped xXShadowXx was watching this from somewhere. I hoped he was watching all his experiments go up in flames. But, even if he were far away, I knew he was evil and would continue doing his terrible experiments. If I ever saw him again, I would kill him without hesitation.

After that cabin was fully engulfed in flame I looked at Wolf and Winter. "Let's go back to where I was ambushed. There might be some clues that will lead us to Slimy." Wolf and Winter collected their llama teams and followed me to the ambush site.

At the ambush site, we found what appeared to be an area of struggle. There were some particles of dried slime goo. And then no more particles, as though Slimy had been lifted from the ground and placed into a bag or a chest.

"It looks like Slimy struggled against his captors before he was taken away," said Winter.

"I agree," I said through teeth clenched with rage.

"I think I see some tracks over here," said Wolf, pointing. "What do you guys think?"

We walked over to the area indicated by Wolf and examined the ground closely. "I agree," I said. "These appear to be the tracks of some sort of illager or a villager. There may have been more than one."

"Do you see any enderman footprints? I don't," said Winter.

Wolf shook his head. "My guess is that Dan the enderman character is not going to be involved in the actual captivity of Slimy. Whoever set this up knew about our investigation. Which means it had to have been someone inside wandering trader HQ."

"Come on, let's see where these tracks lead," I said.

Wolf and Winter led their llamas behind them. I felt almost naked without my llamas. But I was happy to know they had made it back to HQ and that they'd be waiting for me when I returned.

We followed the tracks for about an hour. They went through the forest and then began to enter a swamp biome. Up ahead I could see a tendril of smoke rising to the sky. "A witch's hut? The tracks seem to lead in that direction."

Wolf nodded his head. "It would not be unusual for a witch to be working with illagers or villagers or even wandering traders. We should approach with caution. Let's tie our llamas here."

After securing the llama teams, we slowly made our way towards the witch's hut. We used as much of the natural cover as we could to avoid being seen. Given that we were all trained in the arts of stealth, we easily made it to the witch's hut without being detected. We leaned against the wall of the hut.

I looked at Wolf and Winter and whispered, "What's the plan?"

Wolf thought for a moment and said, "I'll go to the front door and knock. When you hear the door open, you and Winter jump through the window. If Slimy is in there, you should be able to rescue him. But, be careful. The witch may not be alone."

"Agreed," I said.

"Ready when you are," said Winter, removing a diamond sword enchanted with sharpness III.

"Dang, girl. That's a nice blade," I said.

"Yeah, thanks. Winona gave it to me as a gift for being such a good student."

Wolf snuck around to the front of the witch's hut and knocked on the door. I heard startled movement inside the hut and then after a couple of seconds, the witch spoke. "Who is it? What do you want?"

"I am a humble wandering trader seeking to trade with you, madam. Open the door and behold my wares."

I heard more startled movement in the hut. It sounded like there was whispering as well. I looked at Winter. "I think there's someone else in there."

Winter nodded her head and said, "Does it sound like Slimy's in there?"

I shrugged my shoulders.

"Get lost! I don't want to trade with you right now," said the witch.

"But I have such amazing deals," said Wolf. "I'll even give you a 25% discount."

Apparently the witch was a cheapskate in need of some retail therapy because I heard her moving toward the door. I looked at Winter and nodded. "Get ready." She set her jaw and gripped her sword tightly.

The witch arrived at the front door and opened it. That was the signal. Winter and I jumped up and broke in through the window. Meanwhile Wolf grabbed the witch and held his sword to her back, subduing her.

I thought I was prepared for anything when I jumped in the window. But what I saw was shocking. Slimy was bound to an anvil, tied by a half-dozen ropes. I could see the ropes pressing against his slime cube, leaving dents in his gooey flesh. But the abuse of my friend was not the most shocking thing I saw. The most shocking thing I saw was...

"Weston?!? You?!?"

Weston, the villager nitwit turned wandering trader, jumped up and rushed toward Slimy with a sword held out, intent on killing him. I dove at Weston and tackled him to the ground just before he got to Slimy.

I put my knee on his neck and held my sword to his stomach. "Explain yourself!"

He shook his head. "I'm not going to tell you *anything*."

"Oh, I think you will," I said.

"Oh, I think I won't," said Weston.

"Oh, I think you *will*," I snarled.

"Oh, I think I *won't*."

Winter, who had just finished freeing Slimy from his bondage, yelled, "Shut up! Both of you." She rubbed her temples like she had a migraine.

I saw Slimy was free and I rushed to embrace him. Slimy began to cry. "I thought you were dead and that I was next."

I shook my head. "Whoever did this should have killed me. I'm going to track down everyone who did this to you and make them pay!"

Wolf, who had bound and gagged the witch and tied her to a chair in the corner of the hut, approached Weston holding a strange looking dagger that I had never seen before.

"What should we do?" I asked.

"Tie him up. If he doesn't want to talk, I'll make him talk." The way Wolf said those words, I believed him.

"What about the witch?" asked Winter. "Maybe she knows what we want to know. Let's start with her."

Wolf and I looked at each other and smiled. "Good idea," said Wolf.

We walked over to the witch and Wolf pulled the gag out of her mouth. "Why were you harboring the slime? Who set this up?"

The witch looked frightened. "I don't know. Weston's been my boyfriend for a while and he asked if he could keep the slime here. I told him I didn't care."

Wolf leaned down and shook his dagger in the witch's face. "Really? You expect me to believe that?"

The witch began to shake. "I swear. He just asked me if he could keep a slime tied up here. I don't know why."

"How long have you known Weston?"

"About a year."

"Don't tell them anything else," shouted Weston. I grabbed the gag from Wolf and walked over to Weston and shoved it in his mouth. "Shut up."

"What has he told you about the wandering traders?" asked Wolf.

"Not much. He thinks most of you are a bunch of arrogant fools, but I knew that already."

"Did he ever mention someone named Wex?" I asked.

The witch shook her head. "Never heard that name before."

"When was the last time you saw Weston before the last day or two?" asked Winter. That was going to be my next question. If Weston was supposed to be the nitwit who stayed inside headquarters all the time, she should not have seen them for quite a while.

"I don't know. He visits me every couple of weeks. Usually on his way somewhere or another to deliver messages."

I looked over Weston. I saw a combination of fear and anger in his eyes. He was shaking his head trying to communicate to his girlfriend that she needed to be quiet.

"Carrying messages? For whom? For what?" demanded Wolf.

The witch shrugged her shoulders. "I don't know. He never told me that."

The three of us backed away from the witch and huddled in a corner. "I think I believe her," said Winter

"Unfortunately, I do too," said Wolf. "I think we are going to have to get the information from Weston." I walked over to Weston, pulled the gag of his mouth, and put it back in the witch's mouth.

Wolf walked up to Weston and nonchalantly picked his fingernails using the tip of his ornate dagger. "Okay. I am only giving you one chance. Tell me who arranged the kidnapping of Slimy and I won't kill you. But, I will bring you back to wandering trader headquarters for punishment."

Weston laughed like a maniac. "That would be the safest place for me. I have allies there."

I reached down and grabbed Weston's robe and pulled his face close to mine roughly. "Who are they? What's going on? Are you the traitor? Or, are their many traitors?"

Weston shook his head. "I can't tell you. If I did I'd be killed."

"Okay, then," said Wolf. "I guess we'll have to do this the hard way."

But, before Wolf could do anything, an exploding arrow came in through the open window, plunged into Weston's chest, and then exploded. The explosion knocked Wolf backward, slamming into me and slamming us both against the walls of the witch's hut. Fortunately, we weren't rendered unconscious, but we were groggy.

The hut began to fill with smoke as Slimy and Winter rushed to our sides. "What just happened?!?" screamed Winter.

"Winston! Are you alive?" asked Slimy in a quaking voice.

"Barely," I said as I stood up and walked toward the doorway.

I noticed the witch in the corner sobbing. As evil and stupid as she was, I felt sorry for her having to witness the assassination of her boyfriend. I was walking over to her to ask her if she had any idea who might've killed him, when another exploding arrow passed through the open window, landed on the ground near the witch, and exploded.

The explosion blew me off my feet and out the front door of the hut! Although I was groggy and in pain, I scanned the area looking for the source of the arrows but my brain was still too addled from the two explosions to focus on anything very well. I thought I saw some movement in the tree line but I couldn't be sure. And, even if I had seen the assassin, I was in no condition to pursue him or her. None of us were.

Slimy hopped next to me and said, "I'm glad you're alive. Surviving two explosions in less than one minute is pretty dominant."

I grimaced. "I think I'd rather be a little less dominant and not get blown up twice in two minutes."

Wolf and Winter, having escaped the burning hut, approached the two of us. "Winston, we have to talk about Slimy," said Wolf.

"He's right here. You can talk *to* him," I said bitterly.

"Fine. He can't come back to wandering trader headquarters. Whoever set up this kidnapping won't rest until Slimy is dead or recaptured. Since we believe the person or persons behind this are inside HQ, Slimy won't be safe. You probably will be ... as long as we cease the investigation searching for the traitor."

I started to sob. "So, we are just going to give up? Let the traitor win?" I looked at Slimy. He was sobbing too. We hugged again. "But I'm supposed to take care of him. He's my foundling. That is the Way."

Winter and Wolf both intoned, "That is the Way."

Wolf continued. "But the heart of the Way is self-preservation for the *good of the Guild*. The only way for Slimy to live a normal life now is to never return to HQ."

I wanted to argue with Wolf, but I knew he was right. We had to find Slimy some other slimes to live with. I suppose I could visit him from time to time. But if he stayed with me, his life would always be threatened.

"But where will we find a home for him?" I asked.

"He can live with us," came a jolly male voice from behind us. We all looked in the direction of the voice and saw two full-size slimes staring at us.

"Where did you come from?" asked Winter.

"We spawned here. This is our home swamp," said the female slime.

I looked at Slimy. "What do you think? Do you want to live with these two slimes?"

Slimy hopped forward. "Are you sure you want to take me in?"

The two slimes smiled. The female slime spoke. "Of course. Our children are all grown up and have left the home. We have been lonely for a while. You can live with us as long as you need to."

Slimy began to cry. "Thank you so much." Slimy turned around and looked at me, his eyes and mouth quivering. "And thank *you*, Winston. If it weren't for you, those players would've killed me like they killed my family."

I was crying now. I hugged Slimy and said, "You've been a good companion. I wish we could've had more years together."

Slimy nodded his head. "Goodbye Winter. Goodbye Wolf."

Wolf nodded stoically, hiding his emotions. Winter allowed a few tears to fall down her cheeks. It was bittersweet. Slimy had finally found a home but only because he could not return to mine. We watched as Slimy hopped off with the two kindly slimes, his new adoptive parents. He looked back once, smiling at me, and then disappeared over a hill with his new family.

* * *

Wolf, Winter, and I searched what was left of the witch's hut for any clues as to who had ordered Weston to kidnap Slimy and threaten me. But we found nothing. Just the usual witch stuff like potions, bottles, a cauldron, and the charred remains of a crafting table. Any secrets Weston had, he took to his grave.

We then searched the nearby area to try to find where those arrows had come from. There weren't any clues that we could find. No tracks. No telltale debris from the encampment.

"It's almost like the arrows were shot by a ghost," said Winter.

"There's no such thing as ghosts," I said. "It was probably that stupid enderman, Dan, teleporting around the treetops."

Wolf nodded his head. "That's one possibility for certain. It might've also been a ninja. Could've been freelance. Could've been another wandering trader highly-trained in the art of the ninja."

I looked at Wolf. "What do you think is going on? Is it Wickham?"

Wolf shrugged his shoulders. "I don't know. This seems a little too petty for Wickham. If he wanted you to stop investigating something he was involved in, he would just find a reason to have you publicly executed. I think if this *is* someone within HQ, it's someone at a lower level."

Could it be Wes?

"This is crazy," said Winter. "Why would someone do that?"

"Maybe the trader is working against Wickham. Maybe the trader feared that Winston and I were going to uncover his or her identity and destroy the plan."

"Maybe," I said impatiently. "But it's all speculation at this point. Since we can't find a clue as to where the arrow came from, let's just go back to headquarters and see what we can find out. Now that Slimy's free, I'm going to continue my investigation."

Wolf looked at me with determination. "You and I both will."

Chapter 12

Because it had taken us quite a while to track down the witch and Weston and free Slimy, we didn't arrive back at headquarters until the following day. When we entered the headquarters door, Wayne was waiting for us. "It's about time. Get your llamas put away and go to Wickham's chamber ... ***immediately***."

We did as we were told; that was the Way.

When the three of us arrived at Wickham's chamber, we saw Wiggoly the guard knock on the wall of the chamber with his fist. Within a few seconds, Wickham emerged and stood in the front doorway and staring down at us. He spoke to Winter first.

"Because you are a trainee, and your trainer, Winona, gave you permission to stay with Wolf and Winston, your punishment will be mild. You're ordered to work in the llama stables for the next three months. Your wandering trader training will pause. You are not allowed to do anything other than cleanup llama poop."

"But, Wickham..." began Winter.

"Silence!" roared Wickham. "Out of my sight. That is the Way!"

I could tell Winter wanted to offer Wickham some choice insults, but now was not the time. "That is the

Way," she said obediently before turning and descending the stairway.

Wickham stared at us for a minute solid while Winter walked down the stairs and out of sight. When she was gone, he raged.

"Trader Wolf. I ordered you to retrieve the box from the Wolf King and return *immediately*. You completed only part of my order. And while it is a good thing that you found Winston alive, you should not have disobeyed my orders."

"May I speak?" asked Wolf.

"No! You have now made two mistakes in recent memory. The first was your failure to wear a disguise when you assassinated the husk prince. I am still dealing with the fallout from that." *He was?* "Your second was this debacle. As your punishment, I sentence you to be whipped in public with ten lashes."

"You can't do that!" I shouted. Wayne, who was standing nearby, smacked the side of my head with the flat of his sword. My ears started ringing. I collapsed to my knees.

"Don't talk again," growled Wayne.

"Is that all?" asked Wolf, surprisingly calm.

"Yes, it is." Wickham looked at his guard Wiggoly. "Bind him in cuffs and take him to one of the prison cells. Send out an announcement that there will be a whipping tomorrow at noon in the main square. Everyone is *ordered* to attend."

Wiggoly stood at attention and saluted. "Yes, Great Wickham. That is the Way."

Wolf held out his wrists compliantly so that Wiggoly could bind them. That accomplished, Wiggoly walked down the stairs behind Wolf, his spear at the ready should Wolf try anything.

Wickham stared at me and began pacing back and forth. "Winston. What am I to do with you? First, you attack Wes, and now this disobedience? Even though you are a foundling, by all accounts you're an above-average trader. In fact, you have done well for me. Although you seem to be cursed with bad luck. The two times I've asked you to be a messenger there have been ... complications."

"I agree. Maybe you should get someone else to deliver your messages?"

"I'll tell whomever I want to deliver my messages. But, that is not why you're here. You are here because you beat Wes and went after your foundling, the slime. That was *not* the right choice. He is *expendable*."

"He's not expendable! I have to take care of him. That is the Way, right?"

Wickham shook his head. "The Way is for two-legged mobs only. The lower life forms, like the slimes, are not entitled to its benefits. Although I indulged you in your desire to take care of your foundling as though it was a proper application of the Way, that indulgence is over."

"That's not fair!"

"Silence! I decide what is fair, not you. And here's what is fair. Tomorrow, at the whipping, ***you** will be the one* who whips Wolf."

I fell to my knees in anguish. "You can't make me do that. You can't make me whip Wolf."

Wayne reached down and grabbed the back of my robe and lifted me to my feet. "He can make you do anything he wants. That is the Way."

"The Way sounds pretty messed up then," I said.

"You'll find out just how messed up it is if you don't do what I say," said Wickham. "You **will** be there at midday and you **will** administer ten lashes to Wolf. Or else ... I will punish you in ways that you cannot imagine."

I decided to stop talking. I was digging myself a hole that I wasn't going to be able to climb out of. I just asked, "May I go now?"

Wickham stared at me imperiously for about thirty seconds before responding. "Yes, you may. I want you confined in your room until the whipping."

I nodded my head and turned my back and began walking down the stairs. *What was I going to do? How could I get out of this?*

* * *

About ten minutes later, I was back in my room. I saw Slimy's empty bed and felt sad. When we left a couple days ago, he was still a baby slime. Now, he was a young adult with a new family. I was glad he wouldn't be here to see me whip Wolf.

I paced back and forth. *How could I stop this? How could I change Wickham's mind?*

I thought about the possibilities for hours, late into the night. But I always came to the same conclusion: nothing was going to work. Tomorrow, at midday, I was going to have to whip my mentor. In service of the Way, I was going to have to inflict pain on the trader who saved my life and became a surrogate father.

There was no way I could do that.

There was no way I could let Wickham win.

I had only one option.
*I was going **rogue**.*

End of Book 4 of
The Ballad of Winston the Wandering Trader

Book 5

Chapter 1

After making the decision to go rogue and abandon my allegiance to the Guild of the Wandering Traders, I realized that making the decision to leave was the *easy* part. Now, I had to figure out how to escape from headquarters and how to escape from the assassins when they inevitably came after me.

I couldn't ask anyone for help or advice at the risk that they would betray me. I did not think they would betray me because they were evil but rather I thought they would betray me because they hadn't had the time or the experience to come to the same conclusion that I had: The Guild was being run by tyrants for their own gain, not the betterment of wandering traders as a whole. If I *were* to speak with anyone, it would've been Wolf, but he was imprisoned, under guard, and waiting to be whipped by me at noon tomorrow.

As I thought of a way to escape, I began packing. I knew I would need all of my weapons, a crafting table, and a furnace. I packed as much food as I could carry. Unfortunately, I didn't have much food in my room, and I wasn't going to risk going to the cafeteria to get anything. And so, I packed a few loaves of bread and some pieces of fruit. It would be enough until I had the opportunity to purchase food or to kill some chickens or cows.

I wished I had some villager clothes. The last time I wore a villager's robe was when I was ten years old. Even if I had saved that robe, it wouldn't fit me now. I would have to find something else to wear as soon as possible. I hoped that maybe I could blend in as a villager somewhere, buying time to come up with a new life where the assassins would never find me. If I could accomplish that, I hoped that I could elude them for the rest of my life, like Wex.

It was about one o'clock in the morning when I had finished packing. *Now, how to escape?*

The easiest way would simply be to use my pickaxe to mine horizontally until I hit the outside world. Unfortunately, the sound of my pickaxe bashing against stone and ore would alert most of headquarters to my activities. I might not even make it to the outside before I was apprehended.

I couldn't use my llamas. They were too slow and made noise whenever they felt like it. I felt bad for them. I wanted to go and say goodbye, give them an apple or carrot one last time. But I couldn't risk it. I was sure they'd be sad for a few days until they were assigned to a new trader. I hoped stupid Wes wouldn't commandeer them. He had his own llama team but he had wanted Sunny and Pippa so badly when I chose them, I assumed he might try to get them now. I clenched my teeth at the thought of him mistreating Sunny and Pippa, but there was nothing I could do. Not now anyway.

I thought back to Weston and his witch girlfriend. She had said that he visited her every couple of weeks. I wondered, was there a secret passage one might use in order to get out of the headquarters? Even if there were, it didn't matter. I'd never find it.

My options exhausted, I knew there was only one thing for me to do.

But, before I did that, I wanted to make sure that the two people who were most important to me knew why I was doing this. I decided to write notes to Wolf and Winter. I could send them through the intra-headquarters messaging system, which was basically an internal document delivery service. It would take at least twenty-four and probably forty-eight hours for the messages to arrive, so the notes would not give my escape away. By then, it would be well known that I had gone rogue.

I grabbed a few pieces of parchment and a quill and began writing.

Wolf:

Thank you for being my training trader. I learned a lot from you, and not just about how to make emeralds trading with players. I'm sorry I'm going rogue. I hope this doesn't reflect badly on you, the way Wex going rogue reflected badly on Wickham. I just wanted you to know that I'm not doing this because I am a traitor, but because

I respect you too much to obey Wickham's orders to hurt you.

I assume Wickham had someone else whip you, so I'm sorry if you're in pain right now. But at least that will mean that he didn't order you to find me and assassinate me. If someone does assassinate me, I don't want it to have to be you.

It makes me sad that we will never be able to speak to each other again. I wish you the best of luck.

Your friend, Winston.

After sealing that note, I began writing the other one.

Winter (Penelope):

I'm sorry I'm doing this. But, I just couldn't bring myself to whip Wolf, especially since that barbaric act was ordered by Wickham. I hope you understand. They will say I went rogue because I was evil and a traitor, but know that I did it out of my loyalty and respect for my trainer and fellow wandering trader, Wolf. To me, that is the most important part of the Way: Loyalty to one's fellow traders.

I know that you will be under orders to kill me on sight should we ever meet again. I want you to know that I won't be angry at you if you're the one who ends my life. But, you should also know that I will defend myself.

Anyway, thank you for being a friend. Maybe, in another time, another place, or another spawn, we can be friends again.
Yours truly, Winston.

I sealed that note and tucked it into my inventory next to my note to Wolf. I was ready to go.

Chapter 2

I double checked my inventory and looked around my room to make sure there was nothing I'd forgotten. I looked at the dismembered remains of my action figure, Creepy, sitting on my bookshelf. I thought about taking them with me. But, I realized that if someone entered this room and saw them missing before it became known I went rogue, they would know I had fled. Plus, I didn't want to have to constantly relive the moment I found Creepy torn asunder by stupid Wes.

Satisfied that I had packed everything that was necessary, I opened the door to my room and looked up and down the hallway. I was worried that perhaps Wickham might have stationed a guard outside my door. Fortunately, there was no one in the hallway. It was late enough at night that I didn't expect to encounter anyone, but anything was possible. I had to be careful.

I closed my door behind me and turned to the right. The only way I was going to be able to leave the headquarters was through the main door. I walked down the hallway until I passed the intra-headquarters messaging system deposit box. I carefully opened the tilting door and dropped my notes inside before closing the door quietly.

I continued down the hallway until I came to the stairs to the llama stable. I descended the stairs to the bottom and then cautiously looked into the stable area. I peeked around a corner and saw Wenlan, the player turned wandering trader, at the checkout counter. Fortunately, he was asleep.

I drank a potion of invisibility and then used all of my stealth skills as I snuck past him. He didn't even stir. If he had been a full-fledged wandering trader, I might not have been so lucky. But he was still a trainee and was unable to detect me.

I walked down the passageway toward the exit door. Guarding the door was old man Wenceslaus. He was asleep too. I knew that he would wake up when I pulled the lever to open the door. I debated what to do exactly. I needed as much lead time to get away from the headquarters as possible before my absence was noticed.

I felt bad but I *had* to do it. I pulled a wooden shovel out of my inventory bashed Wenceslaus in the back of his head, knocking him unconscious. "Sorry, man," I whispered. I then tied his arms and legs together and put a gag in his mouth. I made sure he was still breathing, and I pulled the lever. The door opened. The mechanism clicked and clacked. It had never seemed so loud before.

Even though I was still invisible I looked behind me to make sure no one was looking. I didn't see anyone. I stepped through the door and waited until it shut behind me automatically. Then I moved off swiftly into the night.

Chapter 3

I dashed away from the exit of wandering trader headquarters as quickly as I could. Although I did not expect to encounter any wandering traders in the middle of the night, it was always possible. Plus, I needed to put as much distance between me and HQ as possible before Wenceslaus was discovered. I figured I had at least three hours and at most five hours.

Right now, however, I was more concerned about skeletons and zombies, whose creepy undead noises I heard nearby. I pulled my diamond sword from my inventory and kept running.

Now that my invisibility potion had worn off, I kept near the trees in order to remain hidden under the surprisingly bright moonlight. Suddenly, a zombie lurched from behind a tree. It saw me and moaned with hunger as it came toward me. I slashed at it, and it backed off. I then rushed past, the zombie's ambling gait much too slow to catch up with me.

As I kept running, an arrow suddenly whizzed by my head. I turned around and saw a skeleton in the distance. I put my sword away and pulled a crossbow from my inventory.

During the time it took me to change weapons, the skeleton launched another arrow at me but I rolled onto my left shoulder, scrambling to avoid the arrow. I came up in a perfect shooting stance.

I let my arrow fly, and it hit the skeleton right in the center of its head, killing it instantly.

The threat neutralized, I tucked the crossbow away, pulled my sword out again, and resumed running. I knew there was a village about thirty minutes away, assuming I ran the entire time. I needed to acquire some villager clothes.

Fortunately, I made it to the village without further incident. I snuck around the outside edge of the village. I was looking for a clothing store. If I had to, I would break into one of the villager homes and steal from them, but I preferred the less risky proposition of simply breaking into a clothing store. I had never been to this village before, so I wasn't sure if there even was a clothing store.

I'd been searching for five minutes and was about to give up and break into one of the homes when I saw a sign that said "Robe Rodeo Round Up." *What a stupid name for a store*, I thought. But, it wasn't stupid in one way: I knew exactly what they were selling.

I snuck around to the back of the store and smashed the wall open with my pickaxe. I darted inside. It was pitch black inside of the store, so I had to ignite a torch. I looked around and found robes representing all different professions of plains villagers. I grabbed clothing for a stone mason, tool smith, and farmer. I figured that I would be able to hide using at least one of these professions. I quickly took off my wandering trader outfit and tucked it into my inventory, then I put on the farmer clothes. I doused my torch and ducked out the back of the store before dashing away from the village.

I knew that I would have to get to another village before sunrise. Villagers were not known for wandering around beyond the borders of a village, unless they were traveling with a group or a caravan, and it would look suspicious if I were traveling alone. If one of the wandering trader assassins found me outside of a village, they might be able to tell it was me even without my wandering trader robe. I knew of another village about two hours away. I could probably just make it before the sun came up.

* * *

After about a half an hour, I came to a river. Now I could execute the other part of my escape plan. I took off my robe and tucked it into my inventory to keep it dry. I was only wearing underwear. I jumped into the river and let it take me downstream for about five minutes. Then I grabbed a rock on the side of the river. But, before I stepped out of the river I put on the shoes I crafted before I left wandering trader headquarters.

When I stepped out of the water, I began walking on the muddy shoreline. The shoes were awkward at first because of what I had attached on the bottom of their soles. But they were doing their job. Instead of villager footprints, I was leaving the footprints of a cow! I had attached carved wooden hooves to the bottom of my shoes.

I put my farmer robe back on, and then I walked in my cow shoes for about twenty minutes until I came to a hard patch of stone where no footprints would be left behind. I took off the cow shoes and tucked them back into my inventory and put on my regular shoes and dashed forward toward the village.

* * *

I was hot and sweaty and out of breath, but just before sunrise, I wandered into the plains village I had been running toward.

I stood next to a tree in the shadows waiting for the sun to come up and the villagers to begin coming out of their houses. Once they did, I began to mingle with them, exchanging small talk and stories about all the emeralds we had made doing one thing or another.

I had to endure some insulting tales about wandering traders, but I said nothing. It didn't matter anyway. I wasn't a wandering trader anymore.

Chapter 4

*(Dearest Reader, Winston here with a quick note. I know that I have been writing my ballad using first-person narrative, but I wanted to fill in some holes so you would understand the entire situation. Obviously, I wasn't present for anything I write in the third-person, but I pieced the story together over many years. So, even if what I wrote below and in some other parts of my ballad isn't **exactly** what happened, it is close. Thanks for understanding, Winston.)*

Wally and William, two wandering trader trainees, met each other in the hallway as they walked down the stairs to the llama stables. They had been assigned to the day shift. Wally was assigned to work the checkout counter while William was assigned to scoop llama dung from all of the corrals.

"Did you hear there is going to be a whipping at noon?" said Wally.

William nodded. "Yeah, I did. I wonder who it is?"

"I wonder what they did?"

William cringed. "I can't imagine getting whipped. It would hurt so bad!"

"It probably would," said a girl's voice behind them.

The two turned around and were surprised to see Winter walking behind them. Wally said, "Trainee Winter, what are you doing down here? I thought you had already served your time in the llama stables?"

Winter sighed. "Wickham's punishing me. I have to work in the stables for three months exclusively on poop patrol."

William gasped. "What did you do?!?"

"I don't want to talk about it. I'm sure you'll hear about it through the rumor mill anyway."

"Well, at least I don't have to scoop as much llama poop as I normally would now that you will be helping me," said William with a smile.

Winter rolled her eyes and shook her head. "I suppose not."

When the three of them arrived at the llama stables, they saw that Wenlan was still asleep at the front desk. Wally walked over and smashed his hand on the desk. Wenlan startled and sat up. "Papers please," he said groggily. Wally, William, and Winter laughed.

"You aren't supposed to fall asleep on the job," said Wally, scolding Wenlan. "What if Wickham or one of his guards came down here and found you like that?"

Wenlan shrugged. "Whatever. No one ever comes down here at night. All I ever do is keep the llamas company and am forced to listen to the stupid stories of the old guys who operate the exit door."

Wally chuckled. "Anyway, you might as well head up to your room. I've got it covered now." Wenlan nodded his head and waved at everyone before leaving the stables.

Wally took his position behind the checkout desk while William and Winter grabbed shovels and went to the corrals to do their morning cleaning.

A few minutes later, old man Wit came down the stairs to take his place as the door guard. "Wally, Wit is pleased to see you. Wit has some good stories to tell today."

Wally rolled his eyes. "Do you have any *new* stories to tell? I think I have heard them all by now. *Twice*."

Wit clucked his tongue. "Wit does not like young trainees giving him sass. Wit will have to think about it and decide what to do."

"Take your time. I'll be at the desk all day."

Wit said, "Bah" before walking to the exit door. He was surprised when he arrived and found no one guarding it. "Wit does not like it when the door is left unguarded," he mumbled.

Wit approached the chair where the guard normally sat and when he got closer, he gasped. There was a drop pile on the ground! Wit kneeled down and inspected the drop pile. It contained a potion of invisibility and a bucket of milk, confirming that it was indeed the drop pile of a wandering trader. Wit's heart began to beat faster as he began to feel panic. He stood up and turned around. "Get the guards! Wit thinks there has been a murder!"

Wally, William, and Winter rushed to where Wit was standing. They saw the drop pile as well. Winter looked at Wit and said, "You don't think that this is Wenceslaus' drop pile, do you?"

Wit nodded sadly. "That is exactly what Wit thinks. Who could've done such a thing?"

"Maybe he died of old age? He was pretty ancient," suggested William.

Wit's face flushed red with anger and he grabbed William by his robe. "Wenceslaus was in good physical health. He wouldn't just die of old age ... not while he was on guard duty."

"Are there any signs of foul play?" asked Winter.

Wit and the others looked around for clues. "Wit's eyes aren't as good as they used to be, but it looks like there might be an extra set of footprints walking behind the chair where Wenceslaus would've been sitting."

Winter nodded her head. "Yeah, maybe. So, do you think someone killed Wenceslaus and then left headquarters?"

Wit sucked his teeth and shrugged his shoulders. "Wit does not know. But we need to tell Wickham and his guards about this so they can investigate."

Winter nodded her head. "I will go the let them know."

* * *

Five minutes later, the stables were a hive of activity. Wickham was by the exit door, pacing back and forth while Wayne and Wiggoly looked for clues.

"Boss, I think Wit was right," said Wayne. "It looks like there are some footprints here."

"Can you tell whose they are?" asked Wickham.

Wayne shook his head. "Just regular wandering trader footprints. I don't see any fresh llama prints, so whoever did harm to Wenceslaus either returned to their room or left headquarters on foot."

Wickham nodded his head, rubbed his chin, and reached under his wandering trader hood to scratch his hair. "Who would have done such a thing? Wenceslaus was loved by all, wasn't he?"

Wayne and Wiggoly both shrugged. "I never heard anything bad about him," said Wiggoly.

Wickham turned toward the trainees. "What about you? Do any of the trainees hate Wenceslaus for some reason?"

All three of them shook their heads. "I thought he was a little goofy, but he seemed nice enough," said William.

"Yeah. He had some pretty good stories. And he rarely repeated them," said Wally, squinting his eyes at Wit.

Wickham turned toward Winter. "I know we have our differences right now, but what do you know about Wenceslaus?"

Winter shrugged. "Not much. He's been a guard since I came here to the headquarters. He's always been nice to me."

Wickham took a deep breath and sighed. He turned his back on the group and walked away, contemplating. He walked down the hall and through the llama corrals looking at the pairs of happy llamas, oblivious that a wandering trader had died near them. And then he got to thinking. If someone held a grudge against Wenceslaus and killed him for personal reasons, he didn't think they would leave the headquarters. They would just want him eliminated. But, the footprints looked like they left the exit door. It could've been a trick to make it look like the killer had left or....

Wickham snapped his fingers. He turned around and rushed back to where his guards were standing. "I want you to search all of the wandering trader and trainee rooms. Make sure everyone is accounted for. If anyone is missing, let me know immediately."

Chapter 5

It was about nine o'clock in the morning and I was wandering around the village in my farmer garb. Several players were milling about. One of them approached me and asked what sort of food I had to trade.

"I have one carrot, one apple, and a bag of wheat."

The player shook his head. "Those are some pretty weak trades."

I shrugged. "That's all I have right now."

The player laughed. "You must not be much of a farmer."

Although I wanted to strike this player down for being such an insulting bully, I played the necessary role of the obsequious villager. "I'm sorry sir. I only recently acquired my farmland. Before this, I worked for another farmer. My farm is just in the beginning stages."

The player flicked his hand dismissively. "Whatever." He turned and left.

I did not feel at ease in this village. I knew that sometime between this morning and noon, when I was supposed to whip Wolf, Wickham would discover that I was missing. It was entirely possible that he had already sent assassins after me. If he hadn't, they would be coming in three hours or less. I figured I had at least a six-hour head start, so if I could keep that buffer until I could get established as a villager somewhere, that would be ideal.

I wandered nonchalantly throughout the village, trying to avoid any contact with players and other villagers. *Maybe I should've grabbed the nitwit robe? No one ever talks to the nitwit.*

A couple hours later, I could not avoid the player coming toward me. I recognized him. It was Glitchmaster, the player who had interviewed me some time ago about the culture of the wandering traders. I hoped he wouldn't recognize me.

"Say there, villager. Do you mind if I ask you some questions?"

"I'm trying to make trades. You're cramping my style."

Glitchmaster laughed. "I've been watching you for the last twenty minutes. You seem to be meticulously avoiding interaction with anyone. Why is that?"

"Why do you care?"

Glitchmaster nodded his head. "Good question. I'm doing a sociological analysis of different mobs in the Overworld. I am primarily interested in the wandering traders and villagers, but I'm open to doing studies of any mobs."

"That seems like a waste of time."

"To some people, it would be. But to me, it's not. I just want to understand everything."

Same old Glitchmaster. "Look, I am quite busy, but go ahead and ask me a couple questions if you want."

"You're a farmer, I can tell by your robes. But, if you didn't have to be a farmer, which profession would you choose?"

I thought about it for a moment. "I suppose I might like to be a weaponsmith."

Glitchmaster noted that in this book. "Even though all weaponsmiths are missing an eye? Would you be willing to give your eye for that profession?"

"I don't think they're missing an eye *because* they chose to be weaponsmiths. I think they're missing an eye because they make some sort of mistake while smithing and damage their eyes. I would try to avoid those mistakes."

"Hmmm, interesting point. I've never thought about that. I'll have to make a note of it. Okay, next question. If you could be any mob other than a villager, which would you be?"

These questions were ridiculous. I was what I was. We are all what we are. Still, I suppose it is an academic exercise that is of some interest. I had to think about this question for a moment. Finally I said, "Probably a wolf. Yeah, I'd be an untamable, wild wolf."

Glitchmaster looked surprised and wrote some notes in his book. "Interesting. Most villagers choose to be passive mobs like squids or chickens, since those mobs are essentially like villagers and have little ambition. But you ... well, you seem to have ambition for freedom and independence."

I shrugged. "Is that what my choice means? I just think wolves are cool."

"Any choice we make actually reflects our inner personality and desires. *Every*one knows that."

This guy was crazy. "If you say so. I'm just a harmless little villager, I guess."

"Well, anyway, thanks for talking to me. I left Zombie Bane at first light and am stopping at all of the villages between there and Creeper Junction. If I stop back this way, I'll try to find you again for an updated conversation."

"Whatever," I said to Glitchmaster before he turned and walked away. His words had sparked an idea in my mind.

Zombie Bane. Of course. It was a small city, but still large enough that I could hide there without drawing any attention to myself. I could open a store. I had enough emeralds with me that I could purchase a good inventory for the store and begin trading. If I stayed inside the store, wandering traders would be unlikely to enter as they don't trade with villagers in the normal course of events.

I slowly began wandering toward the edge of the rural village. I noticed there was an entrance to a cave about fifty blocks from the edge of the village. That was quite a distance for a villager to wander from his village, but not unheard of. I ambled back and forth across the undulating grassland until I got to the cave and ducked inside. After making sure there were no mobs nearby, I quickly changed out of my villager robe and into my wandering trader robe.

It was going to be risky, wandering without llamas, and being out in the open. But, I had to get to Zombie Bane as quickly as possible.

Chapter 6

Wickham sat in a chair in his chamber drumming his fingers together impatiently. He was awaiting the return of his head guard, Wayne, to report if any of the wandering traders or trainees were missing.

"Relax, Wickham. Wayne will be here soon," said a man sitting in a dark corner of the chamber.

Wickham stopped drumming his fingers and looked over at the man. He was a middle-aged villager, dressed in finely-crafted robes. "Robert. I know my business. You know yours. Leave me alone."

Robert chuckled. It was a deep, smoky laugh. "You may know your business, but if the wandering traders get out of hand, my business may suffer as well. I won't let that happen."

Wickham pointed a finger at Robert and shook it angrily. "Don't worry. Your precious Dretsky Empire will be fine. A deal is a deal. The Guild of the Wandering Traders will help to make it great."

Robert Dretsky smiled a sinister smile. "I hope so. My son, Ebenezer, has reported that sales in Creeper Junction aren't growing as quickly as they should be. Without growth, my business will wither and die."

"You don't have to tell me about how to run a business. I am running a giant corporation with hundreds of wandering traders selling goods for me day in and day out."

Robert Dretsky chuckled again. "You think this is a *big* enterprise? You're pathetic. I have hundreds of businesses and tens of thousands of villagers working for me all the time. I'm going to turn the Dretsky family into the richest villager family in all the realms of the world, even richer than the Ender King."

Wickham shook his head in disbelief. "No way. The royal family of the End has been accumulating wealth for hundreds of years *at least*. You can't possibly acquire that kind of wealth before the end of your life."

Now, it was Robert Dretsky's turn to put his fingers together and drum them rhythmically. He bent his head forward and looked up with a flat gaze at Wickham. He smiled a sinister, devilish smile and said, "Watch me."

At that moment there was a knocking on the door. "Wickham? It's Wayne."

Wickham looked at Robert Dretsky and said, "Leave by the secret passage. I'll send a messenger for you when I have any news."

Robert Dretsky stood up slowly, nodded his head, turned to the left, and then pulled a book out of the bookshelf which suddenly rotated, opening a small passageway. Torchlight emanated from the passage. He walked through the secret opening and then pulled the bookshelf closed behind him.

Wickham waited a few seconds to allow Dretsky to put some distance between himself and Wickham's chamber before Wickham turned to face the entry door. "You may come in."

Wayne dashed into the chamber and saluted. "We've searched everywhere. There's only one person missing from all of headquarters. *Winston.*"

Wickham grunted with anger. "Argh! He's run away. Gone rogue, I am sure of it. He disobeyed me because he didn't want to whip Wolf."

"What are your orders?"

"Send assassins after him. But, tell them that I want him brought back **alive**. He needs to be punished in front of everyone."

Wayne saluted. "How many assassins should I send?"

Wickham grinned from ear to ear. "All of them." Wayne saluted and dashed away down the stairs to alert the assassins.

"Wiggoly!" called Wickham. "Get in here."

Wiggoly appeared in the doorway and saluted. "What is it, sir?"

"How long until the whipping?"

"About thirty minutes, sir."

Wickham nodded. "Excellent. Go get Wolf out of his prison cell and bring him to me. I want to have a chat with him before his punishment."

Wiggoly saluted and then dashed away.

* * *

About seven minutes later, Wiggoly returned, pushing Wolf in front of him with the tip of a spear. Wolf's hands were bound in front of him. Wolf walked calmly and steadily up the stairs until they arrived at the door to Wickham's chamber.

"Ah, Wolf. Why don't you come in and sit down?" said Wickham, making it clear that the answer to his inquiry was that Wolf would, indeed, come in and sit down. Wolf did as he was asked. Wickham looked at Wiggoly and said, "You may close the door. But stand ready in case I need you."

"Are you sure closing the door is a good idea, sir?"

Wickham became visibly angry. "Are you questioning my judgment?"

Wiggoly shook his head. "Of course not, sir. That is the Way."

"That is the Way," said Wickham. Wiggoly backed out of the room and shut the door.

"Did you enjoy your prison cell?"

Wolf shrugged. "I've had worse accommodations."

"Well, we aren't savages. We don't have to enforce laws in a barbaric way."

Wolf shook his head in disbelief. "What do you call whipping then? I don't know what else is more barbaric than that."

"Silence. You've *earned* your punishment. There's just one small problem."

"Quit the theatrics," said Wolf. "Get to the point."

"It appears that Winston has vanished. Gone rogue."

A look of shock crossed Wolf's face. "No! Why would he do such a thing?"

Wickham observed Wolf and then nodded. "You really *are* surprised. You had no idea he left, did you?"

Wolf shook his head rapidly back and forth. "Of course not. If I knew he was planning that, I would have tried to stop him."

"Excellent. At least you remain loyal to the Guild."

"I suppose so. I don't like this punishment you've chosen, but ... I did disobey your orders to an extent."

Wickham nodded. "I'm glad you see the light. And for that reason when *I* whip you today in place of Winston, I'll go easy on you. But, not too easy."

Wolf said nothing. He simply stared at Wickham for ten seconds. Finally, Wickham turned toward the door and shouted, "Wiggoly! Take him away."

Wiggoly entered and Wolf calmly stood up and walked out the door.

"Take him directly to the plaza for the whipping," ordered Wickham. "No point in taking him back to his prison cell. I'll be down there shortly."

* * *

At noon, Wolf had been tied to a post in the center of the plaza and all the wandering traders and trainees had gathered as ordered by Wickham. There was mumbling in the crowd and most were not looking forward to the barbaric spectacle. Wolf was friends with most of the traders and trainees, and they were unclear about why he was being whipped.

Wickham took the stage and stood near Wolf. He held up his hands and the crowd went silent. "As you all know, we follow the Way. The Way is what keeps us safe and keeps us together as a group. But when one strays from the Way, one must be punished."

The entire crowd replied with one voice, "That is the Way."

"Depending on the transgression, the seriousness of the punishment will vary. In the case of Wolf, he disobeyed my direct order and because of his cumulative transgressions, which I need not recount here, I have ordered that he receive ten lashes."

The crowd gasped and then calmed down and said, "That is the Way," though with less conviction than before.

"Indeed, I had also punished Winston. His transgressions need not be enumerated either, but my punishment to him was that he should be the one to whip Wolf."

There was mumbling through the crowd. A few scattered voices said, without much enthusiasm, "That is the Way." But, most of the crowd was too stunned and frankly disgusted to respond.

"But you may have noticed that Winston is not present. Do you want to know why?"

The crowd was silent until Wes gleefully said, "I sure do!"

Wickham looked at Wes and smiled. "It seems that Winston has ... *gone rogue.*"

Gasps of shock and horror rose from the crowd. Winter screamed. "No! Why?!?"

Wickham put his hands up to call for the crowd to be quiet. "Order! Order! Silence!" Eventually the crowd calmed down and Wickham was able to continue. "We don't know why he went rogue. But I have sent my assassins after him." Again the crowd gasped. "But, I've asked them to bring him home alive so that he can be punished. And so I say to all of you ... if any of you see Winston during your wonders capture him and bring him back alive. You will be rewarded handsomely."

Wes smiled and rubbed his hands together. He couldn't wait to go out and look for Winston.

"And now, let the whipping begin," said Wickham. He pulled a leather whip out of his inventory and snapped it in the air. He looked at Wolf and said, "Ready?"

Wolf glanced at him like they were just on a walk in the park. "Yeah. I'm always ready."

Wickham smiled and took a few steps back and then snapped the whip against Wolf's back, tearing through the fabric of his robe. Wolf grunted, but did not cry out.

True to his word, Wickham did not put his full force into the whipping ... well, not after the first lash anyway. It was a horrible thing to watch and after the fifth lash, most of the traders and trainees weren't even looking. But Wes *was* looking. He was smiling. He was enjoying this. He was wishing that he could be the one holding the whip.

Chapter 7

I had been walking for about two hours since I departed the rural village for Zombie Bane. To avoid detection, I tried to keep to the denser parts of the forest. I knew that most of the way to Zombie Bane would allow me to hide in the cover of the forest. There were, however, a few open areas which I would have to traverse. I worried about those areas.

At one point in my journey, I happened upon a cow grazing at the edge of the forest. I pulled out my crossbow and aimed at the cow. I snuck as close to the cow as I could before I let fly with the arrow. The cow mooed and started to run away, but I quickly loaded another arrow and it found home, killing the cow. It dropped several pieces of meat. I grabbed the meat and went back into the forest and quickly roasted it using my furnace. I ate one of the pieces of meat and put the rest in my inventory for later.

As I continued in the direction of Zombie Bane, I came to one of the open areas lacking tree cover. I considered changing into a villager robe, but knew that it would be more suspicious to see a villager wandering out here than a wandering trader, so I stayed in costume.

I walked close to rocks and cliffs, doing my best to use my stealth training to blend in with the environment, hoping that anyone who might be looking in my direction would not see me. I was doing very well until I turned a corner and came face-to-face with a player. The player screamed and held out a sword. "Where'd you come from?"

I remained as calm as I could. "Just wandering around, like we wandering traders do."

The player, clad with leather pants and an iron chest plate nodded his head. "Dude, you guys are weird." He tucked his iron sword back into his inventory.

"Are you in need of anything? Maybe I have something you could use?" I said, trying not to sound nervous.

The player nodded his head. "Funny you should ask. Well, maybe not funny. I mean, you are a wandering trader, so I guess it is natural for you to ask. Um, yeah, well, anyway, I am looking for some potions of healing. I almost died several times and would really like to have a couple in my inventory."

As a matter fact, I had a couple of potions of healing. I really didn't want to part with them, but if I refused to trade with the player, I'd be more memorable to him and he might end up giving useful information to the assassins who I knew would soon come after me.

"I have one such potion. I will trade it to you for ... hurrr ... five emeralds."

The player smiled. "That sounds like a good deal, I guess. Here you go." He handed me the five emeralds and I reached into my inventory and handed him a healing potion.

The player tucked the healing potion away and then looked around, confused. "Aren't you supposed to have llamas? Where are they?"

I guess he wasn't as much of a noob as I thought.

"Um, I tied them to a tree a little ways back. They were tired and hungry and so I thought they could graze on the grass for a while."

The player considered my words and nodded his head. "I guess that makes sense. Anyway, what is your name? I would like to know in case we meet again."

I hadn't really thought of this eventuality. I didn't realize someone might ask me my name. "Hurrr ... well, my name is ... Wes."

The player nodded his head. "Wes. A nice name." *Not even close, buddy.* "My name is Tejas."

I reached out and shook Tejas's hand. "Well, nice to meet you and good trading with you. I'll be off then."

I continued in the direction I had been heading but then Tejas shouted after me. "Hey, Wes, aren't your llamas back the other way?"

Netherrack.

I smiled. "Oh, yeah. I was just gonna scout ahead for a little bit before I double back."

Tejas nodded his head. "Oh, I guess that makes sense." I watched as Tejas continued on his adventures. I knew that if he was ever questioned and he mentioned that my name was Wes, I would give myself away. But what could I do? I had to pick a name of a wandering trader, why not use stupid Wes's name?

* * *

It was late afternoon when I reached the summit of a mountain and looked down. I could see Zombie Bane nestled in the plains below. If I hurried, I could get there before nightfall and find lodging.

I began making my way down the side of the mountain, jumping on rocks and avoiding the creatures of the mountain, like sheep, chickens, and pigs. I thought about killing some for food, but I knew that once I got to Zombie Bane, I could buy food. At one point, I saw a wild llama wandering the mountainside in the distance. I felt sad. I missed Pippa and Sunny.

I was descending the mountain quickly, wanting to get off of it as soon as possible so I wouldn't be exposed any longer than necessary. There was a large forest about one hundred blocks below me and once I got into that I would be sheltered for quite some distance.

As I hopped down the side of the mountain, I stepped on a boulder that came loose. I tried to grab a handhold but I couldn't stop myself. I slid down the side of the mountain, flipping a few times, smashing my arms and legs and head against the rocks. I was dizzy and tried to stop myself again, but the pain in my body got in the way of my arms working. I lost several hearts of health. Until, finally, I did an involuntary somersault in the air and smashed my head against a rock, losing consciousness.

* * *

I regained consciousness just as the sun was beginning to set. I moaned in pain as I reached into my inventory and pulled out my one remaining healing potion. I drank it quickly and soon felt much better. I stared in the distance at the village of Zombie Bane as torchlight began to show up on the sides of the buildings as the villagers prepared for the onslaught of nighttime mobs.

"I'll never make it before dark," I said dejectedly. "I guess I need to build a shelter."

It looked like it was only a ten-minute walk to the forest, so I began walking. I worried the assassins would catch up with me soon so I decided to build a completely underground shelter. I dug down into the dirt and carved out a small chamber, sort of like an underground igloo shape. I put torches on the walls to prevent mobs from spawning and I covered up the hole to the surface.

I placed my bed and then pulled out a piece of the cooked steak and ate it. I felt sad. I hadn't thought how lonely it would be to go on the road without my llamas. Sure, eventually I hoped to set up a new identity and live a somewhat normal life, but I would always be worried. I would never be able to be myself again. I would never be friends with Wolf or Winter. If I tried, they might even turn me in to Wickham.

I wished I had brought Creepy with me. Even though he was torn to pieces, he would've been something to comfort me. Instead, I curled up in the depths of the earth to sleep, feeling as though I had been buried alive.

Chapter 8

I woke up the next day, feeling somewhat refreshed, though also a little disgusted by the moist air now filling my small underground "house." I assumed it was the next day and so I punched a hole at the top of my sleeping chamber and the sunlight streamed in. I poked my head out to make sure there was no one around and glanced at the sun's location in the sky. It looked like it was about nine o'clock in the morning. I pulled my head back into the chamber. I punched my bed and put it into my inventory. I pulled out a loaf of bread, ate half of it, and then put the rest away.

I climbed out of the chamber and put a dirt block in the exit hole to make it look natural. I began walking toward Zombie Bane, trying to remain hidden when suddenly a wandering trader appeared in front of me after stepping silently and swiftly from behind a tree.

"I thought I saw the telltale signs of an underground hiding place," she said with a sneer.

"Trader Wendolyn, are you here to assassinate me?" I said as my knees began to shake with fear.

She scowled. "I wish. Wickham has decreed that I capture you alive and bring you back to headquarters."

"Back for what?"

This time she smiled. "For punishment."

I *had to* get away. I knew that she was faster than me and certainly more skilled in all the different types of weapons. But, there was one thing I had to my advantage.

"Put your arms out. I want to put you in handcuffs so you can't try any funny business," she said.

I put my hands out. Then she reached into her inventory to get the handcuffs. But in that moment, she was distracted and not looking at me. I quickly reached into my inventory and ignited a TNT block and put it on the ground and began to run away.

She saw it soon enough and dove away just before it exploded. The block detonated and created a massive hole on the ground, but it did not kill my pursuer. But it was enough. I was able to pull out my diamond sword and sneak behind her while she was recovering from the shockwave of the explosion.

I slashed the backs of her legs twice. She screamed and fell to her knees. She turned around and slashed at me with her sword, but by then I had already jumped in the air. I performed a somersault and landed behind her. This time, I slashed at her back twice and she began to flash red.

Trader Wendolyn turned around and yelled at me. "You're only making this worse for yourself," she groaned.

"I didn't want to kill you, Wendolyn. I didn't want to kill anyone. But, I guess that's the price of freedom from the Guild."

"So, you'll add me to your body count of wandering traders?"

"What are you talking about?"

She coughed. "You *already* forgot that you killed Wenceslaus?!?"

I was shocked. I didn't mean to kill that old man. "How? I didn't kill him. He was just unconscious when I left."

"You disgust me," she said with her last breath as she flashed red one final time before disappearing in a puff of smoke.

Not Wenceslaus? I didn't think I had hit him that hard.

I felt sad as I checked Wendolyn's drop pile for anything valuable. There were a couple of emeralds and a potion of invisibility, so I took those. There was nothing else of any use to me so I dug a shallow grave and pushed it in, trying to cover my tracks.

* * *

The remainder of my trip to Zombie Bane, which took another hour, was uneventful, though I continuously looked over my shoulder, worried that another assassin would be near.

When I was a few minutes away from town, I ducked into a cave and changed into a stone mason outfit. I decided this would be my new identity. I mined a couple of cobblestones and carried one in my hand, trying to look the part. I wandered into town and found the local commercial property rental office.

I walked in and said to the man sitting behind a desk, "Good morning. Hurrr ... I'd like to rent a shop."

The man behind the desk nodded his head and then squinted at me. "I've never seen you around here before. Are you new in town?"

I nodded my head. "Arrived a couple days ago. The village council of my home village said there were too many stone masons in town and asked me to leave, seeing as how I was the youngest. Anyway, I'm hoping to open a stone mason shop here in town."

"Makes sense," said the man as he nodded his head. "I've got just the place for you. The rent is one hundred emeralds a month, but I only need ten emeralds upfront. I know you'll be able to earn the money. We only have one other stone mason in town, if you can believe it."

"In a city this size?!? Wow," I said as I reached into my inventory and handed him ten emeralds. He filled in some blank spaces in a rental contract and then, his quill hovering over the final blank space, said "What's your name?"

I wanted to say my name was Kevin, but that was too risky. If the wandering trader assassins came to Zombie Bane, and *they would*, any villager using the name Kevin would immediately be a suspect. And so I thought for a moment and said, "My name is Doug ... hurrr ... Doug Jones."

The man chuckled as he wrote the name. "Pretty generic name, isn't it?"

I shrugged. "I suppose. But, when your parents are named Chad and Karen Jones, what do you expect?"

The man behind the desk chuckled and then introduced himself. "My name is Gregory Dostoevsky. Come with me and I'll show you to your new store."

I followed the man and he took me to a vacant storefront. Next door was a shop called Slade's Souvenirs and Sundries. It looked like a typical tourist shop, selling curios and memorabilia. I noticed maps for sale showing the locations where the famous Cornelius had killed ten zombies in one night. I smiled. I assumed that a shop like my neighbor's would be getting a lot of traffic and maybe that would allow for me to get some spillover traffic.

Gregory opened the door and we walked inside. There was a counter at the back and a few tables and chairs. There were bookshelves built into the walls. A couple of empty chests lay open behind the counter.

"Looks okay," I said.

Gregory nodded. "It will probably take you a day to get everything arranged before you can open for business, but it's a good location on a well-trafficked street. You should not have any problems making a living."

I smiled and reached out my hand. We shook on the deal and he left me to get my shop ready to operate.

Chapter 9

I worked quickly, and by that same afternoon, I had my shop ready to open to the public. I had crafted a stonecutter and set it up behind my counter. I had placed various items for trade, ranging from clay and bricks to glazed terracotta tiles, on the bookshelves in a pleasing display.

I stood with my back to the door of my shop and looked around to assess the scene. It looked just like the stone mason shops I had visited in the past during my wanders. I knew enough about stone cutting that I would not be a mere novice if I were called upon to cut stone for anyone.

I figured that if I could survive hidden-in-plain-sight in this shop for at least a month, Wickham would back off his attempts to find me and I might even be able to live to a ripe old age. Still, I knew I needed to be cautious.

I was just about to go next door and introduce myself to the proprietor of the Slade's Souvenirs and Sundries when a player walked in my front door.

"Show me what you got," he said abruptly.

"My good sir, may I know your name first? It is only polite."

"Sure thing. My name is SABU6000. Now, show me what you got."

I bowed humbly and informed the player that my name was Doug. I then straightened up and moved my hand in a horizontal arc, gesturing to all the different stones and minerals on display. "Everything I have is before your very eyes. Is there anything you're looking for in specific?"

SABU6000 shook his head. "Just looking for some decorative touches for my mansion that I'm building outside of town. Thinking of getting some terracotta tiles and arranging them in patterns."

I swear ... these players and their houses.

"An excellent choice. I have sixteen different types of terracotta tiles. Priced at only one emerald each."

SABU6000 rubbed his chin. "An emerald each? That seems a little pricey."

"Ah, but there is a *volume* discount. If you buy ten terracotta tiles, then it is only eight emeralds for the lot."

The player did some quick calculations. "A 20% discount. That sounds pretty good. I'll tell you what. If I get twenty tiles will you sell them to me for fifteen emeralds instead of sixteen?"

"Certainly."

SABU6000 rubbed his hands together greedily and began to examine the various tiles. It took him a few minutes to make a selection but once he did, he put the tiles on the counter. I counted them to make sure he had only taken twenty and then held out my hands for fifteen emeralds. He deposited them in my hands, and I tucked them into my inventory. "It was a pleasure doing business with you, SABU6000. Please tell your friends about my shop."

The player tucked the tiles into his inventory. "Yeah, sure, I guess. Thanks for the discount." The player then turned around and left the shop.

My first trade as a stone mason accomplished and not seeing any additional players nearby, I left my shop and went next door. I walked into Slade's Souvenirs and Sundries. I was impressed by how packed it was. You could buy snacks and maps of the town indicating the locations where Cornelius killed the ten zombies. There were numerous books and toys and games for sale to help keep restless children occupied. Lastly, there was a counter where you could order freshly prepared snack foods and drinks.

There were several villagers and a couple of players wandering through the store shopping. I walked up to the middle-aged man standing behind the counter. "Do you own this establishment, sir?" I asked in my most polite villager voice.

The man smiled. "Indeed I do. My name is Jacob Slade."

I reached out my hand. "My name is Doug."

Mr. Slade shook my hand but cocked an eyebrow. "No last name?"

I chuckled. "Well, you might not believe this, but my name is Doug Jones. Boring, I realize."

Jacob Slade chuckled. "Hey, it's a real name. It's not like you are making it up or anything."

"Right. We can't help the name we were born with." I paused and looked around the shop. "Looks like you are doing a pretty good business here. I just concluded my first trade with a player a few minutes ago."

Mr. Slade nodded. "Congratulations. Anyway, yeah, this is a popular shop. It helps that Cornelius, the Bane of Zombies, was a relative of mine a few generations back."

I raised my eyebrows. "Really? That's pretty cool."

"It sure is," said a child's voice.

I looked around. "Sir, is there a child in here?"

Mr. Slade laughed. He reached down and picked up a three-year-old toddler who was wandering around by his feet. The boy was holding a stuffed creeper action figure. I suddenly felt very emotional but then pushed it away so that I wouldn't start crying in front of my new neighbor.

"This is my son, William Slade, but everyone calls him Billy. One of these days, this will all be his."

I reached my hand out and shook Billy Slade's tiny hand. "Pleased to meet you, Billy."

"Okay," said the boy, squirming in his father's grasp.

Mr. Slade laughed and put his son down on the ground. "Run along home. See what your mother's planning to make for dinner." The boy nodded and trotted away.

"Seems like a nice little kid," I said.

Mr. Slade nodded. "Say, you're pretty young to be an expert stone mason, aren't you? What are you like sixteen? eighteen?"

I suddenly realized that my youth might be the one weakness of my plan. Most expert stone masons were several years older than me. I hoped it didn't give me away. "I suppose I am a bit young. My father was a stone mason in my village so he's taught me from a young age. Unlike a lot of villagers who don't know what their profession is going to be when they spawn, mine was chosen for me at birth."

Mr. Slade nodded. "That is exactly what's happening with my child. He is destined to be a shopkeeper."

"Well, I probably should get back to my shop. If you get the customers asking for stone or mineral goods, I'd appreciate it if you'd send them my way."

Mr. Slade smiled. "Sure thing. We don't sell any of that stuff here."

I turned around and returned to my shop.

The rest of the day was uneventful. I made a couple more trades with players and then closed my shop when the sun went down. There was a small living space in the back of the shop, just big enough for a bed and a place to hang my robes. There was also a corner that served as the kitchen. I put my furnace and the chest to store food in that area.

It was going to be a simple life, but at least it was a life. A life where I wouldn't have to whip my friends because some dictatorial oligarch tells me too.

Still, a life on the run was going to be difficult. I knew that wandering trader assassins would be coming through Zombie Bane soon. I just hoped that they couldn't figure out who I was.

Chapter 10

The next morning, I ate a quick breakfast of a half loaf of bread and an apple. My food stores were running out and I would have to go purchase food sometime today. I planned on asking Mr. Slade where a good market was. For now, I put on a fresh robe and opened my shop.

I made a couple of basic trades in the morning with some players that didn't even have leather armor, completely new to Minecraft. It was funny to watch them fumble with their emeralds and purchase things that they could've easily gathered or crafted, if they only knew how.

Just before lunch time, my heart nearly stopped when I saw him: Waldo. Waldo was leading his two llamas through the streets of Zombie Bane very slowly, looking from side to side, obviously searching for me.

I didn't know Waldo personally, which is probably a good thing because he didn't know me personally either and would have no chance of recognizing my face. But I knew him by reputation. We always called him "Where's Waldo?" because he could hide so well. He was constantly hiding in strange places throughout headquarters, waiting for people to find him.

His most legendary act was standing next to Wickham while Wickham was presiding over a ceremony awarding wandering trader status to several trainees. This was a couple years before I became a wandering trader so I didn't personally witness it. But, the story goes that Waldo somehow snuck onto the stage during the ceremony, stood next to Wickham, and no one noticed it until Wickham actually *bumped* into him!

I don't know if the story was actually true, but enough people told it to make it a legend, if nothing else. In any event, Waldo was an extremely dangerous and extremely skilled assassin. If he found me, it was over.

And so, when Waldo passed in front of my store and stared at the door before turning and moving toward my storefront, my heart stopped briefly. My entire body clenched. *Was this really it? I'd only been free for a couple of days? And now, capture or death was about to descend upon me?*

Waldo tied his llamas to the railing in front of my store and walked up the stairs and opened the door. He walked in, glanced around, and then walked up to me. He said nothing.

"Hello, there. Hurrr ... we don't get too many of you guys in the store," I said as I fumbled for words.

"Are you nervous?" said Waldo, staring at my face.

"I mean, no, not really. It's just ... I've never had a wandering trader as a customer before."

Waldo regarded me with suspicious eyes as he rubbed his chin. "Right."

"See anything you like?"

"Not really," said Waldo as he glanced around the store. "Do you mind if I ask you a question?"

I swallowed hard. "No. Go right ahead."

"Have you seen any other wandering traders in the last couple of days? Maybe one without any llamas?"

"Why would a wandering trader not have llamas?"

Waldo shook his head. "That's not your problem. Just answer my question."

I pretended to think about it for a while. I looked to the side and scratched my face. I scrunched up my eyes and put my finger in my ear hole. I thought about picking my nose too, but realized that might be taking the pantomime a little too far. "I can't say that I have. I tend to spend all day in the store so if a wandering trader doesn't actually walk right in front of it, it's unlikely I would've seen him."

Waldo nodded his head. "I suspected as much. Anyway, do you have any bricks? I need to make some flower pots."

I was so shocked by this request that I almost laughed. But then I regained my composure and said, "What kind of a stone mason when I be if I didn't have any bricks?"

"I'm thinking about making four flower pots, so I guess that means I'll need twelve bricks."

I went over to the stack of bricks on my shelf and grabbed twelve of them. I put them on the table in the middle of my shop. "Well, I normally charge one emerald for every ten bricks, but if you want, I'll make you a deal and give you the twelve for one emerald."

Waldo shook his head. "You should never discount trades. If ten bricks is worth one emerald then twelve bricks is worth more. I tell you what. I'll buy twenty bricks for two emeralds. That way I can make six flowerpots and use the left over bricks to trade with some noob player who doesn't realize two bricks are worthless. Or, maybe I can throw them at someone."

I chuckled. "What you do with your bricks is not my concern." I walked back to my stack of bricks and grabbed eight more. Waldo tucked the twenty bricks into his inventory and handed me two emeralds. "Pleasure doing business with you, villager. By the way, what is your name?"

"It's Doug Jones. What's yours?"

"Doug Jones? Pretty generic. Anyway, my name is Waldo. No last name."

"Well, thanks for the business, Waldo with no last name. Feel free to stop anytime for bricks or stone or mineral supplies."

Waldo raised one side of his mouth into a slight smile, acknowledging my stupid joke about his name. He turned around without a word and walked out of my store, closing the door behind him. He grabbed his llamas and began walking slowly away from the store.

Once he was out of sight, I began to hyperventilate, the stress of the encounter finally catching up with me. I sat on a chair and put my head between my knees to try to slow my breathing. After about a minute, I recovered my breath, but my hands started shaking. But soon, I finally calmed down.

Was that it? If he was assigned to search Zombie Bane, then maybe I'm home free? Maybe I can be a stone mason and live out my life here? Maybe.

Chapter 11

The rest of the morning mercifully was uneventful. I decided I would close my shop for the lunch hour and go to a restaurant and do a little shopping for food. But, I didn't know where to do these things in Zombie Bane, so I went next door and asked Mr. Slade.

"What kind of food are you in the mood for?" he asked.

I shrugged. "I don't know ... maybe some pork chops."

Mr. Slade smiled. "In that case, you'll want to go to old man Watson's Pig in a Poke. He specializes in pork products. The smoked pork chop sandwich is amazing."

"It's a strange name for a restaurant. But thanks. How do I get there?"

"Follow the street south and then turn right at the second right. You can't miss it. There is a giant wooden pig sticking out from the front of the building."

"What about a market? I want to buy myself some food to have in my house."

"There is a market on the same street where the Pig in a Poke is located. Farmer Peppers runs it. Just a couple doors past the restaurant."

I smiled. "Thanks a lot. If anyone comes in asking about my shop, I'd appreciate it if you'd let them know I'll be back in about an hour."

Mr. Slade smiled. "That's why I stay open all the time. Don't want to lose any customers. But I'll let them know."

I left Slade's Souvenirs and Sundries and followed the directions to old man Watson's Pig in a Poke. As I turned the corner onto the street where it was located, I could smell the delicious odor of pork being smoked over a wooden fire. My mouth started watering.

When I walked inside the restaurant, a young villager girl who was working there greeted me. "Welcome! My name's Alita. How can I help you?"

"Table for one."

The girl smiled. "Follow me." She led me to a small table in a corner of the restaurant. There was a small window above the table allowing light and fresh air in. "Do you need a menu?" she asked.

"I don't know. Is there something you recommend?"

Her face got bright and excited. She smiled broadly. "Do I! Get the smoked pork chops. It is divine. Almighty Notch himself could not make a better meal."

"Well, blasphemous pork! I'll have to try that. And bring a glass of apple juice to go with it please."

"Sure thing. Just be a couple minutes."

After Alita had left I looked around the restaurant. There were about a dozen villagers of various professions scattered throughout. In addition, there were a couple of players sitting at a table in the corner whispering to each other, probably conspiring about which villager they were going to kill and rob. Typical player nonsense.

When Alita returned with my food, she asked me if I needed anything else. The food smelled delicious. "I don't think so."

She smiled. "I'll check back with you about dessert once you finish."

I laughed. "Okay then."

When I bit into the smoked pork chop, I realized why Alita had given it such high praise. The meat virtually melted in my mouth. I didn't even have to chew it if I didn't want to. The smoke from the burning wood had permeated the meat through and through. It fell right off the bone. The meat was so effortless to eat that it almost felt like I hadn't eaten anything. I washed it down with a glass of apple juice.

As if by a miracle, Alita appeared at the edge of my table. "Good?"

I nodded my head, words not quite coming to my mouth. I was in culinary ecstasy. Finally though, I regained my ability to speak. "Could you bring me another one of those?"

Alita smiled. "Just like all the rest. The first time you have one of these, you gotta have more." She giggled as she walked away and then returned less than a minute later with another pork chop. I ate this one more slowly, savoring the complex and delicious flavors.

I was about halfway finished with the pork chop when I saw the door to the restaurant open and in walked Waldo! And, he wasn't alone. He was accompanied by another wandering trader. I didn't want to stare but I needed to know who it was. If it was one of my friends, I'd have to get out of there. He or she might recognize me even dressed as a stone mason.

I started to look around the restaurant as nonchalantly as possible. As I chewed my pork chop, I glanced in their direction. The other wandering trader was standing behind Waldo and I couldn't quite make out who it was. The two spoke with Alita briefly and then she led them to a table across the restaurant from where I was sitting. It was then I saw it was Trader Winona! She might recognize me. She had spent some time with me but not a lot. Still, I couldn't risk it. I ate the rest of my pork chop quickly and guzzled my apple juice.

Alita, the eagle-eyed hostess, appeared at my table. "How about that dessert?"

I shook my head. "I have to get back to my shop. How much do I owe you?"

"Three emeralds."

I dug into my inventory and dropped three emeralds into her hands. "It really was delicious. I want to have another one but I know I shouldn't." I stood up and began walking out.

"You come back again now, ya here?" said Alita, calling after me. I didn't turn around. I didn't want to risk Winona seeing me. I just lifted my hand and waved it as I walked out the door.

I walked quickly to the nearby market that Mr. Slade had told me about. Before I walked inside, I glanced over my shoulder to make sure the wandering traders weren't following me. They weren't. I breathed a sigh of relief and walked inside the market. I purchased some bread, some meat, and some vegetables. Enough food to make meals for at least a week. I did not want to have to leave my shop again ... not until the wandering traders had cleared out of town.

Chapter 12

And so, my mundane life as a stone mason continued on for weeks and then months. I turned seventeen years old, but there was no spawn day party and no presents. I felt sorry for myself that day and a few days after.

Maybe going rogue wasn't such a great idea?

Thankfully, in all that time, no wandering traders ever entered my shop again, though I did see a couple of them as they passed by the front of my store a couple weeks apart. I recognized them, Wicus and Wikolia, but I couldn't tell if they were looking for me or simply passing through on one of their typical wonders. Nevertheless, I operated under the assumption, which I later learned was true, that all wandering traders – not just the assassins – had been told that if they found me they were to capture me and return me to Wickham for punishment.

One morning, Mr. Slade's wife, Priscilla, walked into my shop. She waved and said, "Hi, Doug. How are you?"

I shrugged. "Fine, I guess. Business has been good lately."

Priscilla nodded. "You seem like you spend a lot of time in your shop. Why don't you get out a little bit? You could meet some people?" I could tell that she was up to something....

"I don't have any real interest in meeting anyone. I'm just happy to have a successful business." Actually, I did miss the convivial conversation I used to have with my fellow wandering traders, but I had to keep a low profile. At least for a while longer.

Priscilla shook her head. "Oh, come on. A handsome young man like you should be out meeting some of the local girls. There's nothing a villager girl finds more attractive than a successful businessman."

I blushed a little bit. "I guess that's nice of you to say, but I'm doing all right here by myself."

"Well, if you ever want to meet anyone, let me know. I have several friends who have daughters about your age. I'm sure they would simply *adore* meeting you."

I could feel myself blushing more. "That's nice of you to say. Um ... hurrr ... so, anyway...."

Mrs. Slade giggled and then waved her hand at me. "Oh, youth truly is wasted on the young. I'll talk to you later, Doug." Then she turned around and walked out of my store.

As nice as it would be to meet some more people in town and maybe even have a girlfriend, I planned to lay low for at least another year. I knew Wickham had yet to give up on killing Wex, even though it had been many years since his betrayal. So, I knew Wickham would not give up on me either. But, eventually, his focus would shift to more pressing matters, and I would be able to get back into the world. Whatever he had planned with the Wolf King, the Spider Queen, the pillagers, and his contacts in

Capitol City was surely moving forward. I wished I knew more about it, but I was out of the loop completely now.

* * *

Just before lunchtime, the door to my shop opened and a player strode in. He was armored head to toe with enchanted diamond armor and walked in like he owned the place. He was the worst kind of player: Arrogant and self-centered.

"I'm here to buy your stone cutter," he proclaimed.

"My good sir, it's not for sale. I need it to run my business."

"Listen here, you stupid villager. I'm gonna take it from you and there's nothing you can do about it."

"My dear player sir, I can't allow you to deprive me of the one thing that allows me to make a livelihood. Without a livelihood, a villager is useless."

The player pulled out an enchanted diamond sword. "And, without your life, you can't do *anything*," he growled. "Now, give me that stone cutter *immediately*, or I am going to cut you down where you stand." For some reason, he reminded me of Wickham.

"I can't let you do that. Got out of my shop, you loser."

The player looked shocked. I'm sure no villager had ever spoken back to him. "How dare you besmirch my honor?!? I am the great DeathCult1978 and all bow before me ... or perish." He slashed at me with his sword, but I ducked it. He was so surprised by my move that when he followed through with his slash, it knocked him off balance. I reached into my inventory and pulled out my own diamond sword and I slashed him on the back. It injured him, but only just, his diamond armor preventing any serious injury.

He turned around and stared at me, his face a mask of shock and anger. "Did you just dare to strike the great DeathCult1978?"

I gritted my teeth. "I'm gonna do more than that if you are not careful. Go on, get outta my shop!"

DeathCult1978 laughed at me. "You think that you, an armorless villager with a diamond sword, can defeat me? You're an idiot. Prepare to die!"

DeathCult1978 bull rushed toward me, but I'd seen his kind before. He was so used to gaining XP by killing passive and weak mobs, that he wouldn't know what to do in the face of a skilled foe. And I *was* one. Just as he was about to slash me across the chest, I jumped into the air and did a somersault over him. I landed behind him and managed to slash across the back of his neck, in between the top of his body armor and the bottom of his helmet. He howled with pain and rage. He turned around and grunted and then rushed back toward me. This time, he managed to land a blow on my left arm, but the cut wasn't too deep.

"That's what you get for messing with the best!" he said.

"Get ready then," I snarled, "because I'm better than you."

DeathCult1978 screamed and sprinted at me. I held my ground and quickly grabbed a crossbow from my inventory with my right hand, shooting him in his diamond chest plate at close range. The arrow penetrated the armor, causing him to buckle over in pain. I quickly jumped up and ran behind him, thrusting my sword into his back.

DeathCult1978 groaned as he reached behind himself, trying to grab the sword and pull it out. I laughed before pulling my sword out and kicking the player down to the floor. He looked up at me with fear in his eyes as he fumbled with his inventory. He tried to pull out a crossbow, but I kicked the crossbow out of his hand before he could shoot me at close range.

I walked up to him and put my hand on his chest plate and held my sword to his exposed throat. "I told you not to take my stone cutter."

"But how? Villagers don't know how to fight?"

I sneered at him. "This villager does."

I quickly finished him. After he flashed red and disappeared in a puff of smoke, I searched his drop pile for anything useful. I kept the diamond armor, a few potions, and some food. The rest of it was just useless nonsense that I would take in the back of my shop and throw in the trash later.

As I was tucking the last bit of useful loot into my inventory, I turned to my left and looked out the window in the front door of my store. I saw a little girl, who could not have been older than two, staring at me. Her eyes were as wide as the ender dragon's wingspan, and she was rapidly sucking her thumb like she was nervous and scared.

Had she seen what I did? Is she old enough to tell someone?

I looked at the girl and put one of my fingers across my lips vertically, indicating that she should be quiet and keep a secret. The girl's eyes remained wide and her thumbsucking intensified. And then, a few seconds later, a woman ran up to her and grabbed her hand and shook her finger at her. "What are you doing here, Cindy? You know you shouldn't go off by yourself." The girl nodded her head before removing her hand from her mouth and grabbing onto her mommy's hand. Thankfully, they walked away.

Had I blown my cover? Would this girl tell her mom what she had seen? Would her mom even believe her? Every villager knows he or she is born a victim for players. No one would believe a little girl who said she saw a villager kill a player wearing full diamond armor. Would they?

I took the remaining items of DeathCult1978's drop pile and took them out the back door of my store and dumped them into a trashcan. I went to my back room and tucked the diamond armor into my storage chest. I decided that I would start sleeping wearing diamond armor. *Just in case.* If I were a wandering trader assassin and heard a rumor that a villager had killed a player, I would come looking for him. And, I would come in the night when he was least expecting it.

Chapter 13

After three days had passed with no mention, either by a resident of Zombie Bane or a wandering trader assassin showing up at my door, of the incident involving DeathCult1978, I began to relax a little bit. Days turned into weeks and after a month had passed with me doing nothing more than living my commonplace life as a stone mason, I concluded that the incident would not come back to haunt me.

I arrived at this conclusion one morning while I was standing behind the counter of my service desk. A few seconds after reaching this conclusion, a player walked in. He was wearing full diamond armor, except, in place of a helmet, he wore a hat cocked to the side at a jaunty angle. He was holding a turtle under one arm.

I greeted him. "Welcome to my shop. How may I help you?"

The player smiled and spread his arms broadly. "My name is Kingtutland. I'm here to give you a big pile of emeralds."

I scratched the back of my neck at the base of my hairline. "Is that so? And *what* do I have to do to obtain this big pile of emeralds?"

Kingtutland smiled. "Oh, something most enjoyable, I assure you."

I took a deep breath and sighed. "I'm waiting."

"You get to make a sculpture of ... me and, of course, my pet turtle."

Oh, goodie. Lucky me.

"I've never made a sculpture before. Are you sure I'm the right one for the job?"

The player chuckled. "Of course, I don't know that. But you are a stone mason and I want a stone sculpture of me in all my glory holding my most cherished pet turtle. Who else could I ask in town to do it?"

"Let me guess, you're going to put it in your mansion so other players can gawk at it, right?"

"Exactly. So here's the deal. I want you to make a statue of me holding a sword in one hand and my turtle in the other. It goes without saying that I should look dominant. If you can get it done in the next couple weeks, I'll give you five hundred emeralds."

Zowie! That is some serious monies!

I may not have been a sculptor, but I could use the money. "Okay. But what if the sculpture looks a little well ... hurrr ... not lifelike?"

"You can cut a straight line, can't you?"

I nodded my head. "I'm sure I can get the basic shape right. It's the details I'm worried about. Like your face, for instance."

The player laughed. "Just get the body and arms right. You can leave the face blank. It makes it more ominous and sinister that way. That's the image I'm trying to project."

This guy was ba-na-nas.

"Okay. I guess I can do that. So just make you look like you look today? Same armor and all? The hat too?"

The player nodded. "Exactly."

"What do you want this thing made out of? Just your basic cobblestone?"

"Oh, absolutely not. I want you to use only polished stones. And, be sure to use stones that are the color of my armor and my hat and, of course, my beloved turtle."

"Do you want me to use actual diamonds for the armor? If you do, I'll have to charge you another five hundred emeralds."

The player shook his head. "Just use nether quartz. Close enough, and it shows I've been to the Nether ... which I have."

"Okay then. I can probably have this ready for you in a couple weeks. Come back then. But I need a deposit of two hundred and fifty emeralds now."

Kingtutland nodded his head and handed me a few stacks of emeralds. I counted them just to be sure all two hundred and fifty were there before tucking them away in my inventory. "Okay, my dear sir, I'll see you in a couple of weeks."

Chapter 14

About a week later I had finished most of the bottom half of the sculpture. I had it in the center of my store because it was the only place big enough to do the work. It had the secondary effect of attracting a lot of attention from potential customers. Several villagers inquired about having sculptures made of themselves. When I told them how much it would cost, they were aghast, but still interested. I had a few players put deposits on sculptures of themselves as well.

It is weird the places life takes you. Here I was, hiding in plain sight in Zombie Bane, worried on the daily that I was going to be found out and captured or assassinated, and I had discovered a new and lucrative business as a sculptor. Weird.

Just before the lunch hour, Mrs. Slade walked into my shop, followed by a villager girl about my age.

"Oh, Doug? Can I interrupt you for a moment?" said Mrs. Slade.

I put down my tools and wiped my hands on a rag. "Sure. What is it?"

Mrs. Slade smiled and then turned around and pointed at the girl behind her who blushed slightly. "Doug, this is Cordelia Lear. She is from one of the most eligible villager families in all of Zombie Bane. Given the success of your business, I was wondering if you might like to go on a date with her?"

I blushed. "Are you trying to get me a girlfriend?" I stammered.

Mrs. Slade clucked her tongue and shook her finger at me. "Oh, not just that. I'm trying to get you *married*."

I turned bright red. "Married?!? Why would I want to get married?"

Cordelia looked a little disappointed when I said that. "All villagers get married, Doug," said Mrs. Slade. "That's what you have to do. It's our way."

Her use of the word "way" triggered me. I suddenly felt stressed and angry. But I suppressed it. I didn't want her to notice anything that might later be used to betray my true identity.

"Well, that's interesting. I hadn't really thought about marriage."

Mrs. Slade gasped. "But *all* villagers think about marriage. We have to keep our family lines going and ensure that the wealth we earn in our lives is passed down to our children and not shared with anyone else."

I'd spent so much time away from villagers during my adolescence inside wandering trader headquarters that I had forgotten how fundamentally greedy they – *we* – were. But, if I were going to hide as a villager for the rest of my life, I had to play the part and embrace my cultural heritage.

"Indeed you are correct, Mrs. Slade." I looked at Cordelia and smiled. "Sure, why don't we get to know each other better?"

Cordelia giggled. "That would be good. Why don't we get lunch together today?"

I shrugged. "Okay. Is there a place you want to go?"

"You two should go to the Steaming Cocoa Bean," said Mrs. Slade. "It's a new restaurant that just opened up a couple blocks away. I hear they have a beverage there that's extraordinary. It's called hot chocolate."

"Oh, I heard my friends talking about that. They say it's amazing," said Cordelia.

I didn't really care about hot chocolate or anything else to be honest. Anytime I left my shop, I worried about being detected by a wandering trader assassin. But I had to get over it. "It sounds great," I said. "Why don't you wait outside and I will put on a clean robe and then we can go?"

Cordelia nodded and she and Mrs. Slade left my shop giggling.

* * *

About ten minutes later I was sitting at a table with Cordelia sitting across from me and fluttering her eyelashes. *Ugh.* We each ordered a pork chop sandwich and a slice of watermelon. And of course, we each had a hot chocolate. I had to admit, the hot chocolate was pretty amazing. I didn't think that cocoa beans tasted that good all by themselves, but when you mixed them with sugar and warm milk, it created a concoction of tantalizing taste.

After she had a couple sips of her hot chocolate, Cordelia asked, "Where did you live before Zombie Bane? You arrived during the last twelve months, right?"

I finished chewing the bite of my sandwich and then said, "Yeah. I'm from the village of ... hurrr ... Gnarled Oak. It's about a five-day walk from here. When I chose my profession, I realized the village was too small to support yet another stone mason. So, I said my good-byes and headed for Zombie Bane."

At least, I think that was my cover story. Had I said a different village name before? Didn't I say that I was asked to leave by village leadership? I was having a hard time keeping my stories straight.

Cordelia nodded. "So you traveled all by yourself? How exciting!"

I shrugged. "I suppose. It *was* a bit scary at first, traveling through the world with nothing more than a few blocks of stone, some food, and a few emeralds. It would sure be nice if we villagers were better at using weapons."

Cordelia nodded sadly. "Indeed. We are at the mercy of players who so very often are merciless."

"Anyway, I made it here and opened the shop and it's been very successful. I'm pleased."

Cordelia smiled. "Well, I spawned in Zombie Bane and I assume I will die here. Maybe, if we get married, we can spawn children of our own?"

This girl seemed pretty aggressive. I knew villagers were all for marriage and family but ... gee whiz, this was our first date!!! Besides, I wasn't going to marry anyone. I couldn't do that to someone. One of these days, I knew I'd be found out and would have to flee.

I was about to respond to her question when I suddenly felt as though I were being watched. I tensed and began looking around the restaurant as nonchalantly as I could. I even added some small talk. "Look at that tapestry on the wall over there. Looks like it's really well put together."

I kept glancing around the restaurant as she responded. "Oh yes, we have a great tapestry maker in town right now. Her name is Athena Adriatic."

At that moment I saw him. There was a villager in a dark corner of the restaurant. He had a mug of hot chocolate in front of him and nothing else. He was staring at me. He didn't even try to hide it. When my eyes met his, he curled the edge of his mouth up in a slight smile, acknowledging that I had seen him and that I knew what he was doing. He didn't look dangerous, but then, neither did I. It seemed like there was something familiar about him....

I turned back to Cordelia and said, "Indeed? Maybe I will have to visit her shop one of these days."

She nodded. "Oh, yes. My parents have one of her tapestries in our living room. It's the centerpiece of our home."

We continued on with the small talk for another ten or fifteen minutes while we ate our sandwiches and drank our hot chocolate. I checked on the villager spying on me a couple times during the meal and he was still sitting there, sipping his hot chocolate and looking at me.

When Cordelia and I got up to leave the restaurant, he sat there, unmoving, and watched us leave. As we walked back to my shop, I kept checking to see if he was following me, but he didn't. *Maybe he was just a weirdo? Maybe he liked the girl I was with? Or maybe, he was a spy for Wickham?*

When we arrived at my shop, I told Cordelia that I had to get back to work. She smiled. "Of course. We all must earn as many emeralds as we can." She paused for a moment and shifted her weight. "Anyway, do you want to have lunch or dinner in a couple of days?"

I shrugged. "I suppose. If you do."

She smiled. "Of course, I do. You're great. And you have successful business, which is really the only thing I look for in a man."

What the ...?

"Um, okay. Why don't you come by in a couple days at lunchtime, and we will eat someplace else? Your choice."

She smiled and clasped her hands together. "Thank you. I will see you then, Doug."

"Okay, bye, Cordelia."

I watched as Cordelia walked down the street and turned a corner. I stood in front of my shop scanning the people passing back and forth in front of me. No one seemed suspicious. I recognized most of them as residents of Zombie Bane, unlike the villager I'd seen in the restaurant a few minutes ago. I didn't recognize him, but he had seemed familiar in some way. Maybe he lived on the other side of town and I had seen him once a few months ago? Or, maybe he *was* a spy? I wasn't sure.

But, I knew one thing: I'd be sleeping with my diamond armor securely fastened on my body and my weapons at the ready.

Chapter 15

I had a couple more lunch dates with Cordelia. She brought up marriage **every** time. It seemed weird considering she was only seventeen years old, same as me. I knew that villagers can be desperate to get their households in order and keep making money, *money*, ***money***, but I was starting to sense desperation. It didn't make any sense either, because she was very nice and I was sure there were many young villagers who would be happy to marry her.

And, villager culture was changing. The kids weren't always interested in making emeralds; they wanted to have adventures and live their lives. They didn't want to get married and be tied down so young. Cordelia seemed like she was more interested in the old traditions.

I realized that I couldn't keep leading Cordelia on and pretending like our lunch dates were going to end in our marriage. It just wasn't fair to either of us. So, I resolved that the next time we met I would tell her that it wasn't working out.

But, there wouldn't be a next time.

On the day that I finished Kingtutland's sculpture, he arrived in the afternoon to take delivery. The statue was sitting in the center of my shop, assembled for his review.

He pulled up in front of my shop with a cart drawn by two horses. Another player was with him. The two of them walked into the store. "Doug, I'd like you to meet Adela2543. She has a house near mine. She has volunteered to help me reassemble the statue when I get to my place. I think she might also want to buy a statue from you."

"That's great," I said looking at Adela2543. "Can you come back tomorrow and we can work out the details?"

Adela2543 nodded her head. "It might be a couple days before I can get back to town, but I'll be sure to stop in."

"Just so you know, there's a waiting list of several other players in front of you, so it may be a few months before I can get your sculpture done."

She smiled. "That's okay. I'm not playing on hardcore mode or anything like that. I'll be around."

Playing? Hardcore mode?

Kingtutland looked at his statue and smiled broadly. "Great work. I love all the different touches of various stones and rocks. Looks very dominant. And, you captured the likeness of my pet turtle *perfectly!*"

He reached into his inventory and pulled out another two hundred and fifty emeralds, to pay the final price of five hundred. He handed them to me and I tucked them into my inventory. "Thank you for your business."

He smiled. "Oh no, thank you. This is just how I imagined it."

"As you can see there are little lines where the stones come together," I said. "You can pull the statue apart along those lines and then put it back together when you get home."

The two players got to work and within five minutes had all of the pieces loaded in the back of the horse cart. Kingtutland thanked me again and then the two of them rolled away.

Although it was still an hour before my typical closing time, I decided I would close my shop early. The two hundred and fifty emeralds was more than I made in an average week, so I thought I deserved to take the day off. Maybe now would be a good time to find Cordelia and let her know that I had no interest in being married ... at least not anytime soon.

I got a broom and swept the spot where the statue had been, making sure that all the little crumbs of rock and stone dust were cleaned. I put the broom away and was standing with my back to the door straightening some of my display items when I heard the door open. Without turning around I said, "Sorry, I'm closed for the day."

"Oh, I think you'll be wanting to stay open ... Winston."

Chapter 16

I turned around quickly as I plunged my hand into my inventory and yanked out my diamond sword. I gripped the sword tightly as I recognized who was standing in front of me: Wes.

"How did you find me?"

Wes laughed. "It doesn't matter. I found you. Wickham's had us all looking for you. He even offered a generous reward of 2,000 emeralds. And, it looks like I'm going to be the one to get it."

I sneered at Wes. "You won't be able to spend it when you're dead." I began to move toward him but then Wes, who hadn't even reached for a weapon, said, "You might want to look out the window."

I stopped and looked behind Wes and saw that Waldo *and* Wind were standing outside. Their llama teams were hitched to the railing a few blocks from the door to my store. And, I saw something else ... Sunny and Pippa!

"You took my llamas?!? How dare you?"

Wes smirked. "They belong to the Guild. The Guild you betrayed!"

"You better treat them right," I said.

Wes laughed. "Those stupid llamas are the least of your worries."

"So that's just it then? You're going to kill me now?"

Wes shook his head. "The condition of the reward is to bring you back alive. Wickham wants to ... make an example of you."

If they weren't going to kill me, I had a chance. I lunged forward and smacked Wes on the side of his head with the flat of my sword. He fell to the ground dazed. Waldo and Wind saw what I had done and dashed toward the door, but I was quicker. I ran in the back room and grabbed my diamond armor that was spread out on my bed. I shoved the armor into my inventory and then ran out the back of the shop.

I ran as quickly as I could down the alleyway behind my shop and then turned left, glancing over my shoulder and seeing that Wind and Waldo were just then exiting the back of my store. I ran through a maze of alleys, putting distance between myself and my pursuers. I ducked into the back of a grocery market and quickly put my diamond armor on and put my villager robe over it. I peeked out the back of the store and looked in both directions up and down the alleyway. I didn't see any of my pursuers, so I ran out the back of the grocery store.

My plan was to get to the edge of town and then go to the local cave system. I could go deep into the cave and find a place to hide. I had enough food in my inventory to last me two or three days, which I assumed would be long enough for me to escape.

But as I was running down one street, suddenly Waldo stepped out from a doorway and stood in front of me. I turned around to run away from him but I saw that Wind had taken a position behind me. I was trapped.

"It's no use, Winston. It's over. You are coming with us," said Wind.

I had to act fast. There was only one thing to do. I reached into my inventory and pulled out a splash potion of slowness and threw it at Waldo. He was so surprised by my boldness that he didn't get out of the way in time. He screamed in pain and yelled at me in slow motion. "You. Won't. Get. Away. With. This."

Waldo temporarily out of commission, Wind rushed toward me but I had already sprinted past Waldo. "Get. Him," said Waldo slowly as Wind ran in front of him.

I knew that if I kept running, Wind would eventually catch me. I hadn't been getting much exercise lately and I could already feel myself getting tired. I had to find a way to confuse his ability to follow me. That was when I remembered.

I turned left at the next street and ran toward the Zombie Bane library. The façade was undergoing major renovations and there were piles of blocks on top of scaffolding. I ran toward the scaffolding. I slowed my pace slightly to allow Wind almost to catch up with me and then I accelerated and knocked a scaffolding down with a slash of my sword. The rocks fell on top of Wind, crushing him. He may have survived, but I was not going to stick around to find out.

I kept running, knowing that Wes had surely recovered by now and would be in pursuit along with Waldo.

As I dashed through one street, Cordelia saw me and dropped the grocery bags she was carrying. She put her hand to her open mouth in shock. "Doug?"

"Can't explain. Not sure I'll be back. Sorry," I shouted as I ran past her. About a minute later, I came to the edge of town and ran into the nearby woods.

Chapter 17

Once I had gone far enough into the woods where I couldn't be seen from town, I stopped by a tree to catch my breath. My lack of physical training was obvious; I hadn't realized how simply walking everywhere when I was a wandering trader was really good exercise.

I really needed to rest more, but I had to get to the cave system. It was at least ten minutes away, even if I ran the whole way. I reached into my inventory and drank half a bottle of water and ate an apple to keep up my energy. I then looked back to the town to see if anyone was following me and saw nothing.

I began running again. But about a minute later, a rock smashed my head, dropped from a tree above me. I wasn't knocked out, but I felt groggy. Blood dripped down my face and I lost two hearts from my health bar. I couldn't walk in a straight line, much less run. Wes hopped down from the tree. "Nice try, Winston."

"How? How did you get here so fast?" I asked, my head spinning. I was seeing stars.

"I rode a horse. Duh. Too bad you didn't have one waiting for you behind your shop. You probably would've gotten away."

I held my diamond sword up, ready to defend myself, but I was unsteady on my feet. If Wes meant to kill me right now, he would succeed. If he meant to capture me, I probably couldn't really put up much of a fight.

"Put that thing away," he said, disgusted. "Waldo will be here in a few minutes and will take you away on the back of one of his llamas. And, you can give me the diamond armor too. I'll be able to sell that for quite a few emeralds."

"Never," I said lurching toward him and slashing my sword. But in my dizzy, weakened state, Wes simply stepped to the side without a problem.

At that moment I heard footsteps approaching. I assumed it was Waldo, but then I heard a girl's voice. "Winston? Is that you?"

I turned around and it was Winter. She was wearing full official wandering trader robes. "Winter? You passed your test."

She smiled. "After I got off those three months of pooper scooper duty."

Wes sneered and said, "Awww. Isn't this cute? What a nice reunion."

Winter shook her head. "You don't have to be mean, Wes. I've had to put up with your attitude ever since we left headquarters. I don't know why Wickham made me come with you and those two assassins."

Wes shook his finger at Winter. "So you could learn your place. Wolf learned his when he was whipped. And you are going to learn yours by seeing your friend and savior punished ... *severely*."

Winter looked down at the ground. "That is the Way," she said sadly.

"That is the Way," said Wes. "Now, tie his wrists behind him."

Winter approached me with a rope and reached for my hands. She held them and was about to wrap the rope around them when her hands began to tremble. She let go of me and threw the rope on the ground. "I can't. He saved my life and freed my village. You tie him up."

"Are you disobeying an order from your superior?"

Winter laughed. "You're not my superior. You've only been a wandering trader for about a year longer than I have. Plus, I'm better at weapons than you."

Wes was taken aback. "How dare you! Wickham will hear about this."

I saw Winter staring at the ground. She was breathing slowly and steadily. She was building her strength, coiling her body and muscles like a snake. Wes didn't notice, but I did. Something was about to happen.

And then, it did.

Winter suddenly removed a long staff from her inventory and smacked Wes's legs with it, knocking him to the ground. He looked up at her in shock. "What are you doing?!?"

"I'm saving my friend," she said as she brought the stick down on Wes's chest. There was a sickening *CRACK* sound as a couple of his ribs broke. He leaned forward in pain, but then Winter smacked the side of his head, knocking him unconscious.

I looked at Winter in shock. "Do you realize what you've just done to yourself? You've made yourself an enemy of Wickham!"

She shook her head. "I don't care. I understand now why you went rogue. The wandering trader hierarchy is broken. Wickham is poison. Wickham is trash!"

"Wickham will execute you for those words," said Waldo who had suddenly appeared behind Winter.

Although she was surprised, she managed to strike him in the arm with her stick. But it was a glancing blow. He moved toward her blocking another blow with his shield and then slashing at her side with his sword, causing a severe wound. Winter collapsed to the ground screaming, dropping her stick and unable to do anything other than writhe in pain.

I looked at Waldo and said, "You'll regret that." I rushed toward him with my diamond sword, my balance mostly regained though I still felt a little weak. He slashed at me with his sword but I managed to duck the blow. I was slashing toward his legs but he was quicker, blocking my sword with his shield. Then he slashed at my arm, opening a big wound. I had to drop my sword and hold my hand over the wound to stop the bleeding.

Waldo shook his head. "What a waste. Both of you? Disgusting. That's why we should never let half-breed, impure mobs become wandering traders. Wickham is going to clean all of you mongrels out. No longer will you disgusting lower life forms pollute our glorious Guild."

Those were the last words Waldo would say. An arrow suddenly embedded in his chest. He stared at it for a moment and then it exploded, blowing him to pieces. The explosion threw me to the ground. When the smoke cleared, I saw that Winter was alive but unconscious and Wes lay on the ground, still knocked out. I scanned the area, trying to see where the arrow had come from.

It reminded me of when Weston and his witch girlfriend had been assassinated. *Was there someone busy killing wandering traders?*

That's when I heard the footsteps coming behind me. I was still holding the wound on my shoulder. Winter had passed out from loss of blood. Suddenly a splash potion hit her body and she regained consciousness, her wound beginning to heal. It had been a splash potion of healing. Then, another splash potion hit me, with the same effect. A few seconds later, I stood up holding my sword and turned around looking for the source of these items.

But I saw nothing. "Show yourself!" I shouted.

Winter and I stood there for a few seconds. I was holding my diamond sword, and she had picked up the staff she'd used earlier.

We heard movement behind one of the trees and were prepared for anything. And that's when Wex stepped out from behind the tree. He smiled. Then he walked toward us slowly, without menace. He held out his hand as though he were ready to shake ours. Then he said, "Come with me if you want to live."

Chapter 18

I looked at Wex's hand and then looked at his face. "What are you talking about? How do we know this isn't a trick?"

Wex smiled and shook his head. "If I wanted you dead, you *would* be dead. Just ask Waldo."

"Did you kill Weston and his girlfriend? They were shot with exploding arrows," I said.

Wex shook his head. "I have no idea who did that. Good riddance, though."

"I suppose you have a point," I said. "Anyway, why should we come with you?"

"I'm not going to tell you anything now *other than* I can offer you protection. It's up to you. I am not going to force you to do anything."

Winter put her hand on my shoulder. "Winston. What choice do we have? The wandering trader guild knows you are in Zombie Bane. There's no way you can ever live here again."

"I suppose...."

"And," continued Winter, "I can't go back either. Well, unless we kill Wes so there aren't any witnesses."

"Maybe we should," I said, looking at Wex.

Wex shook his head. "Don't kill Wes. He's ... useful."

"What do you mean by that?" I asked.

Wex smiled. "I'll tell you later, but only if you come with me."

At that moment I contemplated Wex's face. I studied the lines of his eyes and his mouth. Then I realized ... he was the villager who had been looking at me! "It's you! You were in the restaurant."

Wex smiled. "Yeah, did you have a nice date?"

Winter took a step back and crossed her arms in front of her chest. "Date? What is he talking about?"

I shook my head. "Some villager was trying to arrange a marriage."

"Marriage?!? Why?"

I shrugged. "I don't know. It was stupid." I needed to change the subject. "But, hurrr ... anyway ... Wex, how did you know where to find me?"

Wex shook his head. "I didn't find you. You found me."

"What?"

"I've been living in Zombie Bane for the last few years disguised as a villager. I own the Creeper Cave Tavern." Wex sighed. "Well, not anymore. I'll arrange to have a letter sent explaining that I was killed by a vicious player and that my bartender will inherit the tavern." Wex looked up at the leaves in the trees. "It was fun while it lasted. The tavern was a very lucrative business."

"Sorry about that. So, have you been watching me since I arrived?"

"I discovered you a couple weeks after you opened your store. Once I realized it was you, I was keeping tabs on you just to make sure you weren't some sort of undercover operative sent by Wickham. Soon thereafter, I learned that you had gone rogue. After that, I kept tabs on you for a different reason ... to make sure you weren't found out. I didn't want wandering traders finding me here either."

Winter was shifting nervously from foot to foot. "Should we get going? I mean, Wes might regain consciousness pretty soon. And, Wind might still be alive."

"Here's the deal. I'll take one, both, or none of you with me. Decide now," said Wex.

"I'm coming with you," said Winter with no hesitation in her voice.

I took a deep breath and sighed. Everything I had heard about Wex and even some of the things I'd seen with my own eyes indicated that he was not a good person. But, he *had* saved my life and Winter's life and now was offering to help us even more. I knew that if I had been captured, I would eventually be executed. This was a second chance at life.

I looked at Wex and said, "Okay. Let's go."

Chapter 19

Wex took us deeper into the forest and then to what appeared to be a rock wall. He looked around to make sure no one had followed us and then he pulled a pickaxe from his inventory. He knocked a small hole in the wall and motioned for us to enter.

"Light a couple torches. Here." He handed each of us a torch. We ignited them while Wex backfilled the hole to make sure it would look natural from the outside.

"Where are you taking us?" I asked.

"You'll see. I won't tell you yet, just in case you get captured or killed on the way."

"Is our path dangerous?" asked Winter.

Wex shrugged. "Not any more dangerous than any normal travel through the Overworld. I just can't risk the location of our destination being revealed to my enemies."

Wex led the way through the passage and into the cave system. We made our way down several levels, killing a couple zombies and skeletons. He took us through a maze of passages. I probably could've found my way out, if I had to. But it would take a long time.

Finally we came to a dead end and another wall. Wex again used his pickaxe to make a hole and motioned us to go through. He followed behind us and filled the hole.

Then he walked forward toward an inactive nether portal. He pulled out a flint and steel and ignited the portal. The mysterious purple glow undulating within the rectangle.

"In you go," said Wex.

"You're not just sending us through there to be killed by zombie pigmen or wither skeletons or something, are you?" I asked.

Wex shook his head. "We have a safe place down there. Hidden behind ... well, you'll see when we get there."

I walked through the portal and Winter followed behind me. I materialized in the Nether, its hot, fetid odor assaulting my nostrils. I had never been to the Nether before. I had always wanted to go. Just, not under these circumstances.

When Winter appeared a few seconds later, she took a breath and then pinched her nostrils shut. "Gross."

Wex stepped out of the portal and noticed our distress. "You get used to the smell. It doesn't take long."

Wex led the way through various passages, along lava rivers and over bridges. Zombie pigmen regarded us suspiciously from the corners of the Nether but did not move to attack. As neutral mobs, they watched and waited, preferring to keep their distance.

At one point, we came across a wither skeleton. I was prepared to do battle, but it just stared at Wex, nodded its head, and walked away.

"Are you ... *friends* with that wither skeleton?" asked Winter, astonished.

"Not friends. Allies."

"Allies? Why would you make an allegiance with the wither skeletons?" I asked.

"All in good time, Winston. Let's just get to our safe house."

We followed Wex for another fifteen minutes before we came to a giant lava falls.

Wex turned around and looked at me. "It's a good thing you have diamond armor on. Just in case the lava splashes on you." He looked at Winter. "What about you? You have some armor you can put on?"

Winter nodded her head. "I have diamond armor underneath my robe. Never leave home without it."

Wex nodded. "Good. I advise you remove your robes and go through with just the armor. Usually a few drops of lava will land on you and burn holes in your robe."

We took off our robes and followed Wex behind the lava falls. Several drops of lava hit my armor and one the back of my neck, causing me to grit my teeth in pain, but it was a minor wound and healed quickly.

After we made it beyond the lava falls, Wex looked at us. "You can put your robes back on. Winston, do you want to put your wandering trader robe back on?"

"I ... I'm not sure. I feel more like a wandering trader than a villager, but I hate the Guild right now ... and, I hate Wickham. I think I'll just wear my stone mason's robe for now."

Wex nodded. "I understand. Let's go."

In front of us, there was a small crack in the netherrack. Wex led the way through and we entered a large chamber illuminated by a lava pool in the center and dozens of torches on the walls.

There were several wither skeletons wandering to and fro. A few husks and evokers were there as well.

I looked at Wex in shock. "What is this place? Who are all these strange mobs?"

Wex smiled. "Welcome to the resistance, Winston."

Chapter 20

"Resistance? Who are you resisting?"

"Isn't it obvious?" said Wex. "Wickham and his allies."

"What are they doing?" asked Winter. "I mean, other than the trades and the assassinations, I don't understand why you're using warlike metaphors."

"Wickham cares only about money and power. He will do *anything* to get it and keep it. That is why he asked Winston to whip his mentor, to show that even a powerful, loyal, and long-serving trader like Wolf can be brought low by Wickham's orders. Even if Wolf deserved the whipping, a true and noble leader would never have asked Winston to do it."

"How do you know about the whipping?" I asked.

"We have our contacts within headquarters."

"Who?" I asked.

Wex shook his head. "Not yet. I'm still not entirely sure I trust you. Let's just say, we know almost everything that happens at headquarters within a few days of it happening."

*So there **was** a traitor or traitors within headquarters.*

"Okay then," said Winter. "But, what is Wickham doing that is so different from a maniacal player or a griefer?"

"He's working with a powerful family named the Dretskys. The family is already fabulously wealthy, but they want to acquire evermore wealth. They are insatiable. Their goal is to own all the emeralds in all of Minecraft and enslave *everyone*."

"That's impossible. No one can get everything," I said.

"You think that now but I don't want to risk it."

"Why don't you just kill Wickham?" asked Winter.

"It's not that simple. He has allies everywhere. If he dies, someone will take his place and continue his grand plan."

"Well then, what can you do?" asked Winter. "It sounds more like *futility* than *resistance*."

Wex shook his head. "The Guild of the wandering traders is more powerful than anyone knows. The players don't even know it exists, neither do the villagers. When the leader of the Guild decides something will happen, it usually does. We can't just replace the leader with someone non-evil because that leader will be killed and replaced with a tyrant yet again until the goal is met. That is what happened to Willow."

"So, what are you really saying? What is your plan?" I asked.

"We have to destroy the Guild entirely."

"How could that ever happen?!?"

Wex shook his head. "We're not sure yet. We are working on that."

Winter and I stood in stunned silence staring at Wex when an evoker approached. "Commander Wex. May I speak with you for a moment?"

"Of course, Ebert." Wex looked at us and said, "Excuse me for a moment."

Wex walked away to speak with Ebert where we could not hear what they were saying. I turned to Winter and said, "This is crazy. Do you think he means it? To actually destroy the Guild?"

Winter shrugged. "Probably. He has just as strong of a vision of the world he wants as Wickham does. Sounds like they are on a collision course."

"Dretsky?" I said. "That reminds me. Remember when we were in Creeper Junction and saw that weird guy dressed like a pirate? He was a Dretsky."

Winter nodded her head. "Yeah, I remember. It seems like Wickham and the Dretskys want to turn Minecraft into a land ruled by tyrants and oligarchs. I have to say that I'm with Wex about preventing that."

At that moment Wex returned and I said, "You know, Wex, I've been wondering something. What was in that box that you stole in Capitol City?"

Wex stood there for a moment and tilted his head back and forth. I could tell he was deciding whether or not to tell me. Finally he said, "It was an ancient manuscript. The Dretskys and Wickham have recently become very interested in the powers of the occult. The manuscript was to be delivered to an associate of the Dretskys named Señor Fuego. He owns a bookstore in Capitol City called The Fire Within."

I shook my head. "A stupid book? You killed someone over a book?"

"It's not that simple. It refers to something known as the *creation stone*. Legend has it that if one can possess the creation stone he can control everything and even manifest into being whatever his heart desires. I wanted to capture that manuscript so that any chance they had at finding the creation stone using that book would be lost."

"You don't believe in this occult stuff, do you?" asked Winter.

Wex tilted his head from side to side and shrugged. "I don't necessarily believe in it but I don't necessarily *dis*believe it either. There have been very strange goings-on in Minecraft as you probably know. You've undoubtedly heard of Herobrine, right?"

Winter and I nodded our heads. Everyone had heard of the strange glitch named Herobrine.

"And there is another," Wex continued. "There have been rumors of a strange entity that has been seen roving the land. The rumor says it has white and gray skin, with a red and black face. Our sources within headquarters say it has been spotted inside, but we don't know if that's true and, even if it is, we don't know the entity's purpose. All we know is strange things have been happening."

I thought back to the time I was waiting to speak with Wickham and felt an evil presence. Could that have been this mysterious entity?

"What do you mean, strange things?" asked Winter.

"There's not much I can tell you other than the rumors. There are rumors of strange mobs seen in swamps and in caves, mobs that look like they're made of multiple pieces. There are rumors of villagers being kidnapped and disappearing. Tales of bizarre experiments on mobs and villagers. No one knows where they go or who is kidnapping them."

"And so, if we stay with you, we have to help the resistance, right?" I asked.

Wex nodded his head. "At this point, you don't have a choice. If you want to leave now, I will honor your wish, but I'll have to kill you."

"I get it. You're building a tyrannical guild just like Wickam," I said angrily.

"Not a Guild. An Army." Wex paused and looked me in the eyes. "And war is on the horizon."

End of Book 5 of
The Ballad of Winston the Wandering Trader

End of Season One

A Note from Dr. Block

I hope you enjoyed this book. Please leave a review where you bought it and let me know what you thought about the book.

If you want to continue reading this series, pick up a copy of *The Ballad of Winston the Wandering Trader, Books 6 to 10*, available May 10, 2022.

If you want to be alerted when I release a new book, be sure to **sign up for my email list** at *www.drblockbooks.com* or follow any of my social media platforms. I'm on Facebook, Twitter, and Instagram under @drblockbooks. I am also on *Goodreads*, just search for Dr. Block. I recommend signing up for the newsletter because you will *get TWO* **FREE**, *subscriber-exclusive short stories* as well as a periodic newsletter.

Dr. Block

Mob Coloring Book

This coloring books contains **76 images**, including all current mobs as of version 1.17, as well as the Warden, Alex, and Steve. To help you decide if you want it, check out the sample images below.

Also by Dr. Block

The Complete Baby Zeke: Books 1-9 (**also available in audiobook**)
The Complete Baby Zeke: Books 10-12 (**also available in audiobook**)
The Complete Baby Zeke: Books 13-15 (**also available in audiobook**)

Otis: Diary of a Baby Zombie Pigman, Book 1
Otis: Diary of a Baby Zombie Pigman, Book 2: Konichi Juan
Otis: Diary of a Baby Zombie Pigman, Book 3: Training

Creeptastic (**also available in audiobook**)

Diary of a Werewolf Steve, Books 1-3

Spooky Halloween Tales for Minecrafters

Diary of Herobrine: Origins
Diary of Herobrine: Prophecy
Diary of Herobrine: Apotheosis

Diary of a Minecraft Bat (**also available in audiobook**)

Diary of a Spider Chicken, Books 1-3

Diary of a Surfer Villager, Season One, Books 1-20
Diary of a Surfer Villager, Season Two, Books 21-30
Diary of a Surfer Villager, Season Three, Books 31-35 (*IN PROGRESS*)

The Ballad of Winston the Wandering Trader, Books 1-5 (Season One)
The Ballad of Winston the Wandering Trader, Books 6-10 (Season Two)
The Ballad of Winston the Wandering Trader, Books 11-15 (Season Three; *IN PROGRESS*)

Tales of the Glitch Guardians, Book 1 – Origins
Tales of the Glitch Guardians, Book 2 – Kindred
Tales of the Glitch Guardians, Book 3 – Firestorm

A Notchmas Carol: An unofficial Minecraft holiday story inspired by Charles Dickens' A Christmas Carol (**also available in audiobook**)

Writing as **Matthew Block:**
Shadow Guardians: Seer.

Made in the USA
Monee, IL
09 May 2024

58255883R00267